# XANANA | GUSMÃO

Strategies for
the Future

Speeches,
2007-20

LONGUEVILLE
BOOKS

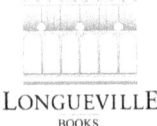

LONGUEVILLE
BOOKS

Published in 2012 by

Longueville Media
PO Box 205
Haberfield NSW 2045 Australia
www.longmedia.com.au
info@longmedia.com.au

Copyright © Kay Rala Xanana Gusmão 2012

All rights reserved. No part of this publication may be reproduced or transmitted in any form or by any means, electronic or mechanical, including photocopying, recording or by any information storage and retrieval system, without the prior permission in writing from the author, publisher and copyright holders.

Cover design: Rebecca Woodward

National Library of Australia Cataloguing-in-Publication entry (pbk)
Author: Gusmão, Xanana.
Title: Strategies for the future / Kay Rala Xanana Gusmao.
ISBN: 9781920681784 (pbk.)
Subjects: Gusmão, Xanana.
         Speeches, addresses, etc., East Timorese.
         Timor-Leste--Politics and government--21st century.
Dewey Number:   959.8704

# Contents

**Poems**
Timor .................................................................................................................. vii
Oh! Freedom! ................................................................................................... viii

**Introductory Essays**
Dom Carlos Filipe Ximenes Belo ........................................................................ 1
His Excellency José Ramos-Horta ....................................................................... 3
The Hon. Michael Kirby AC CMG ...................................................................... 6
Major General (Retd) Michael G. Smith AO .................................................... 15

Biography, Kay Rala Xanana Gusmão .............................................................. 22

**The Speeches**
The Third Anniversary of the IV Constitutional Government ......................... 27
The Ceremony for the Tenth Anniversary of the PNTL .................................. 34
ANP First Year Anniversary, 22 August 2009 .................................................. 41
Eighth Anniversary of the National University of Timor-Leste (UNTL) ........ 44
Strengthening the Private Sector through Business Associations .................... 47
Closing Session of the Timor-Leste and Development Partners Meeting ....... 52
Industry Forum: Customs and Business — a Partnership for the Future
    Development of Timor-Leste ....................................................................... 56
Government and Development Partners Program
    Alignment 2010 Meeting ............................................................................. 59
Opening Remarks to the First International Conference
    on Timor Coffee ........................................................................................... 65
Closing Session of the Seminar on Reform and Development
    of the Security Sector in Timor-Leste ........................................................ 68
Address to the g7+ Ministerial Retreat ............................................................. 74
Launch of the Timor-Leste Transparency Portal ............................................. 80
Launch of the Strategic Development Plan 2011-2030 .................................... 84
The presentation of the Strategic Development Plan,
    2011-2030 to the National Parliament ....................................................... 96

First Graduation of the National Literacy Campaign: 'Yes I Can' ..................114
Awarding of the Order of Vanuatu First Class Medal for Achievement
    of the Highest Service to Vanuatu and Humanity at Large ......................117
Petroleum Fund Management Seminar ........................................................121
First Consultative Meeting on Monitoring Implementation of the
    Principles for Good International Engagement in Fragile States ............125
Closing Remarks for the Second Consultative Conference on Principles
    for Good International Engagement in Fragile States and Situations.....129
National Dialogue on Truth, Justice and Reconciliation:
    Formal and Informal Justice ......................................................................135
Sixtieth Anniversary of the People's Republic of China ...................................137
Inaugural Session of the Bali Democracy Forum .............................................140
Bali Democracy Forum IV – Enhancing Democratic Participation
    in a Changing World: Responding to Democratic Voices .......................144
Redefining Future Relations between Indonesia and Timor-Leste ...............153
Opening Ceremony of the 10th Western China International Economy
    and Trade Fair: Second Western China Forum
    on International Cooperation...................................................................160
Inauguration of the United Nations Educational, Scientific
    and Cultural Organizations' Timor-Leste National Commission —
    Cultural Performance and Reception .......................................................163
Goodbye Conflict, Welcome Development –
    the Timor-Leste Experience........................................................................167
Closing Session of the Díli International Dialogue: Peacebuilding
    and Statebuilding........................................................................................176
Opening of the International Investment Conference .....................................181
Address to the Rio Branco Institute: Lecture for Young Diplomats
    on the Creation of the Timorese State......................................................184
Official Opening of the International Conference on
    Community-based Ecotourism ..................................................................193
Opening Session of the G7+ Meeting...............................................................197
Address to the Pacific Islands Forum, 2011 ......................................................200
Reception Hosted Jointly by the Embassies
    of Timor-Leste and Indonesia ...................................................................204
Timor-Leste's Transition from Conflict to Stability .........................................207

Presentation of Timor-Leste's Draft Penal Code ...................................................... 212
Launch of the Strategic Plan for the Justice Sector ............................................ 215
Swearing-in of Ms Maria Natércia Gusmão
   as Judge of the Court of Appeal ................................................................. 218
Swearing-in of the Trainee Judges and the Trainee Public Defenders;
   III Training Course ..................................................................................... 222
Message to the Nation .................................................................................... 225
Extension of Martial Law in Seven Districts and
   Declaration of State of Emergency ............................................................ 227
Reception for the Indonesian Minister of Defence,
   Mr Purnomo Yusgiantoro ........................................................................... 232
Ceremony Dedicated to the Promotion of Senior Officers of F-FDTL ......... 234
Tenth Meeting of the CPLP Ministers of Defence:
   Review of International Issues and Political and Military Implications
   within the Regional Context for CPLP Member Countries .................... 236
Strategic Framework Module for Timor-Leste within
   the Pilot Course on Defence and Security ................................................ 242
Visit to the National Defence Academy of Japan ......................................... 251
Homage and Recognition by the State of Timor-Leste
   to the Veterans of the Armed Front .......................................................... 256
66th Session of the United Nations General Assembly ................................ 259
Reception by the Council of Ministers to the Special Representative
   of the UN Secretary General ..................................................................... 267
Meeting of the UN Security Council ............................................................. 270
Commemoration of the 9th Anniversary
   of Timor-Leste's Restoration of Independence ......................................... 278
Presentation of the Legislative Proposal
   Concerning the 2012 State Budget ............................................................ 293

Notes ................................................................................................................ 311

**Timor**

where people
are born to die
for hope
in tearings of pain
in tearings of flesh
in tearings of blood
in tearings of life
in tearings of soul
in tearings
of the very freedom
achieved …
through death!

Xanana Gusmão

**Oh! Freedom!**
*(For Sandra Lobo. Lisbon)*

If I could only
in the cold mornings
wake up shivering
beaten by the gale
which opens for me the curtain of the sky
and see, from the top of my hills,
the purple painting
of a disturbed sunrise
east of Timor

If I could only
in the scorching suns
ride in raptures
toward the finding of myself
in the serene plains of the pasture
and feel the smell of animals
drinking from the springs
which would murmur in the air
legends of Timor

If I could only
in the calm afternoons
feel the tiredness
of the sensuous nature
stretching itself in its own seat
and listen to the telling of the wearinesses
within the laughters
of the naked barefoot children
of all Timor

If I could only
at the darkening of the wares
walk by the sand
absorbed in myself
in the wet rapture of the breeze
and touch the immensity of the sea
in a breath of soul
which let me dream the future
of the island of Timor

If I could only
at the song of the crickets
speak to the moon
by the windows of the night
and tell her stories of my people
the inviolable union of the bodies
to raise children
and teach them how to grow
    and how to love
this my Country Timor!

# Dom Carlos Filipe Ximenes Belo

Having led the Timorese People to independence and assuming, for a period, the presidency of the Democratic Republic of Timor-Leste, Mr Kay Rala Xanana Gusmão, in the genuine spirit of serving the common Good of the people, has decided to found CNRT and run for the post of Prime Minister of Timor-Leste.

In addition to presiding over the Council of Ministers and holding the position of Minister for Defence, Xanana Gusmão has sought to ensure that his government holds frequent contacts with the people of Timor-Leste. Such contacts had the form of visits to sub-districts and districts, of meetings with Suco chiefs and with the people in general. Quite obviously, the people in these meetings wanted to hear their 'liberator', their leader of the Resistance, and, above all, their *Maun Boot*.

But there are important occasions in which leaders have to talk to the entire nation. The common good demands that leaders rule properly both in their actions and in their words. The common good requires that, at important and sometimes critical times, leaders should address the people either to call upon their collaboration in the construction of the country, in the maintenance of internal peace and security, or in international cooperation.

Prime Minister Xanana Gusmão has been properly discharging the function of a good communicator with authentic and convincing words. He seeks the well-being of all Timorese, for whom he fought so much during the terrible years of the Resistance and when he was in jail in Cipinang. For this reason, his speeches are full of patriotic love, of a sense to serve the people and of the capacity to mobilise his fellow-countrymen to consolidate independence, peace and reconciliation.

The Timorese will only stand to win if they manage to learn and apprehend properly the true contents of the speeches of Prime Minister Xanana Gusmão.

On my part, I congratulate the publishers for this second volume of Xanana Gusmão's Speeches. I wish that this book does not only reach the shelves of the government or ministries departments, but of all schools and universities, the offices of heads of hamlets and Suco chiefs. And to accomplish such *desideratum*, we hope that the versions in Tetun and Portuguese will soon be published to further benefit the people of Timor-Leste.

**Dom Carlos Filipe Ximenes Belo**
Nobel Peace Prize Laureate 1996
Porto, 12 November 2011

# His Excellency José Ramos-Horta

## O Maun Boot (The Elder Brother)

Let me start by saying: We owe much to Maun Boot Kay Rala Xanana Gusmão. Actually we owe everything. All of us living today in a free Motherland.

I know that Xanana would react to this statement with heartfelt emotion. He would say that we owe everything to the people. It is true that we wouldn't have prevailed over the adversities without the firm foundation underlying our struggle: the People. However, many peoples have resisted throughout history, and continue to resist to-date, raising themselves against tyrannies, too often only to be crushed and see their freedom being denied or continuously postponed.

Peoples who prevail over their enemies are those inspired and guided by leaders with vision; leaders who are capable of eloquently interpreting and materialising the dreams and aspirations of their people, leaders who can indicate the right path to be followed, who can organise and gear their power towards a clear, strategic objective.

Xanana experienced the invasion and occupation, the ideological debate, the internal wars and purges; he saw the people die; he heard fellow freedom fighters dissertations on Marxism-Leninism and 'Class Struggle'. In 1981, FRETILIN's Central Committee had been decimated. FALINTIL was devastated, the people handcuffed, ragged… Everything seemed to be lost.

Xanana survived the sieges and operations that took place in the years 1977-79. He took refuge in the Eastern Zone. From there he sent messengers and he himself risked his own life by walking, blood-soaked, through mountains and hamlets of the country in order to determine the whereabouts of his comrades-in-arms, to hear the people, to find out from the people whether they wanted to continue with the struggle.

And the people said 'yes', they wanted to continue fighting. Maun Boot reconstructed bridges within our divided and estranged communities. He reconstructed bridges with the Church and with all those who until 1981 were considered to be enemies and traitors.

This work is an invaluable and unique contribution to the history of Timor-Leste. It is worth noting that Xanana's political philosophy and vision preceded the end of the Cold War by one decade. And it can be said that from among the national liberation movements, Xanana and FRETILIN were pioneers in the world to renounce the one-party system and embrace democratic pluralism.

In the cases of Angola, Mozambique, Cape Verde, Guinea-Bissau, the Sandinist Front Nicaragua, and in many other examples in Asia, Africa and Latin America, the abandonment of the culture, and suppression, of the one-party system only took place at the end of the 80's and beginning of the 90's, following the implosion of Soviet Union.

When I learned of the decision of Xanana to withdraw from FRETILIN and turn FALINTIL into a non-partisan body, I sent him a message rebelling against such a decision. Still permeated with Fretilin culture, I failed to understand immediately the reason for the decision made by Xanana. A far-reaching historical decision.

As I reflect on such moments from 1981-1983, I had deep admiration for Xanana, who displays an uncommon intelligence and political acumen.

Many years on, in 2001, in a free Timor-Leste, I recall a conversation I had with a simple but experienced member of the Resistance about Xanana's decision to dissolve the then CNRT (National Council of Timorese Resistance).

I used to argue with Xanana that we should have transformed CNRT into a political party all the more because FRETILIN had abandoned CNRT after the August 2000 Congress. Xanana disagreed with my idea and thought that it would be more correct to promote democratic pluralism, to dissolve CNRT and, thereby, free the members of the Resistance so that they could join other political parties or create their own political parties.

A comrade of the Resistance, who accompanied Xanana for many years, replied calmly: 'During the years of the struggle, even at the most difficult times, Xanana would always take correct decisions; he would not fail in his strategic vision. We have learned to trust him'.

Nowadays I always think of what that member of the Resistance said, and of Xanana's decisions which revealed themselves to be of enormous benefit to our struggle and our independence.

This volume gathers speeches by Xanana Gusmão and reveals his vision for the wellbeing of the people whom he loves so much and to whom everything is owed.

**His Excellency José Ramos-Horta**
President of the Democratic Republic of Timor-Leste

# The Hon. Michael Kirby AC CMG

# The Self-determination of the People of Timor-Leste: Success on a Barren Landscape

## An important moment in world history

In 1975, steps were taken to absorb Timor-Leste in the Republic of Indonesia. For 22 years, the people of Timor-Leste resisted. The leader of the resistance movement, Xanana Gusmão, demanded that the people enjoy the right to self-determination of peoples, guaranteed by international law.

A conflict broke out. Xanana Gusmão was captured and imprisoned by the Indonesian authorities. The then President of Indonesia, President Suharto, declared: 'We will not move backwards ... even for one step [in respect of East Timor]. We are ready to face any challenge and hurdle, both from at home and abroad'. The position of the self-determination of the people of Timor-Leste as a former colonial territory of Portugal was contested on the battlefield, in the courts and before international public opinion.

In the last months of 1998, the new President of Indonesia, Bacharuddin Jusuf Habibie, invited public reflections upon the future of Indonesia's rule in East Timor. He referred to the heavy costs then being incurred to maintain subsidies in the province, to support the presence there of the Indonesian military as well as other government officials. He questioned whether such costs were outweighed by any measurable benefit to Indonesia. He pointed to the distinctiveness of the province of East Timor and the fact that it had not been part of the original 1945 boundaries of the Netherlands East Indies, wherein Indonesia had asserted its independence, and that of its peoples, from colonial rule. He raised the possibility of a democratic choice being given to the province as to whether it would remain within the Republic of Indonesia or not. This approach was generally consistent with President Habibie's broad policy of democratisation in Indonesia, following the conclusion of the long Suharto regime.

In consequence of these reflections, President Habibie, on 27 January 1999, made a formal request to the Secretary-General of the United Nations (Mr Kofi Annan) that the UN would supervise a referendum whereby the people of the province of East Timor would be given a choice as to their future. For this purpose, the former colonial power, Portugal, entered into discussions with Indonesia. On 5 May 1999, those discussions produced an agreement providing for the conduct of a popular referendum to afford the people in the province an option between remaining in Indonesia as a Special Autonomous Region or separating from that country.

The United Nations Mission in East Timor (UNAMET) was established to organise and monitor the proposed referendum. Nearly half a million electors were registered to vote, including more than 10,000 electors living outside Timor-Leste, many of them refugees from Indonesian rule. The voters were given two options: whether they accepted the proposed special autonomy for East Timor within the unitary state of the Republic of Indonesia, or whether they opted to separate from Indonesia. When the votes were counted, 21.5 per cent of the electors supported the proposed autonomous participation in Indonesia. However, a clear majority of 78.5 per cent voted for separation. They rejected autonomy within Indonesia. Approximately 95 per cent of the registered voters participated.

On 19 October 1999, the Indonesian government announced its acceptance of the referendum outcome. Indonesia proceeded to repeal the laws that had incorporated Timor-Leste in Indonesia. The United Nations established a Transitional Administration in East Timor (UNTAET), with the intent to proceed to full independence. Xanana Gusmão insisted on protection by the United Nations of the peoples of East Timor 'from a new genocide'. His release from incarceration in Jakarta was brought forward. And from May 2002 until May 2007, Gusmão served as the first President of the new independent nation of Timor-Leste. He now serves as its fourth Prime Minister. These offices constitute a tribute to his leadership of the people of Timor-Leste towards self-determination. The journey to this resolution was a troubled and uncomfortable one. However, it is one that I had the privilege of viewing from close up.

## Peoples' rights in the world

The modern expression of the right of peoples, under the rule of others, to assert, attain and enjoy self-determination has a number of sources. One of them is the *Declaration of Independence* of the people in the then British colonies and settlements of North America in 1776. That *Declaration* famously begins:

> 'When in the course of Human Events it becomes necessary for one people to dissolve the political bonds which have connected them with another ...'

The American Declaration was followed by a prolonged war in which the settlers asserted their independence. They ultimately prevailed against the British Crown. In a world of large and powerful (mainly European) empires, the idea of 'self-determination' was viewed with considerable suspicion.

The idea was, however, included in the *Fourteen Points* declared by President Woodrow Wilson as the Allied war aims in the First World War. The components of this assertion were hotly contested, including within the League of Nations established after the Great War. A committee of rapporteurs in 1919 declared that 'self-determination of peoples' was not a concept known to international law before that time.[1] Nevertheless, the idea gathered force between the two world wars. In a case concerning minority schools in Albania in 1935, the Permanent Court of International Justice gave recognition to a distinction between discriminatory laws and laws that were designed to safeguard the rights of indigenous minorities living within a state.[2]

Under pressure of a later American President, Franklin Delano Roosevelt, the Allied war aims during the Second World War included reference to an international order that would ensure 'self-determination for peoples living under foreign rule'.[3] Doubtless affected by the same influence, the *Charter* of the United Nations of 1945 was declared in the name of the 'peoples of the United Nations'. Its first article asserts that the purposes of the new international organisation included the maintenance of international peace and security and the development of:

> '... friendly relations among nations based on respect for the principles of equal rights and self-determination of peoples ...'[4]

Other provisions of the *Charter* made reference to the goal of the self-determination of peoples.⁵ Thus, Article 76 established a Trusteeship Council and system to promote the progressive advancement of trust territories (mostly colonies of defeated nations) towards self-government or independence, chosen according to:

> '... the freely expressed wishes of the peoples concerned ...' ⁶

In the drafting of the *International Bill of Rights* that, following the *Charter* and its creation of the United Nations Organisation, the Soviet Union repeatedly insisted on recognition of the right of self-determination, although as applicable only to colonial powers.⁷ Other European states demanded a reflection of the generality of the language of the *Charter*. In the end, a common first article found its way into the language both of the *International Covenant on Economic Social and Cultural Rights* and the *International Covenant on Civil and Political Rights*. The common first article of both Covenants states:

> 'All people have the right to self-determination. By virtue of that right, they freely determine their political status and freely pursue their economic, social and cultural development.'

A number of states opposed the adoption of the article in this form. They expressed fears that it would confer rights of secession on domestic minorities. Most experts did not concede such an interpretation or risk.⁸ In 1960, the General Assembly of the United Nations adopted the *Declaration on the Granting of Independence to Colonial Countries and Peoples*.⁹ Without dissent, it was agreed to condemn, as contrary to the *Charter* and as a 'denial of fundamental human rights', 'the subjection of *peoples* to alien subjugation, domination and exploitation'.

Thereafter, the United Nations Educational Scientific and Cultural Organisation (UNESCO) pursued an endeavour to give greater content to the notion of 'self-determination of peoples', so as to clarify some of the anxieties about it that had been expressed by countries with significant minorities in their populations.

This was the point at which I became involved in the attempt of UNESCO to describe (rather than to define) the concept of 'self-determination of peoples' for the purposes of international law. An Expert Group was established by UNESCO, initially chaired by Judge Kéba M'baye, then a Judge of the International Court of Justice, and a series of meetings of the Group was held. I attended in a personal capacity, being invited to be a member because of my background as a lawyer and judge and because I was a Commissioner, and then Chairman-elect, of the Executive Committee of the International Commission of Jurists in Geneva. Meetings of the Group were held in Paris and in Budapest, Hungary. The meetings had before them examinations of the topic of self-determination of peoples, including one by Professor Hector Gros Espiell.[10] Another was edited by Professor James Crawford of Australia,[11] and a further one was produced by Judge M'baye.[12] Ultimately, as a result of the UNESCO meetings, four criteria were endorsed as descriptions of the 'people' in international law who could validly assert a right of self-determination. These were:

1. The right belongs to peoples, not governments as such, and that for this purpose, the people asserting the right must be of sufficient number to constitute a 'people' for international law purposes;
2. The people concerned must have recognised institutions by which they express their identity and the assertion of the right to self-determination;
3. The people concerned must express the relevant determination by manifesting a will as to how the self-determination will be achieved and exercised; and
4. Although self-determination of peoples may, and frequently will, give rise to demands for autonomy or full political independence, this is not essential. Self-determination may be asserted within the political boundaries of a state comprising other peoples, wherein the people concerned may be a minority.

The foregoing descriptions were accepted by an international meeting of experts convened by UNESCO in November 1989.[13] They were reconsidered and refined in a further meeting of the experts held in Budapest in September 1991. It was against the background of these developments, in the 1990s, that I became involved in the legal issues surrounding the claims to self-determination of the people of Timor-Leste.

## Assertions of self-determination

June 1995 was a busy time for the legal question raised by the assertion of self-determination of the people of Timor-Leste. In that month, the International

Court of Justice, on 30 June 1995, decided the case brought against Australia by Portugal, the latter purporting to act as colonial power on behalf of the people of Timor-Leste. By a majority of 12 judges to two, the Court concluded that it could not adjudicate upon the dispute referred to it by Portugal. The majority of the Court held that, in the absence of Indonesia, Portugal did not have the legal standing necessary to maintain its proceedings.

Nevertheless, the Court re-affirmed the importance in international law of the peoples' right to self-determination. Portugal's case had asserted that, by negotiating, and ratifying, a treaty with the Republic of Indonesia governing the exploitation of the continental shelf of the Timor Gap, Australia had violated the rights to self-determination of the people of East Timor, as well as the rights of Portugal, as the lawful colonial, administering power in East Timor.[14]

Whilst dismissing the proceedings brought by Portugal, the majority of the International Court remarked:

> 'Portugal's assertion that the right of peoples to self-determination, as it evolved from the **Charter** and from the United Nations practice, has an **erga omnes** character, [and] is irreproachable. The principle of self-determination of peoples has been recognised by the United Nations **Charter** and in the jurisprudence of the Court ... [and] it is one of the essential principles of contemporary international law.'

Even Indonesia did not contest the principle or the necessity of an act of self-determination in the case of East Timor. It claimed that such an act of self-determination had in fact occurred following its entry into East Timor on 7 December 1975, purportedly to settle civil unrest. Thereafter, Indonesia had convened a 'Peoples' Representative Assembly', constituted of elected members. Indonesia asserted that, on 31 May 1976, the Assembly had decided, on behalf of the people of East Timor, to become independent of Portugal through integration into the Republic of Indonesia. The request by the Assembly to the Republic of Indonesia to that end was accepted by the government and legislature of Indonesia on 17 July 1976. East Timor then became the twenty-seventh province of the Republic of Indonesia.

Few countries recognised the legality of this 'act of self-determination'. The United Nations itself did not accept the 'integration' of East Timor into Indonesia. In 1975, the General Assembly, and, in 1976, the Security Council, condemned Indonesia's purported actions. Over the following years, numerous resolutions of the relevant United Nations organs repeated their condemnation of the act of absorption. The United Nations did what it could during this period, by sending special rapporteurs of the then Human Rights Commission, and by appointing a Special Representative of the Secretary-General for East Timor (Mr F. Vendrell). However, during the presidency of Mr Suharto, no real progress was made.

## Action plan in the Portuguese Parliament

Also in June 1995, just before the decision of the International Court, a large conference was convened in the chamber of the Parliament of Portugal. In my capacity as Chairman of the Executive Committee of the International Commission of Jurists, I attended and addressed the conference. Other Australians participating included senators and members of the House of Representatives of the Parliament of Australia, representing the three major political parties in the Australian Parliament. In all, there were representatives of 33 parliaments in attendance in Lisbon, including six from the former overseas territories of Portugal, whose shields (like that of Timor) decorated the wall of the Portuguese Parliamentary Chamber.

In my address, I collected some practical suggestions, made by the participants, for the way forward. This became an *Action Plan* that was adopted by the Lisbon meeting. It was titled the 'Lisbon Declaration of the International Inter-Parliamentary Conference on East Timor'.[15] The Declaration called on the Republic of Indonesia to abide by relevant United Nations resolutions. It also called on the United Nations to ensure respect for the human rights of the people in East Timor. Specifically, it condemned the sale of arms to Indonesia. And, it demanded an immediate release of Mr Xanana Gusmão and other political prisoners, held in custody in Indonesia and in East Timor.

The *Action Plan* set forth steps that could be taken by other national parliaments to support the cause of self-determination in Timor-Leste. Amongst those steps were:
- The adoption of parliamentary resolutions calling for the true exercise of the right to self-determination of the people of East Timor;

- The proposal of parliamentary missions for the same purpose;
- The establishment of parliamentary committees to receive reports and to focus attention on East Timor;
- The raising of the position of East Timor with major investors in Indonesia;
- The encouragement of common cause with other groups denied self-determination;
- The request to the United Nations Secretary-General to call on the Government of Indonesia to comply with the recommendations of his Special Rapporteur and Representative;
- The request to the newly appointed UN High Commissioner for Human Rights to visit East Timor and to report publicly on his findings;
- The establishment of an information exchange on domestic parliamentary resolutions on East Timor;
- The making of representations to the International Committee of the Red Cross and UNICEF to increase their presence in East Timor;
- The calling on the Inter-Parliamentary Union (IPU) to add the issues of East Timor to its concerns; and
- The encouragement of the establishment of an international Eminent Persons Group to visit East Timor and Indonesia and to consult with relevant actors, especially Mr Gusmão.[16]

The foregoing *Action Plan* was taken up repeatedly in Australia, Portugal and other countries by the International Commission of Jurists, Lawasia, Amnesty International[17] and other civil society bodies. Although the efforts in pursuit of the *Action Plan* did not alter the stance of Indonesia under President Suharto, there can be little doubt that the maintenance of international agitation and objections constituted a factor in the evolving charge of heart within Indonesia. It was that change of heart, together with the pressure of freedom fighters in Timor-Leste, that finally facilitated the change of direction signalled by President Habibie and given effect by the referendum that led to the independence of Timor-Leste.

# Conclusion: a success story

The world is replete with peoples, many of them formerly ruled by colonial masters, who have unrequited demands for self-determination. Often their cries for enjoyment of this basic right of justice in international law go unheard and unfulfilled, except amongst their followers, their families and a few supporters. Against this background, the achievement of self-determination by Timor-Leste is a shining beacon of what can be secured by a combination of political (and military) activism, political and cultural solidarity, media persuasion and civil society engagement.

Through all these efforts, and the ups and downs that they witnessed, the dignity, example and leadership of Xanana Gusmão shone forth. These qualities still constitute a cause for inspiration and encouragement for his own people and for oppressed and neglected peoples around the world. I am proud to join others in paying tribute to Prime Minister Gusmão. But he would surely agree that the greatest tributes belong to the people of Timor-Leste. It is they, and not governments or military or forces or powers, that enjoy the right of self-determination provided by international law. And when they secured the chance, they exercised that right. And the world is witness to the success of the transition that followed.

*The Hon.* **Michael Kirby** *AC CMG*
Justice of the High Court of Australia (1996–2009); International Commission of Jurists, Geneva, President (1995–98), and Chair (1991–95) of the Executive Committee
December 2011

# Major General (Retd) Michael G. Smith AO

Kay Rala Xanana Gusmão was released from custody by Indonesia to return to East Timor on 21 October 1999. He arrived in Díli wearing his military uniform as the former commander of the FALINTIL military resistance movement (*Forças Armadas de Libertação Nacional de Timor-Leste*), and as the head of the political resistance coalition known as the CNRT (*Conselno Nacional de Resistencia*). Whether intended or not, Xanana's return in this dual capacity signalled his conviction that the new nation's future (which included FALINTIL's transition to a regular defence force) would depend on security and political circumstances.

It would take a monumental effort, however, for the country to develop and for its people to earn a sustainable peace. In the violence that had immediately followed the UN-supervised 'popular consultation' (ballot) in August 1999, the country had been almost totally destroyed and the population displaced. It would take time for the international community and the Timorese people to restore security and confidence, and more than two years for domestic political processes to mature so as to enable democratic elections and the proclamation of independence on 20 May 2002. During this interregnum, the International Force for East Timor (INTERFET), so ably led by Major General Peter Cosgrove from Australia, restored security, followed by the United Nations Transitional Administration in East Timor (UNTAET), led by the charismatic Sergio Vieira De Mello, which was assigned the unprecedented and herculean task of governing and preparing a state for independence.

In this uncertain political and security environment, no provision had been made by the international community to recognise and reward FALINTIL for maintaining the nation's struggle for independence, and to transition the resistance movement into a modern defence force. For many months following the ballot, FALINTIL had voluntarily cantoned itself in Aileu and honoured its commitment not to become involved in political activities. Living in deplorable conditions of uncertainty that tested the discipline of its soldiers and strained the leadership of its commanders, the resistance movement was largely ignored by humanitarian agencies because of its military nature. The international community failed to recognise the stature of FALINTIL amongst the people as both the reason and symbol for the Timorese struggle for independence over 24 years. After considerable effort, and demonstrating incredible patience and negotiating skills by the Timorese, steps were finally taken in mid-2000 to commence the difficult transition of FALINTIL to a regular defence force under the capable leadership of its commander, Taur Matan Ruak. That force ultimately became known as F-FDTL (*FALINTIL-Forças Nacional de Timor-Leste*).

With the proclamation of independence in 2002, the newest nation on earth was also one of the poorest and most fragile, distinguished by extremely low literacy and education, and characterised by a multiplicity of languages, poor food security, high mortality rates, a subsistence economy, inadequate infrastructure and appalling health statistics. The initial euphoria of independence and freedom waned as the new Democratic Republic of Timor-Leste struggled to achieve national unity, placate popular aspirations, build the institutions of government and the rule of law, develop its security forces, strengthen internal security, initiate truth and reconciliation processes, confirm and implement a poverty reduction development plan, normalise relations with Indonesia, and implement a 'corruption-free' system for future oil revenues from the Timor Sea, as well as deliver employment, education and basic services to urban and rural communities that had a burgeoning youthful population. These challenges were enormous, and, as is common with countries in post-conflict situations, numerous setbacks occurred along the way. A serious breakdown of internal security occurred in Díli in 2006, caused by disagreement and disaffection within and between elements of F-FDTL and Timor's fragile police force, known as PNTL (*Policia Nacional de Timor-Leste*). This deterioration in security was fuelled by youth gang violence and serious political differences between political leaders and parties. An international assistance force, again led by Australia, was deployed at the request of the Timorese Government to restore security, but the extent of displacement and uncertainty ultimately led to the fall of the Fretilin Government under Mari Alkatiri, and the peaceful election of Xanana Gusmão as Prime Minister, following his decision to step down as President. His place was taken by the internationally renowned Nobel peace laureate, José Ramos-Horta, who had capably served as Foreign Minister and then as interim Prime Minister. An unsuccessful but near fatal attempt on the new President's life in 2008 by a former rogue commander of F-FDTL successfully finalised the re-establishment of security from the 2006 disruption.

I first met Xanana in Díli in January 2000, when I assumed my appointment as the Deputy Force Commander of the UNTAET peacekeeping force, which replaced INTERFET. During and after my time in Timor, I came to know, respect and admire Xanana. A deep strategic thinker of great humility and compassion, he is both a reluctant yet charismatic leader. As shown repeatedly throughout the speeches in this volume, Xanana's unwavering commitment to his people was founded on his passionate conviction of Timor's distinctive political and cultural identity. This driving belief has motivated and sustained him through both triumph and travail. Xanana's repeated references to sovereignty, security and national identity, and the Timorese struggle to achieve independence and eventual prosperity, resonate throughout many of the speeches in this collection.

In our various discussions, Xanana enlightened me on the legacy of 450 years of Portuguese rule. He argued that it was not what Portugal had (or had not) done to develop Timor, but rather that political and social circumstances in Portuguese Timor were distinctive from other parts of the Indonesian archipelago. The Timorese, he argued, were in no way superior, but they were different from their neighbours in West Timor and from other communities in Indonesia. Timor's distinctive identity had been evident throughout the years of Indonesian occupation, particularly by the continued use of the Portuguese language by FALINTIL, the clandestine movement, and the diaspora.

In Xanana's view, it was essential that Timor's distinctiveness be recognised, and more so, given Timor's geopolitical circumstances as a small and poor country located between the regional powers of Indonesia and Australia. Xanana's acute understanding of Timor's strategic situation is repeated in several of his speeches in this collection. As with other Timorese leaders, Xanana is mindful that his small country had twice been occupied against its will by external powers (Japan and Indonesia). Consequently, those who have failed to acknowledge the relevance of Timor's Portuguese heritage also failed to understand the strategic rationale behind struggle of the Timorese people. In many of his speeches, Xanana emphasises the necessity for Timor-Leste to become an active member of ASEAN and other regional fora, but he is also supported by most Timorese leaders in seeking active membership of the lusophone world: this, he explains, will help strengthen Timor-Leste's global connectivity and enhance its standing within the United Nations and other international fora. The importance of this Portuguese connection is a consistent theme that runs through many of Xanana's speeches in this volume, including his presentation in Díli in 2008 to the Tenth Meeting of the Ministers of Defence of CPLP.

The international community may not universally have understood or even fully agreed with the decision by the Timorese leadership at independence to retain its Portuguese heritage, yet, as this collection of speeches suggests, this decision was deliberate and strategic: the country's future security against external aggression, they decided, would be more assured if Timor-Leste's identity could be emphasised and strong international support retained.

Xanana's speeches also reveal, in part, some of his other qualities. His motivational presentation to the cadets at Japan's National Defense Academy, Tokyo, in March 2009, has particular resonance because it is based on the lessons learned from his own military experience. He cleverly explains and emphasises the absolute necessity for military discipline and courage, but at the same time candidly illustrates his true feelings by confessing his reluctance to soldiering. Xanana explains that he and his colleagues put off military service in Portuguese Timor for as long as possible, eventually undertaking it only to 'avoid being conscripted to go to war' in distant colonies. Once conscripted, however, Xanana realised the critical importance of political direction for military success, and he explains how this shaped his leadership of FALINTIL and 'was the turning point for our Resistance'. He talks persuasively about guerrilla warfare, and of the importance of waging this in concert with diplomatic initiatives. Unlike most guerrilla movements, FALINTIL was denied the luxury of geographic sanctuaries across the border, and it was afforded no external pipeline of armaments and equipment. To continue the struggle, FALINTIL had to capture weapons and ammunition from the Indonesians, and it could only survive through the support of the civilian clandestine movement. Xanana displays his strategic acumen by relating these lessons to the challenges ahead for Timor-Leste. He explains that FALINTIL's transition to a regular force needed to be based on 'improved training and education – vital components for our reform', and that this transition would have to be nested within the reform of the entire security sector 'which includes internal security, national defence, intelligence and civil protection'. By linking the past to contemporary challenges, Xanana cleverly emphasises the need for national resilience: 'The current "struggle" that Timor-Leste faces is different from that of the past, but it is not necessarily easier, and once more requires the engagement of all Timorese'.

In this collection, Xanana's messages to foreign audiences are reiterated in greater detail in a number of his speeches to domestic audiences. For example, his presentation on 'Reviewing Resistance and Understanding the Present', delivered in November 2010 to the Pilot Course on Defence and Security, explains in detail the constitutional basis for the country's national security policies and structure. As well, Xanana emphasises the central importance of national unity and sacrifice to the country's future in his speeches that commemorate the deeds of past commanders and in the promotion of commanders to foster renewal.

This collection of Xanana's speeches indicates something about the man, and more about the challenges ahead for Timor-Leste. However, for those of us who already know something of Xanana, this collection is a modest testament to his leadership and character. Like other great leaders, Xanana has shown by example the importance of forgiveness. It is not about forgetting the past or granting impunity to those who have caused suffering; rather, it is about understanding the past and learning how to move forward into the future. Xanana once told me that he had learnt a great deal from his incarceration in Indonesia, partly through reflection of Timor's circumstances but also through understanding the plight of others and the different perspectives of fellow humans. Xanana extols many roles: political leader, military commander, philosopher, poet, husband and father. But mostly he is a listener and a thinker, and a humble and modest fellow human being who is passionate about doing what he can for his country and his people. He understands well the need for Timor-Leste to develop its next generation of political leaders in a democratic manner without the fear of violence or retribution.

*Major General (Retd)* **Michael G. Smith** *AO*

# Kay Rala Xanana Gusmão

Date of Birth: 20 June 1946
Place of Birth: Manatuto, Timor-Leste

Kay Rala Xanana Gusmão was born on June 20, 1946 in Manatuto, Timor-Leste (East Timor). He was raised in the country, with a brother and five sisters. His father was a schoolteacher. He completed primary and started secondary school at the Catholic mission of "Nossa Senhora de Fátima" in Dare and then went on to Díli. He started to work very early in life, mornings as a chartered surveyor and afternoons teaching at the Chinese school. In April 1974 he joined the staff of "A Voz de Timor" (the Voice of Timor).

After the Carnation Revolution in Portugal on 25th April 1974, and faced with the opportunity for self-determination and independence, Kay Rala Xanana Gusmão decided to join the newly formed Associação Social Democrata –ASDT (Social Democrat Association) which was later that same year transformed into the Revolutionary Front for an Independent Timor-Leste (FRETILIN). Having worked as a journalist and photographer, Kay Rala Xanana Gusmão took on the party's job of Deputy-Director of the Department of Information.

On December 7, 1975, after a series of border-armed incursions into the territory of Timor-Leste, Indonesia decided to invade the capital, Díli. Following the death of the then President of FRETILIN, Nicolau Lobato in December 1978, and coupled with the loss of a majority of the Central Committee Members of FRETILIN, Kay Rala Xanana Gusmão was left with the task of reorganising the struggle. In March 1981, he organised the first National Conference of the FRETILIN, during which he was elected leader of the Resistance and Commander-in-Chief of the FALINTIL (National Liberation Armed Forces of Timor-Leste). In March 1983, Kay Rala Xanana Gusmão demonstrated his pragmatism by initiating formal negotiations with the Indonesian Armed Forces (ABRI/TNI) leading to a cease-fire, which lasted until August the same year.

He conceived and implemented the Policy of National Unity that translated into active cooperation with members of the Catholic Church and with the transitional authorities of Timor-Leste. Kay Rala Xanana Gusmão took advantage of the five-month cease-fire to develop the first organised national clandestine network, known in Portuguese as 'Frente Clandestina'. In 1988, the success of the initiative for National Unity prompted Kay Rala Xanana Gusmão to create the CNRM - National Council of Maubere Resistance, as an expression of a non-partisan national command of the struggle; CNRM later became CNRT, National Council of Timorese Resistance.

A year after the Santa Cruz massacre, Kay Rala Xanana Gusmão, after 17 years of guerrilla warfare, was captured on November 20, 1992 in the capital Díli. Faced with international commendation, Kay Rala Xanana Gusmão faced a kangaroo-court trial and was imprisoned in a prison reserved for criminals only, but amid pressure from the international community, the Indonesian authorities were forced to transfer him to Cipinang prison reserved for political prisoners.

In prison, Xanana Gusmão devoted his time to the elaboration of the strategies of the Resistance, while studying Bahasa Indonesia (the Indonesian language), English and Law. He also painted and wrote poetry, cultivating a talent already recognised in 1975 when he won the Timor Poetry Prize with his poem "*Mauberíadas*". Some of his paintings were sold, the payment of which was donated to the Resistance at Xanana Gusmão's request. In 1994, some of his political essays were published in a book, *Timor-Leste - um Povo, uma Pátria*, (East Timor - a People, a Nation) Ed. Colibri, Lisbon.

In April 1998, at the East Timorese National Convention in the Diaspora, which established the National Council of Timorese Resistance (CNRT), Xanana Gusmão was reaffirmed by acclamation as leader of the East Timorese Resistance and President of CNRT.

Following increasing international pressure to release him and the statement by President Habibie of Indonesia on granting independence to Timor-Leste if the outcome of a popular consultation was to reject the autonomy plan proposed by his government, Kay Rala Xanana Gusmão was transferred from Cipinang Prison to house arrest in Salemba, Central Jakarta, on 10 February 1999.

The rapid development of the East Timorese political process and the generalised international recognition of Gusmão's statesmanship and leadership were the reasons for the numerous visits to his prison-house by foreign government representatives, including US Secretary of State, Madeleine Albright, former US President, Jimmy Carter, Australian Foreign Minister, Alexander Downer, and Japanese Foreign Minister, Masahiko Komura.

The UN-sponsored referendum on 30 August 1999, which overwhelmingly rejected the autonomy proposal put forth by Indonesia, signalled the end of the Indonesian occupation of Timor-Leste and the beginning of the transitional process led by the UN in Timor-Leste. This was undoubtedly the first democratic act in Timor-Leste's history.

Kay Rala Xanana Gusmão was released from house arrest on 7 September 1999.

In August 2000, the First National Congress of CNRT, held in Díli, elected Kay Rala Xanana Gusmão President of the CNRT/National Congress. From November 2000 to April 2001, Kay Rala Xanana Gusmão was the Speaker of the National Council, an all-Timorese legislative body of the Transitional Administration of East Timor, comprised of political party, civil society representatives, pro-autonomy groups and representatives from several religious beliefs.

The CNRT/CN was dissolved on 9 June 2001. After the dissolution of CNRT/CN, Kay Rala Xanana Gusmão focused his efforts on the AVR – Association of Resistance Veterans, - an organisation that encompasses former members of the clandestine network and aims to create conditions for their skilled participation in the country's development process.

On 14 April 2002, Kay Rala Xanana Gusmão was elected President of Timor-Leste and was sworn-in as the President of the Democratic Republic of Timor-Leste on 20 May 2002. He served as President of the Republic until the end of his term of office in May 2007.

After leaving the Presidency, Kay Rala Xanana Gusmão was elected President of the newly established political party formed in April 2007, CNRT - 'National Congress for the Reconstruction of Timor-Leste'. For the whole month of June, Kay Rala Xanana Gusmão campaigned during the legislative elections across the country. On 30$^{th}$ June, the legislative elections were held and in the final results, CNRT received the second highest number of votes and immediately formed an alliance with three other parties - PD (Democratic Party) and the ASDT-PSD Coalition called the AMP (Alliance with Parliamentary Majority), thus securing 37 out of the 65 seats in the National Parliament.

On 3$^{rd}$ August 2007, H.E. Dr. José Ramos-Horta, President of the Republic, officially invited the AMP to form the next Government.

On 8th August 2007 at the Lahane Presidential Palace, the IV Constitutional Government was sworn-in with Kay Rala Xanana Gusmão as Prime Minister and Minister for Defence and Security of the Democratic Republic of Timor-Leste. The Government's term of office ends in 2012.

## Prizes

| | |
|---|---|
| 1975 | East Timor Poetry Prize |
| 1999 | European Parliament Sakharov Prize |
| 2000 | Kwangju (South Korea) Peace Prize |
| 2000 | Sydney Peace Prize |
| 2002 | North-South Prize, North-South Observatory (European Union) |
| 2002 | UNESCO Félix Houphouët-Boigny Peace Prize |
| 2002 | 'Honorary Adult Friend', Children's Award, Sweden |
| 2003 | 2003 Path to Peace Award, Path to Peace Foundation |
| 2003 | International Herald Tribune "Leadership with Integrity" Award |
| 2003 | BusinessWeek "Stars of Asia" Award |

## Awards

| | |
|---|---|
| 1995 | Honorary Citizen of Brasília, Brazil |
| 1998 | Order of Freedom, Portugal |
| 1998 | Honorary Citizen of São Paulo, Brazil |
| 1999 | Honorary Doctorate, Lusíada University, Lisbon, Portugal |
| 2000 | Order of Merit, New Zealand |
| 2000 | Honorary Citizen of Lisbon, Portugal; awarded Gold Key of Lisbon City |
| 2000 | Medal of the Vice-Presidency of the Federative Republic of Brazil |
| 2000 | Order of Merit José Bonifácio, Grau de Gran-Oficial, University of the State of Rio Janeiro |
| 2000 | Honorary Doctorate, University of Oporto, Portugal |
| 2002 | Grande Colar da Ordem do Cruzeiro do Sul, Brazil |
| 2003 | Honorary Degree of Doctorate of Laws, Victoria University |
| 2003 | Honorary Knighthood of the Grand Cross of the Order of St. Michael & St. George |
| 2004 | Honorary Law Doctorate Degree, Suncheon National University, Korea |

| | |
|---|---|
| 2006 | Grande Colar da Ordem de Dom Infante, Portugal |
| 2006 | Honorary Philosophy Doctorate Degree, University of Takushoku, Japan |
| 2011 | Grand Cross of the Order of Ipiranga, Brazil |
| 2011 | Order of Vanuatu first Class Medal, Vanuatu |
| 2011 | Honorary Doctorate, University of Coimbra, Portugal |

Last updated: October 2011

- Married Emilia Batista, 1969 (div) 2 Children
- Married Kirsty Sword Gusmão, 2000, 3 Children

# The Third Anniversary of the IV Constitutional Government

Main Hall, Lahane Palace
6 August 2010

>Your Excellency the President of the Republic
>Your Excellencies the Vice Presidents of the National Parliament
>Your Excellency the President of the Court of Appeal
>Your Excellencies the Bishops of the Dioceses of Díli and Baucau
>Distinguished Members of Parliament
>Distinguished Members of Government
>Your Excellencies the Directors
>Your Excellencies the Presidents of the Independent State Bodies
>Your Excellency the Chief of the Defence Force
>Your Excellency the Commander of the PNTL
>Your Excellencies the Members of the Defence and Security Forces
>Your Excellency the Special Representative of the Secretary-General of the United Nations
>Your Excellencies the Members of the Diplomatic Corps and Representatives of International Agencies
>Your Excellencies the Representatives of the Civil Society, the NGOs, the Media and the Private Sector
>Ladies and Gentlemen
>People of Timor-Leste,

First and foremost, I would like to thank you, Your Excellency, the President of the Republic, for your kindness in giving us your time and this venue for this simple ceremony.

Secondly, I would like to express my deep appreciation and thank all of you who have come here today, which demonstrates the sense of collective responsibility that guides us to meet the higher interests of our People.

This ceremony is not a celebration. But it will serve to reflect upon the three years of governance of the IV Constitutional Government. And I can say that an environment of increased national stability and of demonstrated confidence and democratic maturity, factors important and fundamental for our Country, was achieved thanks to the intervention of the President of the Republic as well as the organs of national sovereignty, and especially the role of the political parties as well as that of the Church and Civil Society and, above all, our People.

The AMP Government assumed three years ago the commitment to fulfil a reformist policy agenda that would guarantee to the Country, and above all to future generations, a promising program of social and economic development. And it is in this context that we are gathered here to reflect and evaluate whether or not we have responded in a positive way to the expressed political will for change.

Your Excellencies

Ladies and Gentlemen,

The merging of four political projects into one Government Program (which in 2008 was further strengthened with the addition of UNDERTIM) sought as a priority to systematize structuring reforms in vital sectors for national development, namely:

- The Reform of the Defence and Security Sector in order to ensure national stability;
- The Reform of State Management so as to improve governance;
- The Reform of the Social Justice System to ensure social assistance to the most vulnerable groups and the recognition of the National Liberation Heroes;
- The Reform of Basic Infrastructure enabling, among other things, the start of economic growth; and
- The Reform of the Private Sector promoting strategic partnerships between it and the Government, to promote sustainable development.

The first step for achieving this goal was the creation of a multi-disciplinary team, including a significant number of independent professionals, supported by a series of political principles and values that would bring together two vital aspects for the consolidation of a stable and responsible Government: restoring the confidence of the People in the Agencies of the State as a step to returning the power of decision making to those same People.

Despite the criticisms, which are sometimes unfair but other times needed, I must say that the men and women of this Government knew how to carry out their duties with dedication, having been tireless in the search for solutions to the challenges that they faced. They may not have achieved everything but they did their duty and they gave their best!

It is also with conviction that I can affirm that, without the contribution of a strong opposition and without the participation of an increasingly more sophisticated Civil Society, as is occurring in our country, we would not have taken the leap in the direction of our affirmation as a sovereign State ruled by the values of transparency and good governance.

After three years of continued effort and commitment by the State Agencies and Civil Society, ALL OF US have been moving Timor-Leste from the group of countries in ongoing conflict and with general suffering and attained very significant achievements, which have been acknowledged internationally.

Excellencies

Ladies and Gentlemen,

At this stage, I would like to remind everyone of some the Government's achievements that we accomplished during the three years of the mandate.

Firstly, we have ensured political and social stability, including the resolution of national security problems and the introduction of comprehensive reform in the sector of defence and security.

As you know, security and economic development walk hand in hand, since, without peace, tranquillity and confidence among the People, it is impossible to undertake the necessary steps for the economic, social and political growth of the Country.

Therefore, in 2007 and 2008, and in accordance with our Government Program, we gave absolute priority to the sector of security and defence.

I must give a word of appreciation to the F-FDTL and to PNTL, which, through the creation of the Joint Operational Command during this troubled period in our Country's recent history, acted in a remarkable and extremely cooperative manner, in constant dialogue with the People, and were able to find the best solutions to meet the reality of our situation.

By solving these complex problems, we finally started to see a glimpse of national stability. This, along with the spirit of institutional cooperation and solidarity, enabled us to attain two major achievements: restoring the confidence of the population in State Agencies and restoring the image of Timor-Leste before the international community.

Secondly, we began 2008 as the year of Administrative Reform. And so, we made various legislative, administrative and financial reforms, reformed procedures, systems, processes and governance mechanisms, and established new Commissions to ensure the professionalism and transparency of the Civil Service.

As the Civil Service is a vital component of our economy and promotes economic growth, we focused on its technical capability and administrative competence, i.e., productivity, professionalism, integrity and efficiency in Public Administration.

The primary outcome of this approach was the establishment of the Civil Service Commission, to seek to depoliticize the civil service and to instil a culture of professionalism, merit-based promotion and, consequently, the provision of better services to our communities.

The path is long but we have confidence that we are going in the right direction. And I would like to take this opportunity to express the recognition of the IV Constitutional Government for the contribution of the civil service, and especially the Director Generals and the national and regional directors. Without your efforts, we would never have been able to achieve what we have to date.

Importantly, we also established the Anti-Corruption Commission, which is an independent body reporting to the National Parliament with strong and effective powers to fight corruption. This Commission has a vital role to play in improving governance, which is strategically crucial for us to efficiently mobilise our national resources to achieve economic growth and social development.

In addition, in regard to public administration reforms, we gave special attention to the Ministry of Finance, which has been significantly improving its systems and procedures. And further, the Ministry of Finance is decentralizing its powers and responsibilities in the areas of budget, procurement and treasury to line ministries, resulting, among other things, in a significant improvement in budget execution rates.

Thirdly, we started the process of paying pensions and allowances to our Veterans and National Heroes, our elderly citizens, our widows, our orphans and other more vulnerable groups of Timorese society.

Implementing these measures of social justice, for the first time, is essential for national stability and allows us to, by investing in the current generation, create the conditions for a next generation that is more educated, healthier and more prosperous.

By acknowledging the vital role our veterans played in the construction of the Nation, and by supporting our elderly and other vulnerable groups, we are also investing in our human capital, allowing many families to have access to health, education and wellbeing. And we are also contributing to the creation of small businesses, thereby further alleviating poverty.

Fourthly, we have started an ambitious plan of planning and surveying the need for basic infrastructure that are fundamental to the delivery of education and health services, agricultural and industrial development and employment creation.

Also in this sector, we have started a bold project to generate electricity and energy in order to supply electricity to the entire Country.

Fifthly, at the same time we removed the first of the obstacles to the development of the private sector, i.e., ensuring security and stability in the Country and increasing the confidence to invest. We have started an open dialogue with national businesspeople, listening to their needs and difficulties, and, importantly, we supported the establishment of the Chamber of Commerce and Industry to improve and build this sector even further.

We are also following initiatives for the establishment of consortiums that will give more capacity to our companies.

We have also implemented the Referendum Package, which is a completely innovative measure that, among other things, enabled us to know and evaluate our local businesspeople better, and develop the private sector, particularly in rural areas. This initiative will be continued in the Decentralized Development Package.

This initiative is part of a gradual process to build the capacity of businesses and the local communities themselves, which will have a vital role to play in the identification and implementation of these projects, ensuring the delivery of increasingly more professional and better services.

We need to nurture employment creation, develop the economy and improve basic infrastructure, social responsibility and broad participation in a decentralized manner, as well as encourage development in rural areas.

Employment cannot be created by way of decrees, and it is employment that will enable us to reduce poverty in our Country. Hence, the investments we are making are vital for creating jobs.

Your Excellencies

Ladies and Gentlemen,

During the three years of the mandate by this Government, we have increased public investment, which enabled our towns and districts to grow; the creation of new jobs and the improvement of agricultural productivity; the growth of our tourism industry; the construction of houses, roads, schools and health clinics; the opening of shops and small businesses and the increase in the purchasing power of the Timorese.

And it was because of this public investment that, in 2008, despite the serious financial crisis that affected the entire world, Timor-Leste managed to be ranked as the second-fastest growing economy in the world — after only Qatar — with a growth rate of 12.8 per cent, and continued to have a two-digit growth rate in 2009.

As Prime Minister of the IV Constitutional Government, I would like to give you my word of honour that the Government will not rest on its laurels.

On the contrary, we are encouraged to do more and better, being aware that these last two years until the end of our mandate will require great effort, given the challenges to delivering the commitments we made in the Government Program.

As I travel the Country from East to West, I think all the time about what Timor-Leste wants to be twenty years from now.

I believe it is a Country dedicated to the hydrocarbon industry, supported by other small industries. A Country with an urban expansion that is well distributed throughout the territory, and with rural urbanisation enabling the populations to live in communities where the delivery of basic services reaches every citizen.

The Strategic Development Plan will be essential for improving production, production capabilities and productive employment opportunities, by way of:
- the modernization of agriculture
- the increment of industry
- the provision of social services
- the development of human capital

Ladies and Gentlemen,

It is up to all of you and to the People of Timor-Leste to reflect whether the programs that have been implemented are adequate to respond to the needs of the Nation. It is up to us as Government to correct that which could be better and to continue selflessly to serve the People with boldness and ambition.

When we are talking about serving our beloved Timorese People, of sowing hope for a better future for our children, we can only be ambitious, we can only dream big.

# The Ceremony for the Tenth Anniversary of the PNTL

Government Palace, Díli
27 March 2010

> Your Excellency the President of the Republic, Mr José Ramos-Horta,
> Your Excellency the Speaker of the National Parliament, Mr Fernando Lasama de Araújo,
> Your Excellency the Secretary of State for Security, Mr Francisco Guterres,
> Your Excellency the Chief of the Defence Force, Major-General Taur Matan Ruak,
> Your Excellency the Representative of the Secretary General of the UN, Ms Ameerah Haq,
> Your Excellency the Commander of the United Nations Police, Superintendent Luís Carrilho,
> Illustrious Members of Government,
> Illustrious Members of Parliament,
> Representatives of the Diplomatic Body,
> Your Excellency the Commander of the PNTL, Commissioner Longuinhos Monteiro,
> Officers, NCOs and Members of the PNTL,

Precisely one year ago, at this same location, when we were celebrating the ninth anniversary of the National Police of Timor-Leste, I listed three major challenges that the Police would face and for which they would have to prepare.

The first was appointing a new Commander and a new Deputy Commander, which entered into office at that ceremony. This was a movement towards strong leadership and discipline in the PNTL.

The second concerned the entry into force of the new Organic Law for the PNTL, which included a new police model that was rather different from the previous one.

The third concerned the proximity of the moment when the executive responsibility for the Country's internal security would start to be transferred from UNPOL to the PNTL.

I have no doubt whatsoever, and I think no one else does, that choosing Commissioner Longuinhos Monteiro to lead the PNTL was an excellent decision.

In very little time, Commissioner Longuinhos Monteiro managed to integrate himself in the spirit of a Police Body and to earn the respect and admiration of the men and women placed under his command.

Under Commissioner Longuinhos Monteiro, the PNTL started a process of reorganization and restructuring, and it is clear that in the past year they have acquired rather satisfying levels of operational and intervention capability. These are indicators that they are on the right path.

The last police operations in which PNTL members were included, namely the ones that recently took place in the Districts of Cova Lima and Bobonaro, putting an end to a surge of violent crime that threatened to cause panic among the populations, showed that our Police are ready to take on new responsibilities.

Under the leadership of Commissioner Longuinhos Monteiro, who was in direct command of the operations in the field that led to the capture of the criminals, the PNTL showed the naysayers that they are able to ensure the safety of the populations according to the limits set by Law and in compliance with the most elementary rights of citizens.

I would like to congratulate the Commander for this first year at the helm of the PNTL, and I hope you will continue to be as successful in the future.

The new Organic Law for the PNTL set a new police model based essentially on three aspects: chain of command, hierarchy and discipline.

This last year has shown us that this model is undoubtedly the best for our Police.

The existence of a clearly defined chain of command where the power to make decisions and the accountability for their execution is attributed directly to the leader in the various echelons of command, has given to the PNTL the necessary internal cohesion and esprit de corps needed to meet challenges with greater promptness and efficiency.

A more rigorous discipline, which is consented rather than imposed, as well as accepted and desired by the overwhelming majority of its members, where all those who would soil the good name of the Institution they serve are punished in an exemplary manner, also contributed decisively to make the PNTL stronger and more credible.

I am fully aware that there are still serious disciplinary problems that have been affecting negatively the image of the Police before society. We are aware that the behaviour of a single police member may put into question the credibility of all his comrades, which is why these cases must be dealt with in an accurate and prompt manner.

Situations like the one we saw late last year, where regrettably a human life was lost as a result of the irresponsible actions of a single police member, should not be used to question the capability of the PNTL to take on the responsibility for the Country's internal security.

These are isolated cases that also take place often in security forces of other countries, namely those that present levels of development and stability that cannot even be compared to the ones seen in a State like Timor-Leste, which has only been effectively independent for eight years.

I would like to seize this opportunity to make a request to all PNTL personnel, in particular the officers who are responsible for the behaviour of their subordinates. The Organic Law also states that the PNTL have the characteristics of a community police in terms of policing strategy and philosophy.

This means that a police member must be well integrated in the local community, favouring proximity policing, i.e., in permanent contact with the populations that he is responsible to keep safe.

Patrols cannot be done just by car, as it becomes difficult to take notice of problems this way. It is necessary that police members walk all quarters and distance locations on foot, making direct contact with the local populations.

Only through this close contact, is it possible to identify the problems affecting the communities, to learn what conflicts constrain their safety and to take the proper measures to ensure people to live in peace and tranquillity.

Changing mentalities takes more than merely approving a law. This is the major task that is now given to the hierarchy of the PNTL: to make all officers,

NCOs and members understand that they need to change radically the patrolling philosophy that has been followed up until now, replacing it with effective and permanent proximity policing.

We also hope that UNPOL members will commit to this goal, not only by favouring this type of policing approach against the routine car patrols, but mostly by ensuring its implementation in the district commands still under their charge.

Finally, I wish to speak of the ongoing process for transferring the executive responsibility for the Country's internal security from UNPOL to the PNTL.

In this last year, the PNTL have resumed the mission given to them by the Constitution in the district commands of Lautem, Oecussi, Manatuto and Viqueque, in addition to the Maritime Unit, the Police Training Centre and the Police Intelligence Service.

Going against the voices heard in some sectors that systematically put personal and corporate interests above national interests, insisting on conveying the message that our Police are not yet ready for the new challenges they have to face, the PNTL have been displaying high standards of professionalism, competence and dedication to the public cause in the Units and Services that are now under their responsibility.

Timorese police elements have given us all a lesson in humility and civility, as, despite the scarce human and logistic resources available to them, they have performed their tasks without complaint and have been successfully completing the tasks given to them.

Throughout 2010, we hope that all policing tasks and powers will be bestowed upon the PNTL, which will make the responsibility for the internal security of our Nation rest inclusively in our hands, in the hands of the Timorese.

I wish to seize this opportunity to convey my deep regret for the early disappearance of the person who coordinated with the Government this entire task-transferring process on behalf of UNMIT.

Mr Takahisa Kawakami, who has left us when we were still in need of his services, is responsible for a good part of the success that the PNTL have shown in resuming their tasks as a security force.

Mr Kawakami knew how to speak with us. He understood and respected us, and always acted with intelligence and sensibility. We shall miss him.

I trust that UNMIT, for which this loss is deeply painful and heartfelt, will be able to find another agent soon. This agent, working in close cooperation with the Government, must be able to complete the mission his or her predecessor started.

Officers, NCOs and Members of the PNTL,

My final words are for you.

Today completes the first decade in the history of the Institution to which you are proud to belong. Right from the start, the IV Constitutional Government has vowed to carry out the necessary reforms for strengthening the various Institutions of the State, including the PNTL.

And one of the factors for reforming and strengthening the Institutions was clearly a proper legal framework.

Following this, the Council of Ministers approved on 13 December 2008 the Regime for Promotions in the PNTL, which was subsequently promulgated by the President of the Republic and published as Decree-Law no. 16/2009, of 18 March. This Decree-Law set new categories, subcategories and positions for the PNTL, which until then only had:

- Inspectors;
- Sub-inspectors;
- Members.

The Decree-Law also set the rules to be followed in a normal promotion process, from article 5 to article 35. In the future, promotions shall follow these rules. And I trust that all PNTL elements will study and understand the procedures that rule your professional lives.

The reason I say this is because I have received several complaints and several unjustified comments, in addition to some recommendations, regarding the current promotion process.

Officers, NCOs and Members,

Let us never forget the reasons that required UNPOL's presence here in Timor-Leste.

UNPOL came in 2006 because we were not able to safeguard the integrity of the PNTL as a professional, non-partisan State body and Institution.

We are all living with the pressure of having to re-evaluate you, both individually and as an Institution. This is why we are yet to complete the handover process in the Districts, including Díli.

And this is why chapter V of Decree-Law no. 16/2009 has set a transitional Promotion Regime.

Articles 36 to 48 set all procedures with which you and we have to comply. Throughout the evaluation and testing process set in this transitional Regime, I can guarantee you that there was not the slightest political interference or intervention from anyone.

Therefore, I must say that the promotion process was the best we were able to draft, both for the good of all PNTL members and for the credibility of your Institution.

And this process is not over. There are over 300 pending cases waiting for a solution, which we all hope will come soon.

There are also promotion possibilities according the General Regime, as stated in article 7 and following of Decree-Law no. 16/2009.

For this purpose, the Council of Ministers approved on 24 March, at its last meeting, a Resolution creating a Commission to Monitor the PNTL Promotion Process, which will support:

- The implementation of the promotions already approved;
- The resolution of pending promotions;
- The resolution of cases of PNTL elements who have not been attributed positions;
- The entry into force of the Commission for General Regime Promotions, under article 29 of Decree-Law no. 16/2009, article 7, which sets the following promotion modalities:
    a) Seniority;
    b) Selection;
    c) Appointment;
    d) Exceptional nature.

Officers, NCOs and Members,

I am aware that there have been meetings where discontented people would speak about everything but the results they got in each test.

I want to remind you that the Civil Service Commission was created to ensure the rights of civil servants, but also to strengthen their awareness regarding their duties. The State is implementing meritocracy, so as to put an end to cases of nepotism and promotions resulting from party influences.

And I wish to use this opportunity to publicly convey the Government's appreciation for the integrity, effort and performance of the members of the Evaluation Commission and of the Secretariat for PNTL Promotions.

It is their work that is clearing the path for a professional and non-partisan PNTL that is conscious of its duties.

What I hope from you, what we all hope, is that you will honour the uniform you wear and prove yourselves worthy of the trust the populations have placed on you.

To all those who serve in the PNTL, I congratulate you for this anniversary.

# ANP First Year Anniversary, 22 August 2009

Excellency, President of the National Parliament
Members of the Government
Members of the Parliament
Your Reverence, Dom Alberto Ricardo da Silva, Bishop of the Diocese of Díli
Your Reverence, Dom Basílio do Nascimento, Bishop of the Diocese of Baucau
Members of the Diplomatic Corps
President of the ANP and Directors
Representatives of the Oil and Gas Companies
Distinguished Guests
Ladies and Gentlemen

It is my great pleasure to be here with you today to open this one day seminar entitled, 'The Road to Becoming a Leading Regulatory Authority in the Region', marking the first anniversary of the Autoridade Nacional do Petróleo, known simply as ANP.

Around this same time a year ago, I was pleased to inaugurate the opening of the new office for this institution at the east wing of the Palácio do Governo, and witnessed the swearing-in of a highly motivated young Timorese who assumed the leadership of the organisation. There were high expectations for the organisation, which administers one of the most important resources of the country — petroleum.

Ladies and Gentlemen
Staff of the ANP,

In June 2008, the Council of Ministers passed a Law that established this institution, investing it with administrative and financial independence. The Institute was to formally take office on 1st July 2008 — the day the previous Timor Sea Authority ceased to exist as per the Timor Sea Treaty. The ANP was created as a public institution supervised by the Secretary of State for Natural Resources and falls within the regime of indirect public administration.

Congratulations to you all at the ANP for this first anniversary. You have walked a long way.

One year of existence as an organisation is relatively short. But I am aware of the challenges that the organisation, or you as individuals, faced since day one. Being young (mostly young graduates), your first challenge is managing expectations and to overcome the perception of you being too young for an important job with such responsibilities. This was not only people's perception. There were comments that the 'ANP will not succeed if the Government proceeds with its establishment and places young Timorese in the top leadership positions'. Cynical voices said 'the petroleum industry will fall to pieces within two weeks if ANP takes over the activities'. However, you have proved to everyone that they were wrong. You have all proven to the people of Timor-Leste you can administer a complex and sophisticated industry. This has become an example, a real example with a message that, with appropriate trust and delegation of responsibility and continuing support and assistance from the Government, an institution such as yours can perform its task and duties very well.

Distinguished Guests

Dear ANP staff

Today is your day, a day for celebration. But also a day for reflection — and this is the reason you are conducting this seminar. Reflecting on the past is important. As an organisation, one year is good timing for reflection. The ANP as an institute must reflect about its contributions to the State, contribution to the People, and its contribution to the organisational development itself.

The Government is happy to have had the petroleum sector managed and administered by the ANP under the supervision of the Secretary of State for Natural Resources. Under the ANP administration, Timor-Leste continues to receive a great deal of revenue. Partly, thanks to the high oil prices, but also for your prudent and careful monitoring and control of petroleum activities. I am aware that a number of oil and gas exploration activities are currently undertaken offshore, in Timor-Leste's own jurisdictional areas and in the JPDA. These are important activities to be managed and monitored. The ANP should always strive to strengthen its monitoring capacity and expertise. In all these activities, however, one of the most important aspects is how to develop those resources so that they contribute to the overall economical development of the country. The oil and gas sector must contribute to the creation of jobs and business opportunities. In this regard, I would like to call your attention to the policies and programs of the Government in this sector.

I understand that the ANP will carry out the administration and management of the resources not only in the Timor-Leste's jurisdiction but also in the JPDA's. Following my message a year ago, I urge the ANP to manage the resources in this area carefully and prudently for the benefit of the two countries. As Australia has benefited from previous developments, it is only fair that Timor-Leste should benefit from the petroleum developments to come.

I have no doubt that, as a new organisation, you will face many more challenges and that there is much hard work ahead of you all. However, with perseverance, reflection on past experiences, and openness to learning new things, you will succeed.

With this, I declare open this Seminar and wish you every success.

# Eighth Anniversary of the National University of Timor-Leste (UNTL)

GMT Hall, Díli
17 November 2008

> Illustrious President of the University, Mr Benjamim Corte-Real, PhD
> Distinguished President of the Organizing Committee,
> Mr Agostinho Fernandes
> Distinguished Members of Parliament and Members of Government
> Distinguished Ambassadors
> Distinguished Faculty Members
> Distinguished Guests
> Dear Students,

It is a great pleasure for me to be here, eight years after the creation of the National University of Timor-Leste, to witness and celebrate the success and prestige of this Institution.

University is the main place where scientific and technical knowledge, work methods and professional techniques are honed. It is also the place where critical thinking is developed and where acts and behaviours are shaped, leading to the natural acceptance of others and to the socialization of civic and human democratic values.

University plays an important role in our State under the Rule of Law, as a forum for open and honest discussion on the future of our Nation — it is a place where all points of view can and should be shared — without personal or political agenda, with study, research and investigation being paths towards *Sapientia et Veritas*.

Higher Education Institutions in our Country have a unique dimension, since they represent hope in the future: the academic training of our young (and not so young) people is a vital instrument for national development and an important legacy to leave to the younger generations.

As such, the teachers, staff and students here today represent the hope of our entire People and are also our heroes. The intervention of these professionals and the availability and commitment by students in seeking advanced training will surely have a true impact on national development.

The Country needs its own qualified and qualifying institution of knowledge! UNTL responds to this need, as a place for developing skills to ensure a present and a future with human resources more qualified in scientific, technical and technological terms, and possessing critical thinking and the capacity to make choices, understand matters and make their mark in the Country and in the world.

The challenges that students face in the present and will face in the future, as soon as they complete their academic training, are many. Still, I am sure that they will rise to the occasion and respond to these challenges with responsibility and tenacity — if you have made it this far, with all the difficulties that are inherent to our young Nation, then you will be ready to respond to the national needs with courage and without despondency or giving up.

The courses provided in this University are essential for freeing our People from misery — in the areas of agriculture, social sciences, economy, engineering, medicine and law. Any policy drafted by any Government in these areas cannot be implemented successfully without you, without skilled Timorese citizens!

As such, it is a priority for the Government to make Education accessible to all, even in the most remote areas of the Country. We believe that when our young people acquire knowledge and skills, they will become citizens who are able to contribute to social and economic development and to national stability.

The young students of today are the leaders of tomorrow — the future of the Country!

And these leaders must be responsible; they must be able to overcome the obstacles that our young Country faces. They must have sound knowledge and strong moral character.

It is important that you are aware that you will have to be able to provide clear guidance in the areas of expertise where you are presently being trained, while making room for others to have initiative and participation. This will contribute to a more tolerant, more dignified and more democratic country.

UNTL is a reference in this goal, and as such I would like to convey my appreciation to the staff and teachers — both national and international — of this University, as well as to President Benjamim Corte-Real. Your dedication and commitment are key elements for achieving quality education and for serving our dear Fatherland.

Lastly, I would like to request a strong round of applause for the students gathered here today, who are making a valuable contribution to our Nation. The challenges placed by national development require great dedication from you, but there is no nobler and more necessary purpose.

# Strengthening the Private Sector through Business Associations

Ministry of Foreign Affairs Building, Díli
14 March 2009

> Mr Peter McMullin
> Government Members
> Dear Businessmen and Businesswomen,

This meeting, the first of many we hope to schedule this year with the private sector, is especially important as it seeks to help overcome the obstacles that have been slowing down our economy.

The Government of Timor-Leste is committed to having the private sector boost the economic growth and the sustainable development of the Country.

Today, national businessmen and businesswomen are invited to speak openly with the Government, in order for us to create instruments and mechanisms that enable the private sector to become a Strategic Partner of the Government, so as to:

- generate employment;
- increase national productivity;
- increase income; and
- develop and strengthen the business capacity of the Country.

The difficulties in starting or developing businesses in Timor-Leste are not new. What is new is the fact that problems are being identified and that the Government is implementing measures to alter this situation, together with the very agents of this change, that is, the private sector.

We start off with the conviction that the Timorese are among the most skilled people in the world in turning resources into major achievements. This makes it possible for us to realise our dream of creating a Timorese industry that can sell our products in local and international markets.

We also start off with the belief that, in today's world, it no longer makes sense for the Government to be the main driving force for economic growth. The strategy of the past, where companies depended upon projects presented by the Government, has proved not to be the best way of developing a strong economy.

The Government must cooperate with the private sector, not rule it.

However, both have great responsibilities, and the Government's first responsibility is to create favourable conditions to enable businesses to develop.

In this sense, the first obstacle to the development of the business and industrial sector of Timor-Leste has already been removed. Today, our people have a sense of security and national stability, which gives more confidence to private investors.

Security and economic development go hand in hand. To invest in security is to invest in development!

On the other hand, the reforms started in public administration, and in particular in the Ministry of Finance, have been improving systems and procedures significantly, including the procurement system and the improvement of the efficiency of public spending and of budget execution rates.

This is a vital condition for nurturing the development of the private sector. We all know that our private sector still has difficulty in accessing bank loans and guarantees, unlike foreign businessmen and businesswomen. Therefore, good management of our public finances to ensure that businesses are paid on time contributes to providing a level playing field between national and foreign businessmen and businesswomen.

The tax reform already adopted by this government was another vital measure for promoting private sector development. The simplification of the tax system and the lightening of the tax load, which was inadequate and excessive in view of the Country's reality, were vital measures for developing our businesses and industries.

Presently, our tax system has very low rates for every type of tax, and the former lengthy and complex procedure for paying taxes is now simpler and more transparent.

The Ministry of Tourism, Commence and Industry has developed regulations to support the new company registration system, in order to make the process of creating companies faster and less bureaucratic. The new system reduces processing time from 92 days to a maximum of three days.

The Government has also started a process to provide greater judicial security concerning property rights. In short, these efforts can be summarised as follows:

- the existence of a legislation to support business, such as the Commercial Societies Code, the Commercial Registry Code and the regulation on extractive activities;
- the development of a Building Registration Code and the capacity building of Timorese staff for the Building Registration Department;
- the completion of the draft Civil Code, regulating, among other things, rights in real estate and property rights;
- the development of a National Mapping Service, which will enable the identification of every land parcel; and
- the revision of a new legislation package on Investment.

These are some of the steps we have already taken, but the Government is aware that there is still much more to be done.

We acknowledge that one of the reasons for such a low private investment rate in our Country is the state of our business environment. This is why we are giving priority, during this year, to improving this situation.

To improve our business environment we are undertaking efforts to create conditions for private businesses to have access to credit, including through support of microfinance institutions, especially in rural areas.

We will also be accelerating short-term measures, including:

- eliminating the minimum capital required for starting a company;
- reviewing labour rules in order to increase flexibility;
- developing construction rules;
- continuing to simplify procedures for creating companies;
- improving coordination among the various stakeholders; and
- strengthening the capacity of institutions, including technical, human resource, financial and training institutions, and of businessmen and businesswomen.

Ladies and Gentlemen,

The start of infrastructure projects, set for 2009, will be fundamental for improving the competitiveness and efficiency of the private sector.

The production and distribution of electricity to the entire Country, the improvement of the road and harbour networks and the improvement of telecommunications are some of this Government's priorities.

This is indeed an opportunity for the private sector to develop and to assist the transformation of our society, leading to better lives for all Timorese.

What we ask of the Private Sector is for you to join these efforts by the Government to develop our Country as a national cause.

All Timorese are called upon to participate in our nation's building and development. When we all suffered with the crisis that jeopardised public order and security, all Timorese agreed that the institutions had to cooperate and work closely to overcome this national challenge.

Fortunately, we were able to do this, and there can be no better example than the excellent contribution that F-FDTL and PNTL, working together, made towards national stabilisation.

At this time, it is the private sector that is being called upon to contribute to this national cause of combating poverty. We know that the only way to deliver our People from misery is to achieve economic growth, and for this we will be requiring joint efforts by the public sector and the private sector.

And what can the private sector do now?

It can view its participation in our economy's development as a mission. It can work with dignity, professionalism and transparency.

It can join with the Government in the fight against corruption, reporting irregularities found in the system and acting responsibly in every situation.

Dear Businessmen and Businesswomen,

The private sector must also seize the opportunities brought by foreign investment. This Government has a strong policy that the Country's openness to foreign investment must be repaid through the capacity building of our national private sector, which means that you must also act to enable the establishment of joint venture arrangements.

Even if, at first, Timorese companies and industries can only make use of limited financial resources, they will have the opportunity to benefit the most from the imported know-how. The benefits they receive from these partnerships will in time enable them to invest more and more, and to collect the respective dividends — this is how you build a strong private sector.

Ladies and Gentlemen,

Lastly, one of the main reasons why we are here today is the identification of means for improving the organization and leadership of the private sector.

Experience in other countries tells us that the creation of business associations has been a success. By businesses organising themselves to provide one voice, and to share experiences and knowledge, companies and industries have been able to develop more successfully.

On the other hand, business associations enable the Government to provide focused support with greater effectiveness — this will promote a better environment for business operations.

A collective effort is a more effective effort. Companies and industries, by developing businesses associations, have greater ability to overcome business challenges.

The success formula of our struggle for freedom is precisely in this spirit and in the strength of the whole to pursue common goals — if we have been learning from our mistakes, then we should learn even more from our achievements!

The presentation we will now watch will contribute towards a better understanding of how a Chamber of Commerce and Industry works, and what advantages it brings. I thank our friend, Mr Peter McMullin, for collaborating with us in this effort to strengthen our private sector. I hope this is the beginning of a successful and constructive partnership between us.

Ladies and Gentlemen,

Progressing means action and sacrifice! It means understanding the challenges ahead of us and choosing the most effective means for overcoming obstacles. It means genuine cooperation to reduce the chances of wasting the great opportunities for development we have in our Country.

Let us have the private sector's help to develop our country and to serve our poor!

# Closing Session of the Timor-Leste and Development Partners Meeting

Díli
13 July 2011

>Your Excellencies
>Ladies and Gentlemen,

It is with a mix of satisfaction and motivation that I now bring to an end this meeting with the Development Partners of Timor-Leste.

Once again the International Community, friends and partners of Timor-Leste, and the various components of our Civil Society — Private Sector, NGOs, Churches, Media and others — have contributed with valuable interventions, in an atmosphere of cooperation, friendship and honesty, seeking to make this young Nation a more prosperous place with greater opportunities to improve the living situation of the Timorese People.

The Strategic Development Plan that I had the opportunity of launching during this meeting was awaited with great expectation by all those who are interested and who want to contribute to the development of the Country.

These two days of debate, mostly to discuss this new Plan, lead me to conclude, with a renewed sense of responsibility, that we have not failed to meet these expectations, and that, today, we have mustered the conditions for successfully implementing a new strategy for developing the Nation.

In fact, the Financial Agreement signed just now between the Government of Timor-Leste and the International Development Association is an excellent indication of this and the perfect way to conclude this meeting, as the implementation of the Strategic Plan will start immediately.

>Ladies and Gentlemen,

There is now an additional factor that makes us believe that this Plan will be successfully implemented: the way in which it was received by our Development Partners!

I say it again: it is with great satisfaction and particularly with great motivation that we have entered this new stage for Timor-Leste. The clearly positive input we received in relation to this Plan — the express will to support and contribute to its implementation — gives us great confidence.

Receiving this support and solidarity also gives us great responsibility. The drafting of the Plan is an important step, but it is its implementation that will determine whether the effort was worth it.

The presentation of the Plan is not an end in itself, but, rather, a new start for Timor-Leste, a new opportunity!

There are many challenges to the implementation of the Plan, as we could see during these two days of round-table discussion.

We accept and appreciate the various recommendations made here by the various representatives of our Civil Society, particularly the valuable contributions of the Private Sector, the NGOs, the Churches and the Media, and by the representatives from various foreign countries and international agencies in attendance.

Today we are here to take on a new commitment.

We have learned a lot during the drafting of this Strategic Development Plan. We have learned a lot from our People and its will, which is stronger all the time, to contribute towards the construction of our Country. We have learned a lot from our development partners, which never refused to provide data and opinions to give coherence and even consistence to this Plan. We have also learned a lot from all those technical officers, civil servants and advisors, who were directly involved in the drafting.

Most of all, we learned that we still have a lot to learn during the implementation of this Plan, which is ambitious but clearly doable.

We appreciate the various recommendations made here. We are aware that transparency and good governance during the implementation process are fundamental factors, and that this requires efficient verification and monitoring mechanisms.

We know that we will have to fine-tune some programmes, to research new data and to constantly update the obtained data, particularly in productive key sectors such as the agricultural sector.

We are aware (thus, the focus on social capital) that without skilled and trained human resources, it will be extremely difficult to implement this Plan.

We are aware that we still have to draft several legislation and regulation pieces, as well as to speed up administrative procedures in the various components of this Plan.

We are also aware that, in order for us to achieve this goal, we must always — and I mean *always* — work in a duly coordinated manner.

This means coordination between the various line ministries, coordination between the various Sovereignty Bodies, coordination between these State Agencies and Development Partners and, obviously, coordination and constant and open dialogue between the Government and Civil Society, and between the Government and the Timorese People.

Ladies and Gentlemen,

The national Private Sector will be essential for starting the economic growth described in the set strategies. We will continue to invest in this sector; however, we will also urge it to control its frustrations, often regarding funding and know-how, particularly when compared with the international private sector. It is important that the national Private Sector displays honesty and accountability beyond reproach, so that it can be a true agent of national development.

Your Excellencies

Ladies and Gentlemen,

It is with great hope for the future that I bring this meeting to a close. The way in which the Strategic Development Plan was received encourages us not to rest for a single moment until we can truly move forward with the sector programmes we presented.

I must also thank the Ambassadors and representatives of various International Agencies in attendance, including Scholars and members of International Non-Governmental Organizations, for their words of support and for their will to actively participate in this development journey of ours.

I do not need to tell you that, once again, we accept with humility and gratefulness all assistance that will be provided in order for us to achieve this goal.

The Díli Development Pact defines the new paradigm through which this new form of cooperation will be established. The new commitment between Timor-Leste and its Development Partners strengthens the need for a more articulate, responsible and dynamic partnership, based on the following core principles:

- National ownership, with greater responsibility for the Timorese, and the commitment of strong leadership regarding the destinies of the Nation and the People.
- Greater articulation and transparency in the set assistance and cooperation mechanisms, moving gradually from a stage of development assistance to a stage of development investment.
- As partners towards the 'best possible investment in Timor-Leste', working together in order to reinvent synergies focusing on the expansion of the private sector, the creation of employment and investment in key areas, enabling the sustainable development of the Country.
- Timely reform and reorganization of the set cooperation systems and mechanisms so as to ensure the implementation of the goals and a better service delivery to the Timorese People.

Ladies and Gentlemen,

Lastly, I would like to pay homage to His Excellency the President of the Republic, José Ramos-Horta, for once again displaying his exceptional leadership during these two days in which he listened and reflected on the strategic Plan alongside us. He is undoubtedly a magnificent example of our Country's commitment to move forward towards development and to provide our People with a better future.

I conclude this meeting by saying I am very happy to see that we have managed to link the vision of the Timorese People with the vision of our international friends and partners, so as to enable the successful development of Timor-Leste.

# Industry Forum: Customs and Business — a Partnership for the Future Development of Timor-Leste

Díli
19 March 2010

>Members of Government
>Business Representatives
>Members of International Organisations
>Members of Non-Government Organisations
>Ladies and Gentlemen,

It is with great pleasure that I am here today to welcome you to this important Forum, which heralds the beginning of what I am confident will be a successful partnership between Customs and the business community.

Timor-Leste's future depends upon the development of a strong private sector to achieve long-term economic growth and create jobs. It is not sustainable for the Government to continue to be the primary driving force for economic growth. To build a strong Timor-Leste, we must build a strong private sector.

And the Government recognises that it must support the private sector to secure Timor-Leste's future — that we must act together, in partnership. Working together, we have already made great progress. In 2008 and 2009, we successfully managed the impact of the worst global economic crisis in almost 100 years.

Our economic growth in 2008 was the second highest in the world, with a rate over 12 per cent. We overcame the world economic turmoil, and achieved an unprecedented level of economic growth as a result of the sound economic management of the Government, the trust and confidence of the People, and the hard work and initiative of the private sector.

But one of the main drivers of our economic growth has not been given the recognition it deserves. It is the tax and financial management reforms of the Government and the Ministry of Finance.

These reforms have ensured that the Government now operates more efficiently and effectively, resulting in the improved delivery of services, the increase in public spending and budget execution rates and the promotion of economic activity and national development projects.

These reforms have been vital for nurturing private sector development. The Government and the business community must operate in partnership to support the development of our nation. Central to this relationship must be an effective partnership between Customs and business.

The growth in our private sector will require the import of goods and productive equipment. And in turn, this growth will allow the increased production and export of goods that can compete on the international market.

Customs recognises that it has a central role in supporting this national economic growth and improved processes for international trade.

And this is why Customs has embarked on an ambitious reform and modernisation program, which involves restructuring its operations and management in line with best practices guides published by the World Customs Organization.

It is important that Customs continues these reforms and fully embraces its obligation to facilitate international trade. It must use the latest technology and adopt business-focused work practices.

This Forum today is a recognition of the need for Customs to consult more widely with all stakeholders — including business — to ensure that your needs are taken into account in Customs' reform program. The results so far have been positive. Duty collection is at record levels and, in the next few months, Customs will be introducing new procedures to reduce the time it takes to clear shipments.

These improved procedures have resulted from the adoption of new technology, including the ASYCUDA declaration processing system that I was pleased to launch in June last year, as well as new x-ray technology at Díli Port. The Ministry of Finance has also made substantial investments in improving the professional standards of Customs staff.

Ladies and Gentlemen,

Customs is working hard to meet its responsibilities to support trade and economic growth and the business sector must also play its part, working together in partnership with Customs.

In an era of unprecedented transnational criminal activity, from which Timor-Leste is not exempt, business must recognise that, from time to time, cargo will need to be subject to intrusive inspections by Customs.

Border protection and national security are critical responsibilities of Customs. To meet these challenges, Customs will be trialling the electronic reporting of cargo, the application of intelligence-driven assessment techniques and other risk reduction strategies.

We ask that you work with Customs — and understand its responsibilities — as these important reforms are implemented. And I urge you to recognise that it is your responsibility to give Customs confidence that cargo does not pose a threat to our security or community welfare.

You can help by training your staff in both Customs procedures and your obligations, just as the Ministry of Finance is training its staff to improve customer service.

Ladies and Gentlemen,

I am pleased that the business community is collectively coming together. You are founding an independent and representative Câmara do Comércio e Indústria that will speak for the interests of business with one voice.

A Câmara do Comércio e Indústria, which operates with an effective executive management, will not only become a strong lobby group for your interests and address the skill and training needs of the private sector; it will become a strategic partner of Government in the development of our country.

And so I ask that, in this spirit of partnership, that business and Customs work together to build our economy — and Timor-Leste's strength — through improving our ports and supporting trade and private sector development.

Progress depends upon taking action, making sacrifices and working together to overcome obstacles. It also means genuine cooperation to make sure that we do not waste the great opportunities that we have for economic growth and job creation.

Let us all work together for the long-term development of our Country.

# Government and Development Partners Program Alignment 2010 Meeting

Díli, 15 June 2009

> Vice Prime Minister
> Ministers
> Heads of UN and World Bank Agencies, Mr. Antonio and Mr. Finn
> Ambassadors and Heads of Delegations
> Heads of Agencies
> Ladies and Gentlemen
> Dear Friends,

Good morning and welcome to this meeting, marking yet another milestone in the forging of a closer and more effective partnership between Development Partners and the Government of Timor-Leste.

We, as a Government, have made considerable progress in enhancing the quality of our programs over the past year and a half. This progress has not been without its challenges and set-backs, however, we feel that, at each and every stage, we have overcome these potential stumbling blocks, not alone, but with the support of our Development Partners who, most recently, at the Timor-Leste Development Partners Meeting (TLDPM) in April 2009, re-committed themselves to the development of Timor-Leste as a Nation and as a people.

In April, you came together in this very room to underscore your willingness to better align your assistance with Government priorities, and I am grateful that many of you have made good on your pledges and responded quickly. Let us gather here today to bring with us this same energy and dedication displayed on previous occasions, for what we will achieve here today will undoubtedly have long-term ramifications as to the success of this and subsequent governments in providing the best quality support to the people of this Nation.

2009 is an auspicious year for celebrating many anniversaries regarding the independence of our young Nation. Yet as detailed at the first Consultative

Conference on Fragile States last March, we learned that post-conflict countries such as Timor-Leste take an average of ten years to make the difficult transition from fragile state to developing nation, often with a series of struggles and challenges along the way. Our experiences have shown this to be an accurate depiction of events. It has been just over a year since this country's most recent threat to stability, with Timor-Leste experiencing serious bouts of instability on average every two years since regaining independence. Each time we have recovered — with the help of the international community. The challenge faced by us all here today is how best to make this hard-won sovereignty work, so state institutions can deliver for the great majority of Timorese people throughout the country.

As you are all no doubt well aware, this Government is currently involved in a comprehensive and wide-ranging reform process. Such a process does not begin and end within the space of one year, within a budget cycle, or even within the term of one administration. Reform processes such as ours are and must be ongoing. Our reform process is as pragmatic as it is constant. We knew that what we wished to achieve would not be completed in the short term and now, as we find ourselves in the second year of this reform process, having learned many lessons, some difficult, we take this opportunity to re-commit ourselves to the continuation of this very necessary and worthwhile endeavor.

Throughout this reform process, we have learned that sometimes it is laws that must be reformed, whereas other times it is practices. While some reform can be done through the passing of legislation and the creation of regulatory bodies, other types of reform are of a much more personal nature. Reforming work ethics and similar attitudes takes time, however, achieving success in all these areas will ensure that the institutional reform we are attempting will be maintained into the future.

In this journey of constant improvement, both personal and institutional, we must seek to work together and learn from each other.

While reform must take place in terms of practice and thinking, similarly, reform must take place at both an international and at a local level. The Government of Timor-Leste, through the Ministry of Finance, is committed to international agreements such as the Paris Declaration on Aid Effectiveness, the Accra Agenda for Action and the Principles for Good International Engagement in Fragile States, amongst many others. We see our efforts in these high-level initiatives as demonstrated on the ground through events such as the Annual and Quarterly Development Partners Meetings, National Priority Working Groups and others — these occasions represent but one frontline of our reform process.

Ladies and Gentlemen,

Much has been achieved in the last 10 years, and we could not have made this progress without our friends and supporters represented this morning here in this hall. We are determined to move forward with equal speed and increase the pace of development over the next decade.

We have already achieved some strong markers indicating success. Last year we committed ourselves to securing peace and stability for the citizens of Timor-Leste — and we have done so. We announced that we wished to better align budget preparation to planning — and we did. Now, in 2009, we have made the decision to starting our planning for 2010 early, allowing us to better allocate resources in order to maximize impact.

Dear Friends,

As agreed to in March at the first Consultative Meeting on Good International Engagement in Fragile States, it is the responsibility of this Government to engage in a strategic development planning process, in order to guide alignment efforts between both Ministries, and between Government and Development Partners. This Government is committed to honoring this responsibility and my Office is currently doing so in the production of the Strategic Development Plan, a document which I know many of you are eager to see.

We wait for the day when this document is ready to be released, but, as my Office works toward this goal, we must not forget that documents such as the Strategic Development Plan require time, patience and foresight.

And so, let me update you briefly on where we stand on our preparations for the medium- to long-term Strategic Development Plan (SDP).

My Office, the Strategic Planning and Investment Unit, has been working hard with all Line Ministries and, as promised, I will present this SDP to the National Parliament by September 2009.

Meanwhile, the National Priorities 2010 that you have before you is the result of a collaborative exercise with distinguished members of the Council of Ministers and will be a guiding instrument for all of us. A series of Strategic Workshops titled, *Timor-Leste's Yellow Brick Road* were held on 16 and 23 May

2009 at the Health Sciences Institute in Comoro, Díli, to determine the structure of the National Priorities for 2010. As a result of discussion and reflection, the National Priorities for 2010 were approved at an extraordinary Council of Ministers meeting. It is now my pleasure to share with you, our Development Partners, the outcomes of this workshop:

The National Priorities for 2010 are:
1. Roads and Water
2. Food Security (with a focus on Productivity)
3. Human Resources Development
4. Access to Justice
5. Social Service and Decentralized Service Delivery
6. Good Governance
7. Public Safety

These seven National Priorities for 2010 are linked to the overarching themes of medium- to long-term job creation and cross-cutting human resources development. These two areas represent the themes upon which further goal and target setting will be based.

While these new National Priority areas may appear similar to those we selected for 2009, this time they will also serve as a strategic bridge to longer-term planning, into 2011 and 2012.

This National Priorities process has matured within the space of one year, and so, in 2010, we will be increasingly able to look more and more at the quality and impact of targets that will be developed for each of these seven National Priorities.

While we are committed to providing strong leadership in this area, the Government would also like to listen and consider your feedback when determining our focus areas for next year and for future years which, as we know, is a key principle found within the pages of the Paris Declaration on Aid Effectiveness.

Ladies and Gentlemen,

I am aware that many may have differing views on our priorities. However, I would like to state for the record that these priorities were chosen because we believe that their impact will provide the type of environment that will enable other activities to take place, which are also important for the development of the country, such as the private sector development.

We must not forget that we are still very much a fragile state. All that we have worked so hard to build can still be taken away from us if we do not continue to address the numerous daily struggles they face.

To illustrate this situation clearly, consider that, only this week, IDPs from Metinaro camp on the outskirts of Díli will begin the long and sometimes difficult journey to return to their communities, or in some cases, to new homes in new communities. We must realize that the emergency phase may have passed but there is still work yet to be completed.

To maintain this, the government has embarked upon two parallel processes — a two-track approach. We are addressing both the short-term needs of our population while at the same time transitioning to addressing their medium- to long-term needs. This is why, for example, you will see that, for 2010, human resources development and job creation underpin all of what we have prioritized. Clearly, a capable work-ready population with a strong and committed work ethic will benefit the private sector in years to come.

We seek from you an exchange of ideas and input for Timor-Leste's future. I appreciate the help we receive from the international community, both in terms of substantive assistance and planning support for reaching the MDGs — they remain a medium- to long-term goal of the Government, and they are indeed part of everyone's agenda, including that of civil society.

I call upon you here, the Development Partners, to look closely at your programs, as we are looking at our own programs. I ask that you ask yourselves what can be done to fast-track alignment so that they complement the National Priorities for 2010.

We know all too well that we, as a Government, cannot do everything, nor do we seek to at this point. We are conscious that many countries the world over, including some here with us today, are feeling the effects of the global financial crisis. While Timor-Leste has, in many respects, been shielded from some of the more devastating effects of this crisis, we are still vulnerable through future estimated revenues, to give just one example. This is why we have sought to ensure that our overall fiscal envelope for FY2010 (637M) is sufficient to achieve our objectives on poverty reduction.

Considering this international financial climate, it is our aim to make the most of our Development Partner's contributions. To do this we say: here is our guidance, look at your priorities — let us highlight and build upon those programs that are already aligned with this Government's National Priorities, while taking the time to address programs that fall outside these priority areas.

I would like very much if Development Partners could hold these conversations with Line Ministers over the next two weeks so that our the Budget Committee can make an informed final decision, taking into consideration, for example, the location of various programs to ensure that spending is done with a geographic spread equal to need.

To give an example, last year, I asked you to consider rural development as a focus, and very little changed in this regard, as rural development continues to be a focus of this Government. And, so, it is important that, in your discussions with Line Ministries, you are able to get into the nitty-gritty details to avoid program duplication and overlapping. When we make decisions with the help of the Ministry of Finance as to which of our development initiatives should go ahead, this type of information gained from your conversations with Line Ministries will be critical. For example, if we wish to build a road, we must know, so that we can ensure that roads that are distributed equally.

Ladies and Gentlemen,

Dear Friends,

I am convinced that we can continue to make a difference in reducing poverty, given that we are not just catching up on the aftermath of the 2006 crisis but we are doing so within a context of centuries of oppression.

The challenge this Government faces can be summed up as follows: how can we best allocate our limited resources in order to provide essential services to the population? The solution, of course, lies in our ability to align development programming so that our programs complement each other.

Complacency has no place in this Government! We must not allow ourselves to be sidetracked by our own success! Our sense of achievement must be tempered with consideration as to the work that still lies ahead.

In conclusion, I wish to state my thanks to all those present here this morning. Our mission is clear and our vision shared.

Let us all contribute here today in a spirit of mutual respect and appreciation of the fact that the sometimes difficult work we must set for ourselves today will no doubt result in a better future for the citizens of this nation.

# Opening Remarks to the First International Conference on Timor Coffee

Díli, 3 April 2009

>Minister for Tourism, Commerce and Industry
>Minister for Agriculture and Fisheries
>Excellencies
>Members of Government
>Mr. Néstor Osorio, Executive Director, International Coffee Organisation
>Members of the International Coffee Community
>Distinguished Guests,

It gives me great pleasure to welcome each and every one of you to the First International Conference on Timor Coffee. And I would like to commend the Minister for Tourism, Commerce and Industry, together with the Minister of Agriculture and Fisheries, for hosting this conference about Timor-Leste's most important agricultural export.

I would also like to recognise the presence of Mr Néstor Osorio, Executive Director of the International Coffee Organisation.

The International Coffee Organisation is well known as the primary body that brings together exporting and importing countries to address the challenges of the world's coffee sector, while at the same time, making practical contributions towards improving the living standards in developing countries. I thank Mr. Osorio for his support and participation today.

>Ladies and Gentlemen,

For Timor-Leste, rural and agricultural development is national development. And with coffee being by far our largest agricultural export, the coffee industry will be important to our nation's future.

The coffee industry already makes a huge contribution to our country and to our People. Through working together to improve and increase our coffee production, we can achieve our dream of rural development in Timor-Leste.

As a result of the work of our People, the international coffee community and our development partners, the production of coffee is already well developed in Timor-Leste.

Coffee has an important place in the culture and tradition of our country, and the five districts of Timor-Leste that produce coffee — Emera, Aileu, Ainaro, Manufahi and Liquica — are distinctive for their abundance of coffee trees.

Our coffee culture adds to the diversity and beauty of our land, with coffee trees growing through our rural and mountainous areas.

And the production of coffee makes a huge difference to many of our People. Coffee production supports around 50,000 Timorese families, and, in the coffee-picking season between May to October, around 15,000 jobs are created.

Coffee is, of course, also a huge export earner for Timor-Leste and is by far our number one agricultural export. This boosts our economic growth and has flow on economic benefits for Timor-Leste.

We also benefit from the fact that half of all our coffee is exported as organic and fair trade, which brings higher prices to our farmers and ensures greater care for our natural environment.

While Timor-Leste produces an estimated 0.2 per cent of the world's coffee production, there is scope to improve and increase our coffee production. This will bring more export dollars back to our rural areas, stimulating local economies and increasing the living standards of our farming communities.

To achieve this, and to develop our rural areas, we must work together.

In my humble opinion, Timorese coffee is the best in the world!

But we must work together to make sure that we can compete on the international market; a market that has been growing since the revival of coffee drinking in the 1980s, with its emphasis on specialty gourmet coffee.

I would like to offer some food for thought for your deliberations over the next two days — that is, that we can achieve sustainable development through working together to develop specialty coffee in Timor-Leste.

The specialty coffee of Timor-Leste deserves greater respect on the international market. And I ask that the international coffee community continue to assist Timor-Leste and help us to explore the unique characteristics of our coffee that is found throughout our coffee growing areas, with their varied soils and micro-climates. In doing this, we can identify unique flavour profiles and characteristics for our customers.

In this task, we must also remain focused on the development of our farming communities. We must realise the dreams of coffee farmers and their families with improved housing, clean water, education and opportunities for better standards of living. After all, these are the same dreams we all have and our relationship with farming communities must reflect our common dreams for our shared benefit.

How can we work together for common benefit?

Working together can begin with coffee buyers sharing information and resources with their farmer partners.

Additionally, roasters and importers can share technical skills on harvesting and processing, on picking the best beans, and on cupping coffee. And they can share information on what qualities are desired by consumers and how changes in growing, harvesting and processing can impact on these qualities.

Timor-Leste is looking for international partners who believe as we do, that the quality of our coffee is linked to the quality of life of our growers.

We are fortunate to have the ongoing assistance of our development partners, such as the United States, Portugal, Spain and Japan, who have being making a significant contribution to the development of our coffee industry.

And we hope that the great coffees of Timor-Leste will continue to find their way to the markets and the consumers of the world.

In closing, agricultural and rural development will be vital to the development of our nation — and as our most important agricultural export, coffee will be fundamental to this future.

Our coffee industry already makes a large and important contribution to our nation. And it provides great opportunities for our People. Through working together to improve and increase our production of coffee, we can help fulfil our common dreams for the rural development of Timor-Leste.

I encourage you to make the most of the opportunity that this conference provides, urge you to work together to build our coffee industry, and hope you enjoy many delicious cups of Timorese coffee!

# Closing Session of the Seminar on Reform and Development of the Security Sector in Timor-Leste

Lahane Palace, Díli
12 December 2008

Your Excellency the President of the Republic

Your Excellency the Vice Speaker of Parliament
Your Excellency the Chief of the Defence Force
Your Excellency the Interim Commander of PNTL
Your Excellencies the Representatives of the Diplomatic Corps
Your Excellencies the Representatives of the International Organizations
Dear Representatives of the Civil Society
Ladies and Gentlemen,

I must start by extending my congratulations for the excellent organization of this Seminar, particularly the special commitment by His Excellency the President of the Republic and his Task Force for the Reform and Development of the Sector of Defence and Security, Working along with UNDP, you have enabled this first of a kind reflection in our Country.

Although I could not participate as much as I would have liked in these two days of hard and fruitful work, I know that the varied inputs provided here by the various forces of our society were extremely important for continuing this vital process. I would also like to thank all those who travelled great distances to be here today, contributing to this national project.

Ladies and Gentlemen,

Reforming the Security Sector is undoubtedly a vital need for the Timorese State and a very demanding challenge! Reforming is always more difficult than building from scratch.

This is so because there are installed habits, practises and perceptions, and naturally because it is easier to accommodate to a situation that one knows, even if it is imperfect, than to have the courage to transform and repair that which needs to be changed.

Unfortunately, the challenges put to the young democracy of Timor-Leste, which has seen setbacks and situations of conflict every two years, leading up to the attacks of last 11 February, showed the fragility of our Defence and Security Sector. As such, all Timorese Sovereignty Bodies, Institutions and representatives of the Civil Society have recognized, **in time and not too late**, the need to revise our national policies and the need to change.

No matter how committed the Government is to this reform, this is not a task that the Government can or should perform by itself.

Well, the Government is not alone. On the contrary, this motto of Reforming the Security Sector has already added a chapter to our recent History: the commitment, involvement, solidarity, participation and institutional cooperation of all national bodies — Presidency, Parliament, Government, Defence Forces, Security Forces, Non-Governmental Organizations — that we have seen in this process are already the Reform!

Ladies and Gentlemen,

I would like to comment, or strengthen, some of the aspects mentioned here already, namely by His Excellency the President of the Republic.

1. Our Independent Nation celebrated its sixth birthday in May. Therefore, it is evidently young and consequently fragile, however, this does not mean at all that Timor-Leste is or will become a failed State. The reflections and conclusions made in this Seminar prove that it is not so;
2. Our independence was gained within a context that presents serious risks for national stability. I am referring to the consequences of the struggle against the Indonesian occupation and also to the Country's economic characteristics: low income, low growth and extreme dependency on imports of essential commodities;
3. I have once said that a researcher of such matters has compared this situation to a game of Russian roulette. In other words, the probability of a country with these characteristics to fall into civil war within five years is one in six — the same risk one has playing Russian roulette!

4. These are weaknesses that we must address as challenges and without pessimism. Our past, our cultural characteristics, our transition process, the timings required to enable the sustainability of any project and even the experiences of other countries must be considered, which is why we have been giving so much importance to the security sector and to the consolidation of stability.
5. Lastly, in democracy, the various development sectors are not isolated. Timor-Leste has obviously a legacy of poverty and, if poverty, unemployment, hunger and social injustice lead to the overall discontent of the population, then this naturally threatens national security and stability. As such, the processes are too integrated, and perhaps this is one of the main internal threats we face and the main factor of internal destabilization.
6. Consequently, the strategic development of the Security Sector, providing its officers with the tools to operate efficiently and effectively, will enable the populations to enjoy the peace, tranquillity and trust they need for the development of the vital activities for the economic, social and political growth of the Country.
7. Underdeveloped countries must equip themselves with conditions for fighting today's multidimensional problems in terms of security. They must protect themselves, precisely because they are more vulnerable to crises and more affected by their impact. Therefore, Security and Economic Development are closely interconnected. To invest in Security is to invest in the Future!

It was said here that this investment is extremely costly. We are aware of this, as well as of our natural budget limitations. We also know that the multilateral and bilateral support from development partners has been precious.

However, and once again not immune to the international experience, we have been learning that there is only one way for making this Reform successful: finding the right model for Timor-Leste, respecting the steps and times suited to our reality. This is the model resulting from Timorese consensus, implemented under Timorese leadership.

As such, we created the Task Force for Reform and Development, under the Office of the President of the Republic, involving the various bodies of society. We have been carrying out extensive work in terms of studies, planning, legislative reforms and improvement of infrastructures, equipment, logistic means and human resources — both in the Defence Sector and in the Security Sector.

Ladies and Gentlemen,

Another aspect covered during this Seminar is that today it is difficult for a State to separate between external and internal threats. It is complex to determine clearly if a certain threat is to be met by National Defence or by Internal Security.

Additionally, in today's globalized world, the expansionistic interests of States use more accurate resources, such as actions carried out inside the very borders of the Country to be dominated. As examples of this we have the methods used by terrorist organizations, which in various parts of the world seek to overthrow legitimate governments, undermine internal institutions and make States weaker and consequently more vulnerable to their goals.

Threats to internal stability in today's global world are shared with concern at international levels. Subversive actions against national identity and cohesion, organized crime such as the trafficking of drugs, people and weapons, as well as smuggling, must be dealt with in an integrated manner.

An effective fight against these new threats must imply a conjugation of efforts between the forces responsible for ensuring national defence and those tasked with safeguarding internal security.

Therefore, it is imperative for States today to create cooperation and coordination mechanisms between defence forces and security forces, with both being able to carry out missions that would normally be carried out by the other.

The purpose of this is not for the military to start carrying out police operations, thereby taking the place of the security forces. Instead, the military should be prepared to assist the police in certain specific missions and vice versa.

In view of this new reality of non-conventional threats and in view of the specific circumstances and history of the Armed Forces and of the Police in our Country, the Government made a decision that is surely innovative in the region of the world where we are inserted: to concentrate the areas of National Defence and Internal Security into a single Ministry.

This also enabled both Institutions to coordinate their relationship and to develop their activities in close cooperation, in the pursuit of a common goal. The success with the creation of the Joint Command is a practical example of this.

We see National Security within a broader perspective that, in addition to national defence and internal security, also includes other components, such as civil protection and foreign policy, thereby ensuring cooperation and solidarity between forces as a way to ensure the stability, unity and safety of the populations against any type of threats or risks.

The first steps have already been taken. We have achieved the coordination needed at political level, both with F-FDTL and PNTL. We have also been producing structuring documents for these Institutions to consolidate and develop.

Ladies and Gentlemen,

All the right words have been said throughout the past two days. Now we must do the right actions. We owe it to ourselves and also to the International Community, as a State that is part of the Community of Nations. We, the Timorese State and population, must be able to have effective and efficient military and police institutions.

One way to show this is proving that PNTL can succeed without being guided by the United Nations. I have confidence in PNTL. I know that many officers feel that they are ready, and now they must prove it while not losing sight of the difficult lessons we learned in the recent past.

2009 will be a crucial year. The Secretary of State for Security is finalizing the negotiation of a plan with UNMIT to achieve this goal, whereby PNTL will resume its tasks in full already in the next year. This means that PNTL will assume its rights as well as its duties and responsibilities. PNTL must show strong discipline, administration and operational capacity, healing the wounds of the past.

Additionally, 2009 will be the year in which Force 2020 will effectively begin to be implemented. We expect nothing less than perfect coherence and articulation between the Armed Force members, so as to enable the necessary restructuring, reorganization and professionalization of F-FDTL.

A defence policy cannot be improvised or done overnight. It must be coherent and prepared appropriately. This restructuring process obviously includes the veterans and their demobilization process.

I hope that all those who have patiently waited, with great personal sacrifice, to see the dream of an entire People come true, and all those who have been waiting for so long to see their most elementary rights as National Liberation Heroes recognized, will continue to contribute to this reform process.

The Government is aware that any reform process that did not include the future Military Condition Status and the rights and duties of all military, and naturally of the veterans, would not be good enough for Timor-Leste.

I could go on speaking, but I understand that at this time all of you must be very tired. As such, I will bring my address to a conclusion.

I would like to thank the international lecturers and participants who have travelled over continents and oceans to be here today, sharing your experiences and your best practises with us.

I would also like to thank our international friends in Timor-Leste for the confidence and support they have always shown to our country, as is evidenced by renewed partnerships.

As for us Timorese in attendance here today, the best way in which we can repay this confidence is by making this Reform more than a mere set of good intentions. Let us make this reform a collective success for all Timorese — men and women — who, in a spirit of cooperation and unity, will ensure a bright future for Timor-Leste.

# Address to the g7+ Ministerial Retreat

Juba, South Sudan
18 October 2011

> Honourable Kosti Manibe, Minister of Finance and Economic Planning, South Sudan
> Ministers
> Brothers and Sisters,

It is a great honour and a privilege to be here to speak at the opening of this g7+ Ministerial Retreat.

First, I would like to thank our hosts, the Republic of South Sudan. We are here today not only for this g7+ Ministerial Retreat but to show our solidarity and support for South Sudan.

To be here at this time, a few days after the 100-day milestone since independence, where South Sudan became the world's newest nation, is special for us all. We not only congratulate South Sudan on its independence; we also celebrate the birth of this new nation. We commend the people of South Sudan for their courage, their sacrifice and their determination to achieve independence. And not only do we wish this new nation a bright future, but we also pledge to do all that we can to support South Sudan in becoming a strong, successful and peaceful State. I commend the President and the government of South Sudan for hosting this international event and give thanks for the warm welcome we have received.

> Ladies and Gentlemen,

Please allow me to give a very brief overview of Timor-Leste's experiences, as a new nation, of Peace building and State building.

Following our Referendum in 1999, when our people voted courageously for independence, we became trapped in a vicious cycle of violence. About every two years, we suffered violent outbreaks, which resulted in deaths and the destruction of property. And, in 2006, just four years after we assumed sovereignty from the United Nations administration, we suffered our worst internal conflict. This violent period threatened to tear our nation apart, the nation that we had fought so hard, and suffered so much, to achieve. We had to break this cycle of violence. To do this, we had to take a painful step and admit that we had failed. We had failed to address the root causes of our problems and failed to build our State institutions.

When our Government came to power in 2007, we set about reducing our fragility. We focused on reforms to our security sector to build capacity and professionalise our police force and our military. We introduced social policies to address the underlying causes of our fragility and to support our veterans and elderly, who had sacrificed so much in the struggle for independence. We restructured the public sector, implemented public financial management reforms and established bodies of independent oversight to promote good governance. And, we tackled poverty and encouraged economic growth to underpin our development. In 2009, on the Tenth Anniversary of the Referendum, the Government launched a new motto, 'Goodbye Conflict, Welcome Development', which was embraced by our people who were tired of suffering, tired of fighting each other. We are now enjoying stability and security and strong economic development.

This period of stability has allowed us to prepare a 20-year Strategic Development Plan that focuses on three vital areas: social capital, infrastructure and economic development. This plan represents the hopes and wishes of the Timorese people and it will be the cornerstone of our nation-building efforts as we move further and further away from our fragile beginnings to become a secure, peaceful and well-governed nation.

Next year will be very important for us. In 2012, we will hold presidential and legislative elections, the third democratic elections in Timor-Leste. We are confident that they will be conducted peacefully but we must remain vigilant. While we are confident that we are now becoming a more stable, peaceful and tolerant society, we remain fragile. We know, from painful experience, that it is easier to burn down a house than to rebuild it, just as it is easier to derail a State than to develop it. And that is why we are here today.

Friends,

Today we meet to discuss our future. We may meet as fragile and some of us as conflict-affected States, but we also meet with unity and strength. Together, we have so much experience and so much wisdom to share. Our common experiences give us natural bonds of solidarity and understanding. Our different experiences add depth and value to our group. Here, we can be open about our problems. We can be honest about our failings. And we can share and celebrate our successes.

This meeting of fragile, conflict-affected and post-conflict States is the most important step for the consolidation and the future, of the g7+. Whether this body succeeds in its goals or fades away over time is up to us. I am a great supporter of the potential of the g7+. That is why I have promoted this body to the United Nations General Assembly and its Security Council and all other forums I attend. It is only together, speaking with one voice, acting as one group, that we can bring about change to the way that aid is delivered. And it is only through learning from each other, and supporting each other, that we can move beyond fragility and conflict.

In this way, the g7+ can be seen to have two roles. The first is external, representing us all collectively to the world. The second is internal, allowing us to learn from each other to inform our own approaches to Peace building and State building.

Ladies and Gentlemen,

One of our key aims is to improve the transparency and effectiveness of international aid. It is to re-acquire ownership of the development program and to ensure that it does not weaken our self-determination. We did not fight for our independence just to lose ownership of our development. But it has been our experience that aid has the potential to weaken or avoid our internal processes, to actually inhibit institution building. It has been our experience that aid can result in expensive, foreign-controlled programs; where most of the funds find their way back to donor nations with limited benefit to our people. And it has been our experience that aid delivery can be inflexible and process-heavy, resulting in funds being spent in the wrong places and not able to be used to prevent emerging conflict that threatens the State.

We have also had to deal with development 'experts' seeking to impose their supply-driven or template solutions with little regard for our culture, our context and the reality of our country. And, worst of all, when aid programs fail, the blame for this failure is often located not with the donor, but with our people — with us. But achieving development is not a matter of merely following some easy and universal steps, like following a recipe in a cookbook.

All fragile States are different and require different approaches. But we have not come to this retreat to criticise foreign aid. We are here to work towards making aid more effective, both for our people and for the donors who provide it. It is up to us to exercise leadership, set priorities and take ownership, and with ownership accept accountability. It is up to us to make sure we transition from traditional approaches of aid delivery to more effective models. It is up to us to make sure that development assistance responds to the demands, needs and aspirations of our people.

We need a new aid deal. This deal must recognise that fragile States cannot meet most of the Millennium Development Goals. It must recognise that it is first necessary to embark on an inter-related process of peace building and State building before the MDGs can be achieved. We need to advocate the importance of peace building and State building goals as a necessary foundation for meeting the MDGs. And we must be the ones responsible for measuring our own fragility and not have it done for us. To do this, it is critical that the voice of fragile States be heard, that our experiences are considered, and that changes are made to transform the politics and policy of international aid.

In the future, we must focus on results and not inputs. We must explore how the global technology and telecommunications revolution can be harnessed to develop our nations, how health care, education and economic opportunities can be provided through new technology. And we must take advantage of the historic global political and economic structural changes that are taking place.

Not only are we witnessing the transformation of much of the Arab world, but we are also experienced the rise of great emerging economies. Many African nations are already benefiting from the rise of China and the potential it provides for cost-effective infrastructure building. Many of us are already sourcing professional and technical assistance from India rather than from traditional, developed countries. And we are looking at training our people, to build our skills, knowledge and human resources, in the emerging economies of South East Asia, as well as India and Brazil.

With this shift in economic and political power we will also see changes to global governance and our international institutions. These trends will continue and we must not be passive in the face of these structural changes, we must make sure we benefit from them. We must not continue to be the third class citizen of this chaotic and globalised world.

Friends,

The Fourth High Level Forum on Aid Effectiveness in Busan, Korea, begins next month. This is a critical meeting for the g7+ and this retreat will determine whether we will be successful in Korea. At this Retreat, we must develop our priorities and determine the position that we will take to Busan. This will include working on an effective and sophisticated communications strategy. We must make sure that our voice is heard in Busan. We must make sure that the future framework of aid delivery takes account of our needs and our situations. And we must make sure that our experiences define the terms of the discussion about international aid, rather than having those terms dictated to us.

While the g7+ was born out of the global debates on aid effectiveness, that does not mean we should be limited to this single issue. This group provides a unique opportunity for us to pursue an agenda that supports our nations and our people. There are many issues, beyond aid, that shape our progress and our future. These include global trade, finance, labour, health, environment and development policies. The g7+ provides a collective voice for us to be heard on international issues that impact our people. But to be heard, and to be recognised as the global voice for fragile nations, we must have unity.

We must also have credibility, and to have credibility, we must have substance. I urge the Policy Working Group of this Retreat to set a foundation for us to develop a shared set of priorities and policies. There will be a need to undertake research, prepare case studies and discussion papers and to critically evaluate how global actions impact local communities in our countries. The advocacy of a substantive policy agenda provides great scope for the g7+ to influence global change into the future, and, through those changes, improve the lives and wellbeing of our people.

Brothers and Sisters,

Before I finish, I would like to speak about the internal role that the g7+ can play. This role allows us to speak as friends in a spirit of solidarity and support about the progress of own countries. We can share our experiences, both sweet and bitter, with people who understand our circumstances.

We face many common challenges. These challenges raise questions and together we are more likely to find answers. These questions include:

- How do we turn a subsistence economy into a modern economy?
- How do we develop our human resources?
- How do we build basic infrastructure?

- How do we manage aid without forsaking our sovereignty?
- How do we ensure security when we are fragile?

Such questions are not easy. But we are the ones who are best placed to find the answers. This is because it is our people who live the experience of fragility. It is our people who have to find the courage, determination and spirit to move from fragility to strength. And we understand the realities of our nations and what it means to live with extreme poverty, with insecurity and with struggle. This Retreat gives us all the chance to further develop our bonds of trust and friendship. I urge us all to make the most of this rare opportunity.

Friends, thank you for giving me the time to speak to you all today. It is a true honour and a privilege. In this room, we have a group of people from across many countries, whose expertise on fragile States is unsurpassed. There is, however, much work to be done and this Retreat will establish the foundation for the future of the g7+. I look forward to working together with you all in the future as we take the outcomes of this Retreat to the international community.

# Launch of the Timor-Leste Transparency Portal

Díli Convention Centre,
15 March 2011

>Your Excellency the President of the Republic
>Honourable Members of Parliament
>Honourable Government Members
>Honourable Members of the Diplomatic Corps
>Distinguished Members from the Church
>Distinguished Director-Generals and National Directors
>Distinguished Civil Society Representatives
>Distinguished Guests
>Ladies and Gentlemen,

It is my pleasure today to welcome you to the launch of the Timor-Leste Transparency Portal. Since the IV Constitutional Government came to office, on 8 August 2007, we have been walking a long path to strengthen the institutional capacity of public administration, so as to better protect the interests of the State, to improve public service delivery and, of course, to promote good governance. As such, it is a great honour for me to be here today at the launch of the Transparency Portal, which will enable real time data on State expenditure, that can be accessed by the public through a website.

>Ladies and Gentlemen,

This Portal represents much more than the development of a mechanism for promoting transparency, accountability and control in regard to the public accounts of the State. This Portal represents the true transformation of our State, particularly in Public Administration, which, step-by-step, has been adopting new efficiencies, innovation and accountability standards. This was the commitment we made when we accepted the challenge of governing the Country for five years, that is, to implement bold policies enabling the social and economic development of the country and the reduction of poverty. This goal can only be achieved with a strong Government that is transparent and that does not favour one party over others; when we have the necessary instruments to oversee Government members, Directors and other public servants, so that they do not misuse the financial resources that belong to the People and that they never put their individual interests above the interests of the whole.

This oversight, this control over the public accounts of the State, can now be performed by ALL Timorese citizens, regardless of whether they reside in Timor-Leste or anywhere in the world! Timor-Leste is, therefore, leading one of the most progressive systems in the world, enabling any person to have access to the Timor-Leste State General Budget process, as well as to its tax execution, in real time and in an interactive manner.

Your Excellencies

Ladies and Gentlemen,

We have achieved reforms in the area of Public Finance Management that resulted in efficiency improvements, including a significant degree of decentralisation to enable better service delivery to our People. The reform and improvement process continues every day, step by step, as we continue to build on the foundations that have already been set.

Civil servants are first, with front line responsibility for providing services to the entire population, and have the potential to contribute to improving the living situation of the Timorese People. Therefore they must — or, rather, all of us in attendance must — perform our duties with greater efficiency and professionalism, making better use of the available tools and mechanisms that support integrity and productivity. Given their management and administration of public investment, the establishment of the Civil Service Commission is vital to our economy. The public services are currently the main driver of economic growth.

It was also in pursuing greater accountability in the national development process that we established the Anti-Corruption Commission. We have also begun a process of reform to Public Finance Management and started to set up a Superior Audit Agency, which, for the time being, is the Chamber of Accounts. This Chamber will constitute part of the Court of Appeal, with the mandate of promoting transparency in public accounts and ensuring accountability in regard to reporting.

I say all this to put in context this reform, to show that the Transparency Portal is just one more measure from this Government to achieve the goals set out in our Five-Year Program, particularly in regard to:
- Fighting corruption in Government and Public Administration;
- Implementing the principle of Good Governance, including encouraging the People to take part in political decisions and their execution;
- Creating transparency mechanisms;
- Establishing an efficient and transparent system so that the entire population knows how the executive carries out the tasks given to it.

The Government is also committed to managing the revenue flow with accountability and transparency, investing in the development of the Nation.

In July, last year, we became the third country in the world to be given full compliance status with the Extractive Industries Transparency Initiative. In October, last year, we were recognised in the first ever Revenue Watch index as a Government with Comprehensive Revenue Transparency. Further, and as we have done since the beginning of our mandate, this year we held a full parliamentary debate on the State Budget that was conducted transparently and televised to the public. This degree of public accountability is something that is not seen in many countries in the world.

I said it then, and say it again to you now, that, as we see people across the globe crying out for democracy, this type of transparency proves that our people have reasons to be proud of their Democratic Institutions. And indeed, we all ought to be proud of our Nation's democracy.

Your Excellencies,

Ladies and Gentlemen,

Public Administration Reform is already in full swing. With this reform, the Principle of Bringing Public Services Closer to the Population and the Principle of Participation by All Stakeholders in Public Administration, particularly Civil Society representatives, has already been realised! Through the Transparency Portal, we provide an innovative way of calling upon all Timorese to be involved in the very operation of public administration and, in as much as possible, participate in Government decision making.

Starting today, people will be able to go on-line and monitor the books of public expenditure, with information updated daily. People can see how the budget is being executed, what is being spent in each Ministry, Department and Directorate and on what category of items. For a Government that is committed to broad development throughout the country, it is important that the public has access to this information. At a time when we are preparing to make significant investments through the Infrastructure Fund and Human Capacity Development Fund, we now have an important instrument for monitoring our expenditure. As we work towards achieving the Millennium Development Goals through the MDG Suco program, we can see what is being spent and where. Furthermore, the expenditure information concerning the Decentralised Development Programs will be updated daily.

This innovative Portal will also be strengthened with the launch of the Procurement Portal, which will take place in Díli, on 25-27 August, on the occasion of the large Regional Conference on the Extractive Industries Transparency Initiative (EITI) that we are currently organising, and where we hope to see each and every one of you. We are aware that the Timor-Leste Transparency Portal will raise many questions, and some of these may require some time and some knowledge of public accounting to reconcile. But we also know that this is part of the process for reforming and improving our Institutions.

I urge you to use this Portal for the good of Timor-Leste, as I believe that it will contribute:

- to detailed research on the country,
- to foster knowledge and understanding, and
- to bolster our national development.

As such, I cannot but thank the Minister of Finance and her entire team for their commitment and hard work in this difficult task that is the promotion of Transparency and Good Governance, particularly in regard to the management of the public finances of the State. That being said, and since, in this case, images speak louder than words, let us all log on to the Transparency Portal and witness another major step in our Country's path towards development.

I officially launch the Timor-Leste Transparency Portal.

# Launch of the Strategic Development Plan 2011-2030

Díli
12 July 2011

>Your Excellencies
>Ladies and gentlemen,

First and foremost, I want to salute all of you who have come a long way to take part once more in this important meeting, the main purpose of which is to strengthen strategic partnerships to develop our Nation.

We all know that the future of the Timorese and of Timor-Leste is closely associated with the relationships that we have established through these meetings. As such, in my name and also on behalf of the Government and the People of Timor-Leste, I would like to welcome you and to thank you all for coming.

>Ladies and gentlemen,

Everyone knows that, since the first donors meeting held in Tokyo in 1999, we have had the good fortune to be able to rely on international aid to build our State under the rule of law and to mitigate extreme poverty of our People.

Therefore, and despite the difficulties, we have already walked a long path since 1999.

We are proud to have established a structure of democratic governance, setting as an initial priority the consolidation of our State agencies and the promotion of a fair and participative political system.

Aware that the triumph of democracy is not easy in a country that is mostly poor and deeply traumatised, the perseverance of our young, our men and our women enabled us to walk a path full of aspiration and achievement, and to break with the curse of cyclical violence and crisis that affected Timor-Leste.

Taking inspiration from our difficulties, and from the experiences of other frail nations that take around 10-15 years to recover stability, we focused on a strong investment in initiatives with direct impact on the lives of the people, earning greater participation and trust by the population in regard to the solving of conflicts and consolidating unity and national stability.

It was under this spirit of union, and celebrating the safety we began to feel throughout the country, that in 2009, on the occasion of the 10$^{th}$ Anniversary of the Referendum, we chose as a motto for our Nation: 'Goodbye Conflict, Welcome Development'.

On 31 December 2010 all people celebrated the new environment of security and stability, and our trust in the future, with joy and enthusiasm. Finally we stopped our cycle of conflict and violence that was occurring every two years.

The various setbacks and serious crises we faced during these years became important lessons for our future, of learning how to deal with the fragility of our State. And it was with your help that we have been working together to align our national priorities every year to achieve progress.

Consequently, Timor-Leste became a safe country in less than a decade, benefiting from peace, stability and a clearly growing economy.

Your Excellencies

Ladies and gentlemen,

Today we witness another landmark towards our future, launching in this Timor-Leste Development Partners Meeting the Strategic Development Plan (SDP), which was endorsed only yesterday by the National Parliament.

And for those of you who recall last year's Synopsis, the Strategic Development Plan sets a vision for the next two decades and starts a new stage of bold national development.

## Setting of the Strategic Development Plan

Allow me to start by explaining the writing of this plan, that mobilised every piece of knowledge, resource and effort available to understand the will of the Timorese People and set the path down which we want our country to head.

In May 2002, I and the Government of RDTL launched the National Development Plan as a response to the aspirations of the People of Timor-Leste and their 20-year development expectations.

In this document the Timorese People set, in a simple but multifaceted vision, the challenges to nationbuilding and the developmental needs of the country.

The National Development Plan of 2002 was designed to cover a period of five years with a special focus on the establishment of institutions that previously did not exist; the recruitment of civil servants, including those in the justice sector. It also defined strategies, identified goals and adopted guidelines for its period of execution and included performance indicators.

Many political leaders, and even some international agencies, asked: 'If there is already a National Development Plan, why make another?'

Well, as for the need for a new plan, the 2002 NDP stated:

*This is Timor-Leste's first Plan and, consequently, it is important that it is reviewed at certain times to see if the overall strategic direction remains valid or if changes should be made.*

Indeed it was recommended that *'because the Plan is Timor-Leste's first, it should be subject to a full review after its first year of operation.'* This review never took place, despite the warning that planning for the future should be an ongoing concern and that the planning process itself should evolve, change, mature and improve systematically.

More than enough time has passed to justify a new plan, for the good of our People. This plan must be duly adapted to the new circumstances of a country that is changing and growing, responding to needs through a coordinated development framework that enables harmony and sustainability at all levels: economic, social, cultural, political and institutional.

This was undoubtedly the ideal moment to undertake this mission.

At the time we drafted this Strategic Development Plan we benefited from the recent political and social stability.

Additionally, we were able to make use of the institutional and structural reforms being implemented, which resulted in a period of unprecedented economic growth.

The Strategic Development Plan is informed by:

**First:** The outcomes of the 2010 Census, which updated statistical information on demographic, economic and social aspects of the nation – allowing us to take 'a real and objective picture' of the population. As such, the SDP was informed by accurate data in order to substantiate real progress and to define the necessary policies and programs, without being based on wrong assumptions.

**Second:** The outcomes of the public consultation in the 65 sub-districts, including villages in *sucos* throughout the entire national territory.

Therefore, in addition to the exhaustive technical work by all those who contributed to the drafting of this project, including the active participation of the Ministries and Timorese civil servants, this plan relies on the participation of an entire People.

This plan gives voice to our women, our young and our elders. To our farmers, our health professionals, our businesspeople and our teachers. It gives voice to consumers, patients and students. The plan gives voice not only to those who live in our capital, Díli, but also to those who live in remote villages, from the Oecusse enclave to the eastern tip of Lospalos.

## The philosophy of the Strategic Development Plan

I believe that planning and development are not ends in themselves. Planning is just a method for structuring ideas and ideals, containing a socio-economic political philosophy that all leaders of the country must adopt.

The philosophy guiding these ideals is translated in the provision of better living conditions for the entire Timorese population, within a feasible and tangible period of time.

Under the country's current conditions of poverty, needs are still many and large. As such, responses must themselves be multi-dimensional and integrative so actions have continuity and, more importantly, have the necessary positive impact in households, communities, areas, regions and ultimately all the territory.

This plan's main underlying premise, ladies and gentlemen, is that the current situation of the nation requires the leaders of this country to assume their historical responsibilities without hesitation, and to be brave when making the decisions that will enable a brighter future for the People of Timor-Leste.

## The Strategic Development Plan seeks integrated growth

There is no doubt that the country needs to grow its economy, so that society obtains and retains benefits. Only continuous economic growth can support social and human development:

- in terms of creating jobs,
- in terms of improving service delivery,
- in terms of equity in the distribution of national wealth,
- in terms of improving knowledge,
- in terms of changing attitudes and behaviours, and
- in terms of national confidence and stability.

As such, we present an integrated package of policies to be implemented in the short term (1-5 years), medium term (5-10 years) and long term (10-20 years), serving as guides for inclusive, sustainable and long-term development.

Despite the complexity of its history and the fact that Timor-Leste is defined as a Least Developed Country (LDC), our country has four essential attributes that make development possible:

### 1. Political Will

The centuries of colonial domination never destroyed the Timorese dream of autonomy and emancipation. In the same manner that this national cause united the People around a common ideal, so now does the current fight for prosperity nurtured by all with conviction, courage and determination.

### 2. Economic Potential

Thanks to the petroleum wealth and Timor-Leste's position in East Asia, a coherent and strategic plan will enable us to boost our economy by using oil revenues to invest in productive sectors, infrastructure, education and health, turning an economy that presently is fully dependent on oil into a non-oil dependent economy.

### 3. National Integration

Timor-Leste has a land area of around 15,000km$^2$ and a population of little over one million. Timor-Leste has every requirement for successful national integration, through the establishment of effective connections among its population, between rural and urban areas and between the Government and the People. In a relatively short period of time, we can change our economic distance in terms of suppliers and markets by improving the road system, telecommunications, and transportation and power distribution, without neglecting planned urbanisation that enables us to achieve balance between rural and urban areas.

**4. Dynamism**

Timor-Leste also has a very young population. Although this causes some challenges to the State, it also opens great opportunities for the future. We have the potential with this young population, to transform the social and economic fabric of Timor-Leste and, with initiative, innovation and access to new technologies, create a better life for the country.

Your Excellencies
Ladies and gentlemen,

Every strategy and action considered in this Plan seeks to transform Timor-Leste from a low income country to a medium-high income country by 2030. This is intrinsically associated with a healthy, educated and safe population and a society that is prosperous and food self-sufficient.

This is the yearning of our People, to which we must respond. So now we must ask ourselves: how are we going to achieve this? How will the SDP respond to these aspirations?

Ladies and gentlemen

The Strategic Development Plan covers three key areas: **social capital**, **infrastructure** and **economic development**.

While the goals of the Strategic Development Plan are consistent with the Millennium Development Goals, they are tailored to reflect the unique history, culture and heritage of Timor-Leste — our goals recognise that nationbuilding and peacebuilding must first be addressed in order to achieve other social and economic objectives.

Education and training are crucial to improving the life opportunities of our young and to Timor-Leste's economic development and growth.

Our plan will ensure that all Timorese children have the opportunity to attend school and receive quality education. It is our aim to give all our children the knowledge and skills necessary for their future and for our nation's development.

A training and vocational education system will be developed to build the capacity of our people to take on new challenges and to provide Timor-Leste with the skilled people we need.

Our plan also addresses our desire for a healthy population and our aim is to ensure that by 2030 we will have comprehensive, high-quality health services accessible to all Timorese people.

Our plan to provide quality primary health care services for all focuses on the needs of children, women and other vulnerable groups, and the development of hospital services that are able to respond to our people's need for specialist care.

Ladies and gentlemen,

Since independence in 2002, successive governments in Timor-Leste have made assisting the poor and vulnerable a national priority. While almost every second person in Timor-Leste still lives below the poverty line, modest subsidies and other in-kind support to our most vulnerable people have dramatically improved the lives of many families.

We must also continue to provide appropriate recognition and assistance to ensure our veterans and their families live with dignity.

Ladies and gentlemen,

For generations our ancestors depended on the environment for food, clothing, building materials and everything else essential for life. But over our history there has been extensive exploitation and destruction of our environment.

The Strategic Development Plan is based on the assumption that our social and economic development requires healthy forests, rivers, and marine and animal life. Our plan therefore aims to renew the strong bond between Timorese people and the environment.

Our plan also recognises Timor-Leste's incredibly rich and diverse cultural heritage. In each part of our country, there are languages, dances, music and other forms of social and artistic expression that cannot be found anywhere else in the world.

We have managed to maintain our traditions that date back thousands of years and we are proud of what makes us uniquely Timorese. By 2020 Timor-Leste will have a vibrant creative industries sector that is making a significant contribution to our economy and our sense of national identity.

Ladies and gentlemen,

After social capital, the next key focus of the Strategic Development Plan is the building and maintenance of core and productive infrastructures. We also need core infrastructure to connect our people and drive our emerging industries.

The plan sets out strategies to improve the quality of our roads, build efficient commercial ports, improve water and sanitation, and provide affordable energy and a modern communications system to our people.

Roads will be improved and a national road network will be developed to connect our communities, provide access to markets and government services and support rural development, industry and tourism.

In summary, our plan for road infrastructure in Timor-Leste is to:
- rehabilitate all rural roads to a minimum standard by 2015; and
- fully rehabilitate all national and district roads to an international standard by 2020.

Another important element in the economic and social development of Timor-Leste — and in the health and wellbeing of our people — is access to safe drinking water, sanitation systems and improved drainage.

We will continue to take action to overcome the many challenges involved in improving access to clean water, sanitation and drainage across Timor-Leste so that by 2030, all citizens in Timor-Leste will have access to clean water and improved sanitation.

Ladies and gentlemen,

Access to electricity is a basic right and the foundation for our economic future. We are taking action to ensure that by 2015 everyone in Timor-Leste will have access to reliable electricity 24 hours a day.

This will be achieved through investment, already made, in new power plants and upgraded transmission and distribution systems, along with the rapid expansion of renewable energy systems.

The expansion of the Timor-Leste economy, and the increased demand created by the Strategic Development Plan infrastructure program, will generate an urgent need for greater sea port capacity on both the north and the south coasts.

The plan provides for the establishment of new sea ports at Tibar on the north coast and Suai on the south coast to meet our future industry and freight demands. We will also embark on a regional ports construction program over the next ten years. Our plan also provides a much needed program of airport rehabilitation and construction.

Improved telecommunications are also essential to Timor-Leste's future development. The vision of the Strategic Development Plan is that by 2015 we will have a modern telecommunications network that will connect people in Timor-Leste to each other and to the world, and that will allow us to take full advantage of global telecommunications advances in such areas as education, health, local governance, information technology, security, justice and vocational training.

Three quarters of our population live in rural areas. Over 50 per cent of our rural population is under 19 years old.

The economic development section of our plan therefore focuses on rural development and sets in place policies to ensure there will be jobs for these young.

To build our nation and grow our economy we will focus on three critical industries – agriculture, petroleum and tourism.

Seventy per cent of families in Timor-Leste rely on some sort of farming activity for their survival which is why the plan aims to increase productivity in our agriculture sector. Increased agricultural productivity will also be essential to achieve the Strategic Development Plan goal of food security by 2020.

The petroleum sector is another key industry in the Strategic Development Plan. This sector is critical not only to our economic growth, but also to our future progress as a successful, stable nation.

While developing the sector, we must ensure that Timor-Leste's natural resource wealth is used to build our nation and support all our people.

We will make the most of our oil and gas wealth by establishing a National Petroleum Company, TIMOR GAP, developing the Tasi Mane project on the south coast and giving our people the skills and experience they need to lead and manage the development of our petroleum industry.

Ladies and gentlemen,

Tourism is the third key industry that will be developed to help build our nation and provide jobs for our young people. With Timor-Leste's natural beauty, rich history and cultural heritage there is great potential to develop tourism as a major industry to underpin our economic development.

A successful tourism industry will contribute income to the national and local economies, create jobs, build businesses and improve regional economic imbalances.

The Strategic Development Plan also sets new economic policy directions to support private sector development and build our finance industry in Timor-Leste.

This includes undertaking a reform program to improve our business environment and establishing a National Development Bank to support our entrepreneurs, a Timor-Leste Investment Agency and transforming the Timor-Leste Microfinance Institute to become a small commercial bank, which was launched yesterday at 5pm to support small companies and cooperatives in rural areas.

Ladies and gentlemen,

We know from experience that stability and security are necessary preconditions to social and economic development. After many years of conflict, our people want to live in a stable and secure nation that recognises the rule of law and provides access to justice for all our citizens.

Our plan aims to achieve this through the development of transparent, accountable and competent institutions across our civil service, our security sector and our justice system.

It also acknowledges the need for the development of a professional, respected defence force that has the capability to defend our nation and contribute to regional and global peace and stability.

Over the next 20 years we will adopt an outward looking, collaborative approach to foreign policy to encourage stronger cultural, economic and trade relations with other countries and be an active, contributing member of the international community.

Ladies and gentlemen,

The strategies and guidelines presented here seek above all to alleviate agriculture and the public sector as the driving forces of our economy, by focusing on a growing private sector, on industries and on other services.

To start this new paradigm we require strong public investment and great dynamism by our private sector. It is comforting to know that, despite the serious economic crisis, many emerging economies have been consolidating.

Timor-Leste may be one of these economies, particularly if it knows how to use the fact that it is a part of Asia. Joining ASEAN gives us great market potential, while the good relationships with countries like China, Japan and Indonesia make this ambition even more promising.

On the other hand, counting Bayu Undan, our main petroleum field, and Kitan, which should start generating revenues for the country soon, the conservative estimates indicate that we will generate around US$22 billion in oil by 2025. The Greater Sunrise field and other potential discoveries will also increase revenues substantially within the next 20 years.

As such, we are reviewing the Petroleum Fund Law, which we have already submitted to the National Parliament for consideration. We will be diversifying Petroleum Fund investments, with greater balance between bonds and equities, so as to safely protect and produce more wealth for the country.

We are also exploring new mechanisms to fund infrastructure programs included in this SDP, such as Public-Private Partnerships and concessional loans. These will have the additional advantage of enabling the expansion of the private sector in Timor-Leste, namely in larger projects such as roads, bridges, seaports and airports.

Timor-Leste is also fortunate to have a vast number of generous development partners that continue to provide support and financial assistance to all sectors and line ministries. This assistance is vital in what concerns the development of our human resources, without which implementing this strategy to develop the Nation would be impossible.

Ladies and gentlemen,

Before I conclude, I must mention our recently established National Development Agency, which will transition into the Economic Policy and Investment Agency and which will be primarily responsible for the implementation of the Plan.

The Economic Policy and Investment Agency will plan, design and monitor the strategic programs and projects and supervise the ministries responsible for the projects, ensuring the integrated coordination of the entire Government, the implementation of this Strategic Development Plan, good governance and quality and timely execution.

Additionally, we will be creating a National Procurement Commission, which will recruit an international firm of acknowledged competence to carry out the entire procurement competitive process, ensuring high quality and cost efficiency.

We will, of course, also rely on the excellent sector plans prepared by Ministers and Departments to aid implementation, and the annual budget process will continue its pivotal role.

Ladies and gentlemen,

We are aware that this is an ambitious plan and that the challenges to its implementation are enormous. However, as leaders of this Nation and having extensive knowledge of the needs and yearnings of our People, we know that this is a feasible and timely plan.

We are inspired by the Monterrey Consensus on Financing for Development, which declared that:

> ... *effective partnerships among donors and recipients are based on the recognition of national leadership and ownership of development plans.*

All this was reaffirmed at the C8 Summit at Gleneagles, in 2005:

> *Developing countries and their governments are responsible for leading development. They need to decide, plan and stage their economic policies in order to adjust them with their political strategies, for which they will be accountable to their peoples.*

This is the future that we will decide for ourselves.

The People deserve it and the People are waiting for action! They have fought for 24 years because they believed independence would bring greater benefits. They have been waiting for 10 years to be rewarded for their sacrifices.

I believe that the Development Partners are supportive of our development decisions and that once again they will align their priorities with the priorities of the Timorese People.

As His Excellency The President, put so well in the Preface of the document distributed today: 'the drafting of our Strategic Development Plan was led by our people, belongs to our people and reflects the aspirations of our people'.

Consequently, we Timorese have no doubts that this is one more battle we can win. After all, the success in implementing the plan will ultimately depend on the will of the Timorese People.

# The presentation of the Strategic Development Plan, 2011-2030 to the National Parliament

Díli
11 July 2011

>   Excellency, Acting Speaker of Parliament
>   Excellencies, Presidents of the Benches
>   Excellencies, Presidents of the Committees
>   Distinguished Members of Parliament
>   Dear colleagues Members of Government
>   Representatives of the Civil Society
>   Representatives of the Media
>   Distinguished guests

On behalf of the Government, I want to thank this Sovereign Body for its availability to provide us with this opportunity to present the Timor-Leste Strategic Development Plan for the next 20 years.

Today is a good day for reminding everyone that, in the five-year Program of the IV Constitutional Government, we made the commitment to present a Development Plan for the country. As such, I have the honour to come before you today in order to present the guidelines that will lead our policies in the future, seeking to ensure the wellbeing and prosperity of our People.

We all remember that Parliament, in its I Legislature, approved a Resolution, the National Development Plan, also for 20 years, by 2020.

In any evolution process, one would do well never to lose sight of the need for a permanent, realistic and current review of the conditions involved, the difficulties and constraints, and the large or small achievements made. No review is objective if it neglects these two sides of reality. Sometimes we are made to exaggerate only the good side of things, while other times we tend to assume a defeatist attitude and look only to the negative side of things.

Any process has the same potential: to either collapse upon itself or to bloom into something great.

A political and socio-economic process will obviously present complex factors that must always be taken into consideration, not only individually but more importantly in terms of their interconnection, as it is the latter that determines whether the process moves forward or not. And this is the challenge for the Timorese. Either we face the future with optimism or we just look at our indecisiveness. That is why I will present the presuppositions of the Strategic Development Plan.

Consequently, I will now explain the assumptions of the Strategic Development Plan.

This SDP results from a critical review following the National Development Plan launched in 2002; this review enabled us to understand the evolution of our State building and Nation building process.

The review highlighted the vision of the leaders of the time in the fight against poverty, but stated that since the NDP was *Timor-Leste's first Plan ... it is important that it is reviewed at certain times to see if the overall strategic direction remains valid or if changes should be made.*

Our review also considered the recommendation in the NDP that, *because the Plan is Timor-Leste's first, it should be subject to a full review after its first year of operation (meaning that the review would be in July-August, 2003).*

Indeed, in the aftermath of the destruction of 70 per cent of our infrastructure, and starting an administration from scratch, the NDP reflected the current circumstances of the political moment, with activities focusing on the establishment of human resources and institutions, some of which did not yet exist. Another factor to be considered was the enormous shortage of financial resources, a *sine qua non* condition for effectively implementing any plan. Our review did not put aside our full dependence in terms of support funds from the international community, to which we are all deeply grateful.

Ladies and Gentlemen, this SDP is, as I have said, also the result of the commitment made by the IV Constitutional Government, prescribed in its Program and presented to this National Parliament in September 2007. Consequently, and after dealing with the most pressing problems of the country, all ministries and secretariats of State, together with their directors and heads of department, were directly, actively and fully involved, in 2009, in drafting the sectors to which they all belonged.

In this participative exercise, the Government's task was only to integrate the various sector plans in a single framework, highlighting the interdependence of the various components of the life of the State and the Nation.

This SDP is the outcome of a magnificent work done by dedicated Timorese citizens, that traveled all over the country, to every home throughout the national territory, in order to accurately collect the data we required to learn about the actual living situation of our people and the state of our Nation.

The 2010 Census was of the utmost importance, and the National Statistics Directorate is to be praised for its outstanding work.

This SDP results from the collection of our people's aspirations under a broad national consultation. This was the second one in which I took part, with the first being in 2001, to draft the NDP.

When we presented the Summary of the SDP, titled 'From Conflict to Prosperity', we understood that our people were waiting for more decisive actions that would mitigate their daily suffering and remove them from the miserable conditions in which they dwell.

We could also see joy in the eyes of children, hear cries of hope from youngsters and note benevolent smiles in the wrinkled faces of the elders.

I am proud to say, and I believe that all of you in attendance share this feeling, that this Strategic Development Plan is 100 per cent Timorese.

Some might say that we do not require a SDP, since we already have a plan and what we need now is to continue implementing the NDP. The answer to this is more 'no' than 'yes'. No, because of the grounds that supported the NDP, which no longer apply today — goals that were too vague and that contained macroeconomic uncertainties.

Any reality is in constant evolution and the rapid change of balances between challenges and skills is always reflected in new processes, in processes that start because of the inherent circumstances.

The ability to deal with processes comes from the clear notion of the changes made in the situations of those processes. And today our State and our Nation are in a new situation.

In this new situation, it is absolutely essential that our State defines, as clearly as possible, the stages and phases for our country's development. It is necessary for the State to define national priorities, to determine the vital sectors for solving the problems of our people. The State must determine the sector or sectors that are to become the driving engine of economic and social development.

We are a democratic country, but no State lives on freedom of expression or on physical development alone. Democracy is vital for the integrated and sustainable development of a country, but without development there is no democracy.

Both components are interlinked, supporting and consolidating one another. In our case we can even say that our People have waited too long. Together we have succeeded in breaking the cycle of violence and skirmishes of the last few years. Now we all have the duty to meet the aspirations of our People.

And the Nation already has the basic and essential conditions to provide the country with the boost it requires.

Timor-Leste is part of the 40 countries called LDCs, or Least Developed Countries, and a member of the group of so-called Fragile States. The definition of Fragile States has connotations both political and socioeconomic.

If we look at a Libya, an Egypt, a Syria or even a Yemen, the process we see in those countries is the demand for political democracy. In our case, what we need is economic democratisation, where our society must be able to participate in order to improve its living situation.

This is what the SDP wants to focus on. The Strategic Development Plan provides an accurate picture of the state of the Nation and an objective perception of the challenges ahead in the various spheres of life.

The Strategic Development Plan is a thorough and reliable instrument for identifying and assessing priorities and is a means we can use to understand the necessary strategies and the consequent actions deriving from the adoption of policies, both in global terms and in terms of each sector.

The Strategic Development Plan sets a special framework that protects the country from regional imbalances and that makes use of the entire potential of Timor-Leste, providing equal opportunities to all the people to benefit from the wealth of the country.

The 2020 vision of the NDP is as relevant today as it was back in 2001. And this is the vision that the Strategic Development Plan pursues for 2030, since all of us here want that:

- Timor-Leste will be a democratic and prosperous society with adequate food, shelter and clothing for all.
- People will be literate, knowledgeable and skilled. They will be healthy, and live a long, productive life. They will actively participate in economic, social and political development, promoting social equality and national unity.
- People will no longer be isolated, because there will be good roads, transport, electricity, and communications in the towns and villages, in all regions of the country.
- Production and employment will increase in all sectors – agriculture, fisheries and forestry.
- Living standards and services will improve for all Timorese.

After overcoming the economic circumstances that earlier Governments faced, during the difficult period when it was necessary to set the bases for a democratic State, the Strategic Development Plan today presents a safe path for us to achieve the goals set in 2002.

As such, I will now focus on the Strategic Development Plan.

The SDP, of which you have all received copies, is a document covering three essential areas — Social Capital, Infrastructure and Economic Development.

Ladies and Gentlemen

The SDP places the person, the Timorese, as the central point around which all our considerations, strategies and actions revolve. A State can only exist if there are people living within a territory. Throughout the centuries our People have shown their strength and their determination to achieve their goals. Consequently, the People should be the target of the policies made by the State. The people are the greatest wealth of any nation. A nation can only move forward if its people evolve in terms of practices and behaviour, evolve in knowledge, evolve in their adaptation to the new technology that they require for their development. Educated and healthy people, with strong principles and ideals, make a strong and dynamic State and make a prosperous and modern nation.

Regarding Social Capital, we insist on educated people that are able to rise to the challenges and to handle their own problems.

The State must set the way to make this possible, and the SDP shows this way.

In the Education sector, the SDP sets benchmarks to achieve in the short (by 2015), medium (from 2016 to 2020) and long term (from 2021 to 2030).

In terms of Social Capital, we want to have healthy, energetic and dynamic people who are able to get actively involved in the development of their own country from the villages, *sucos* and municipalities. As is the case in the rest of the world, from America to Africa, from Asia to Europe, the State has the duty to look after the health of its citizens. The SDP presents a framework for the provision of health services.

In the Health sector, the SDP sets equally the benchmarks to achieve in the respective timeframes of implementation.

Concerning Social Capital, we advocate that an egalitarian society is the basis for a fairer society and that it provides the conditions to raise the spirit of solidarity between people and communities — which constitutes of the stronger points of the character of our People. The State must look after everyone and the SDP provides the means to do so. The disabled, the elderly, the chronically sick, vulnerable people, including women and children, will be protected and receive support. The Veterans deserve a special place, in the sense that the State must continue to provide opportunities for them to participate in small projects and allow them to feel that they are contributing to the development of the Nation, for which they fought.

The State must look after everyone and the SDP provides the means to do this.

In the Social inclusion sector, the SDP sets equally the benchmarks to achieve in the respective timeframes of implementation.

Regarding Social Capital, we have expressed our concern as to the degradation of our environment. The birds, whose melancholic chirping announced the rainy season, and the swallows that flew low as to attract the heavy rain clouds, have disappeared from the annual ritual that sets the calendar for farmers. Gone too are our springs and our bushes, the hiding place of our guerrilla fighters. Enter floods and out-of-control erosions, causing immeasurable damages to every home, to every community.

The State must strive to correct this, and the SDP presents the guidelines.

In the Environment sector, the SDP sets equally the benchmarks to achieve in the respective timeframes of implementation.

In terms of Social Capital, we look inside our People, to their identity and culture. In short, we look at their soul. People do not live on bread alone, meaning that any social and economic progress counts for nothing if people cease to know themselves. The effects of globalisation cannot make the Timorese citizen just one unit among billions. The effects of the new technology are a threat to the identity of our people if our children, wearing suits and ties, will hesitate to say that they have a wealthy patrimony.

The State cannot minimise this danger. The SDP presents the solutions.

In the Culture and Heritage sector, the SDP sets equally the benchmarks to achieve in the respective timeframes of implementation.

To conclude my address on this area, I want to say that the primary investment of our State must be in human capital, in our Country's human resources.

Ladies and Gentlemen

Another vital area is Infrastructure. Without schools, children cannot have classes. Without clinics, patients cannot receive treatment. Without roads, the people cannot have access to basic services and markets. Without power, we continue to need firewood for cooking. Without water, there is no hygiene and no agricultural production.

After the Second World War there were 13 countries that emerged from nothing or from nearly nothing and which developed quickly. They are known as 'economic miracles'. They had the courage to focus on infrastructure because they knew that without infrastructure the country could not move forward. Today we feel the same in Timor-Leste; we feel that infrastructure must accompany development. Today, in Timor-Leste, we have reached the conclusion that rehabilitation alone only makes costs higher and unsustainable.

If we want to accelerate economic development in our country, we have no other alternative but to stimulate construction on a larger scale, of necessary infrastructure to support the development of all other productive sectors in the country's economy.

Regarding Infrastructure, we have looked at the condition of our roads and bridges. We established a road network, defining its size and importance. We sought to understand the causes for its deterioration and the options in terms of its repair and safe maintenance. It is vital that the national road network provides access to the population in its daily needs. It is necessary to break the isolation of communities, while needing to deal with the growing volume of traffic, with safe roads. The State must make decisions, and the SDP drafts this strategy.

The State has to decide and the SDP develops this strategy.

In the Roads and Bridges sector, once more, the SDP sets the benchmarks to achieve in the respective timeframes of implementation.

Concerning Infrastructure, we took the care to look at our people's needs in terms of improving hygiene and the supply of safe water. The lack of latrines and sewage systems, even in urban centres, as well as the unreliable supply of water to the people, are among the main causes of child mortality and overall poor health condition of our people.

The State is clearly aware of this and the SDP points to an integrated solution.

The SDP sets equally the benchmarks to achieve in the respective timeframes of implementation for the Water and Sanitation sector.

In terms of Infrastructure, we acknowledge the great importance of electricity in the lives of people. Social benefits are huge. Energy will also promote the development of other industrial sectors. Studies have also been conducted regarding our alternative energy potential. More importantly, our people need their poor homes to have light at night, since this will make a huge difference in their lives.

The State must assume this priority and the SDP will provide the means.

The SDP sets the benchmarks and the respective timeframes for implementation to ensure electrical energy supply in the Country.

Regarding Infrastructure, we have also examined the Díli port, which can no longer respond to the increase in the cargo volume, along with the other constraints we all know. We also looked at the importance of other regional ports that can provide better sea connections for our country, making transportation easier and supporting the fish and meat industry for exportation.

The State is aware of this and the SDP has the planning.

The SDP presents the benchmarks and the timeframes of the building of Bridges sector.

In terms of Infrastructure, we noticed that the Díli international airport requires immediate attention, lest it becomes unable to respond to air traffic requirements. We cannot also imagine Timor-Leste without air connections that cover the Country. The development of our FFAA will also require an air base in Baucau, to support our sea control activities.

The State must assume this programme and the SDP can implement it.

In the Airports sector, the SDP expresses the benchmarks to achieve in the respective timeframes of implementation.

Finally, concerning Infrastructure, the subject of telecommunications has shown the urgent need to liberalise the sector, lest it hinder the development of the Country. A small country such as ours, well served by an accessible, fast and affordable communications system, will enable the introduction of new methodologies in sectors such as education, local government, health, vocational training, national and international markets, tourism, travelling agencies and other areas requiring the adoption of new technologies.

The State knows it must change this situation and the SDP provides access to this change.

In the Telecommunications sector, the SDP articulates the policies, the benchmarks in the respective timeframes of implementation to be considered in this sector.

In conclusion, without basic infrastructure providing easy access to the populations and opportunities for the sectors or services and industries to grow and to create employment, the Country will not move forward.

The third area that the Strategic Development Plan focuses on is Economic Development, which encompasses Rural Development, Agriculture, Petroleum, Tourism and Private Sector Investment.

There is no doubt that the Country needs economic growth so that society obtains and retains the consequent benefits. Only continuous economic growth can support the development of the social and human components:

- in terms of employment opportunities
- in terms of better service delivery
- in terms of equity in the distribution of national wealth
- in terms of improving knowledge
- in terms of changing attitudes and behaviours
- in terms of trust and national stability

Development is the gradual, consequent and tangible outcome of the efficient implementation of this way of thinking, this philosophy, for a relatively long ongoing period.

The philosophy is that Timor-Leste will build a modern and diversified economy based on agriculture, tourism and the petroleum industry, with an emergent private sector and with opportunities for all people.

Regarding Economic Development, we took into consideration the fact that 75 per cent of our population lives in rural areas, which means that rural development must be a priority concern. It is in the rural areas that the millennium goals are to be achieved. However, this requires populations to have access to roads, water and sanitation, power, schools and health. The development of rural areas is directly associated with the improvement of infrastructures throughout the Country.

In rural areas, all efforts will focus on creating and developing micro, small and medium companies. While the PDD I and II are focusing on the area of construction, the ongoing creation of cooperatives will enable communities to conduct their own business activities.

In rural areas we must encourage the creation of agricultural companies, which will require vocational training. As such, we must also identify agricultural production and forest preservation areas. Additionally, the land law is vital for supporting farmers.

In order to project harmonious, integrated and sustainable development for Timor-Leste we drafted a National Spatial Planning Framework. This will enable each area of the country to know exactly what its potential is and to explore it, as well as to be informed regarding the potential of other areas, so that there can be an ongoing balance between regions. The National Strategic Areas set the context of specialisations, which each one can develop.

Another factor that is not less important is Decentralisation to local governments. However, in preparing for this, the priority must be the training and preparation of human resources in the areas of administration, treasury and finance, planning, budgeting, execution and monitoring.

The State is aware of all of this and the SDP points towards implementation.

Regarding Economic Development, agriculture is the most important sector for reducing poverty, ensuring food security and promoting economic growth. In terms of subsistence agriculture, it is vital to continue assisting farmers concerning training and expansion of new cultivation and treatment techniques, since this is the only way we can increase the productivity of staple foods and improve our people's nutrition. It is essential to rehabilitate and expand irrigation systems.

An exhaustive survey was conducted on the conditions in which our staple foods such as rice, maize, cassava, potatoes, beans and vegetables are cultivated. This survey also included the potential of cash crops such as coffee, coconut, cashew nut, nutmeg, vanilla, peanut, etc. We did not neglect Timor-Leste's potential in terms of fruits, which we must improve in order to at least replace imports. This survey will serve as a guide for strategies and actions regarding the identification and expansion of production areas and the care to be provided, as well as support systems to farmers for using improved technologies, financial advices and trading assistance.

The sector of livestock has also received due attention. Radical changes are required in terms of breeding practices, and training is needed on basic animal care. New practises must also be introduced. The goal is to replace the import of meat, eggs and poultry with productive employment.

The fisheries sector has also provided data on the potential regarding diversified and developed aquaculture, as well as the need to perfect coastal fishing and a training and capacity building strategy for deep sea fishing, so as to boost employment and exports.

Additionally, we considered the problems of our forests, which require a Management Plan to enable sustainable exploration of forestry products and wood. We will also be implementing a program to plant 1 million trees per year, in order to save the country from ecological destruction. We also considered bamboo, not only to prevent soil erosion and degradation but also as a raw material that generates employment and income.

The State is aware of these needs and the SDP provides the proper answers.

In terms of Economic Development, the petroleum sector appears today as a vital cornerstone of our future development. The petroleum sector is already the largest revenue source for the State General Budget. We must be able to use petroleum revenues wisely so as to invest in a petroleum industry and in that way nurture other economic, industry and service activities, as well as activities to support the sector. It is necessary to invert the State's dependence on petroleum revenues and to use petroleum to create other revenue sources and to generate productive employment for the Timorese.

Timor-Leste will be a country directed to the hydrocarbon industry. In order for this to be possible, Timor-Leste must invest in the human resources that will participate in, manage and work in that industry. We will create the National Petroleum Company to lead and manage this sector development process. We have established the South Coast corridor, with a highway linking Suai, where the Supply Platform will be located, to Betano, which will house the Oil Refinery and Petrochemical Industry, and to Beaço, where the LPG facilities will be located.

All of this requires vocational training and the enhancement of agriculture and livestock, resulting in the creation of employment and income opportunities for our People.

The State is aware of the project's size, with the SDP setting the goals.

Regarding Economic Development, Tourism is a sector with enormous potential to contribute with income to the national and local economies through the creation of companies and employment, thus reducing regional economic imbalances.

We can explore various types of tourism, such as ecological, maritime, historical, cultural, religious and adventure tourism, as well as tourism in terms of conferences and conventions. Taking into account the diversity of landscapes, we have set three Tourism Areas, indicating the potential to be explored in each one.

As our economy grows and our tourism industry becomes stronger, it will be necessary to develop a marketing strategy promoting Timor-Leste as a choice destination.

The State is aware of this magnificent potential and the SDP sets the ways in which this potential will be explored.

In the Tourism sector, the SDP presents the benchmarks and the respective timeframes of implementation.

Still on the Economic Sector, the Private Sector will assume the role of creating employment in Timor-Leste. In order to build the Nation, we will have to attract investors to our main industrial sectors, establish partnerships with international companies for building our infrastructure, support the growth of national companies and boost the ongoing improvement of local companies.

This requires capacity building Timorese businesspeople and supporting those who need opportunities to start and expand their businesses. However, in order to succeed in business, many require financial support and training in good business practices.

Therefore, while Timor-Leste must provide a healthy business and investment environment, we must also create the National Development Bank to make long-term loans to our private sector. Concurrently, the Microfinance Institute will be transformed into a Commercial Bank, so as to provide credit to citizens in rural areas wanting to create micro or small companies.

Special Economic Areas may be created to attract foreign investment, being ruled by laws and regulations that make them more attractive.

In all of this, the goal is to create more employment opportunities, to encourage the participation of the Timorese in the various economic activities and to diversify the economy, which will slowly move towards the Country's production and service sector.

The State is aware of these challenges and the SDP sets the strategies to follow.

On the issue of the Private sector, the SDP presents the benchmarks and the respective timeframes of implementation.

Chapter V gives particular and detailed attention to the subject of the Institutional Framework. Timor-Leste is a very young State. We are no longer the world's youngest state, and I invite you all to salute the new State of South Sudan, wishing great prosperity to their people.

In terms of the Institutional Framework, the sectors of Security, Defence, Foreign Affairs, Justice, Public Sector Management and Good Governance are seen as the pillars of this democratic State under the rule of law. A State without capable security and defence is vulnerable to all sorts of threats and pressures.

Stability and security are pre-requirements for social and economic development.

Thus, concerning the Institutional Framework, we focus on the sector of security, indicating the current challenges from the legal regime to human resources, from public safety and conflict prevention to the necessary infrastructure and logistics. The goal is to make the PNTL a professional, non-partisan and competent security force, with respect for human rights, so that it can fulfil its mission to serve our people and ensure peace, security and stability of the Nation.

Under the Institutional Framework, we acknowledged the specific role of the F-FDTL, while giving due priority to geostrategic and maritime security, particularly in our Exclusive Economic Zone.

We also conducted a review from the legal framework to possible force engagement scenarios, from human resources to the development of infrastructures, from the setting of priorities to an integrated vision on national defence.

The State is aware that its sovereignty depends considerably on these two forces and the SDP ensures their development.

Regarding the Institutional Framework, we considered the fact that Timor-Leste is a young member of the community of nations, and as such the goal of our foreign policy is to protect and promote the vital interests of our people, while safeguarding and consolidating the independence of our Nation.

Foreign Affairs will lead a cooperation approach seeking to encourage strong cultural, economic and commercial relations with other countries. We consider multilateral relations, starting with the UN, regional organisations, including the CPLP, and bilateral relations.

In the world of LDCs and fragile States, Timor-Leste is taking part in the dialogue forum promoted under the initiative of the OECD and with the support of Australia. After the Díli Forum in April 2010 on 'Peacebuilding and Statebuilding', Timor-Leste is co-presiding over the Dialogue and leading the g7+, which covers 17 nations and 350 million people. The purpose is to guide fragile countries so that they may discuss their own internal problems, set goals for solving them, and align the funding received by donors with the programmes created by those States, so as to ensure efficiency and a better use of foreign aid monies.

On the other hand, our foreign policy needs to look at strategic, economic and political developments for the next 5-10 years. If necessary, laws and regulations on the development of the diplomacy sector must be revised. Additionally, it is equally important to continue training qualified professionals.

Our choice is for economic diplomacy, at the same time we will continue participating and contributing to peace and stability in the region and in the world.

The State acknowledges the importance of diplomacy; and the SDP ensures that the mission will be carried out. In the Foreign Affairs sector, the SDP sets the benchmarks and the respective timeframes of implementation.

Concerning the Institutional Framework, we have set the goal, after many years of conflict, to make Timor-Leste a stable and safe nation, recognising the rule of Law and ensuring access to justice for all citizens.

Despite the efforts made in this sector, we must admit that we still have a long way ahead of us. Meanwhile, we will adopt a comprehensive strategy for building the justice system and improving its capability to fulfil its mandate and tasks.

We cover the development of Timorese legislation, the legal framework of which is still far from being complete. We require an integrated and coordinated system that can be strong, efficient and fair. The development of human resources is vital, which is why we call attention to the need of supporting private lawyers and of extending justice services to the Districts.

The State has the duty to look after the justice system and the SDP points the way to make that possible. In the Justice sector, the SDP expresses the benchmarks to achieve.

Distinguished Members of Parliament

Ladies and Gentlemen

In order for our Nation to move towards a fair, cohesive and confident society, we need transparent, accountable and competent agencies in our public service, security sector and justice system.

The public sector will be essential to instil confidence in the Government. At the start, the public sector will be the main driver of economic growth. It is necessary to develop a culture of responsibility in all levels of public agencies. We must continue to nurture a culture of commitment and good governance. We must continue to develop our human resources and the professional management mechanisms for programmes and activities.

We conducted an extensive review of the challenges faced by the State and the steps taken in order to reform mentalities and behaviours. We must acknowledge that we are still starting to establish the mechanisms we need to ensure good governance in our Country.

We have covered the tasks of the Civil Service Commission, the need for greater authority in the Office of the Inspector-General of the State and the continuous capacity building of the Anti-Corruption Commission.

In all areas, we highlight ongoing training and capacity building in the areas of leadership and management, in addition to the need to introduce information technologies. We also suggest creating management public entities with greater independence from the Government, so as to ensure better commitment, greater professionalism and better management in some public areas, such as ports, electricity, airports, water and others.

The Institutional Framework also covers Public Finance Management, the Statistics Department and the Central Bank.

The Institutional Framework further explains the measures to be taken to ensure that the SDP and the infrastructure projects are duly implemented.

The National Development Agency, which is working hard to assess the efficiency and accuracy of costs, as well as being responsible for supervising projects, will become an Economic Planning and Investment Agency.

The Economic Planning and Investment Agency will plan, design and monitor strategic programmes and projects, supervise ministries responsible for projects and ensure integrated coordination within all the Government, among other tasks.

The most important task is ensuring good governance and good value for money, which entails having projects at proper costs, with good quality and in good time.

The Government has planned to create a National Procurement Commission, which will hire an international firm of acknowledged competency to carry out a complete procurement competitive process seeking to ensure quality and value for money.

The State knows that it must consolidate these agencies and the SDP presents the actions to be taken. Regarding the Public Sector and Good Governance, the SDP presents the actions to be undertaken.

The SDP, Ladies and Gentlemen, is defined as Strategic because it seeks to radically change the current structure of the country's economy, going from a petroleum-based economy to a non-petroleum based economy. In order to have more sustainable growth and to eradicate poverty by creating social income, we need effective national development strategies.

The SDP presents its paradigm, which is focused on:
- production;
- production capacities; and
- productive employment opportunities

As such, the strategies and guidelines presented in the previous chapters will enable us to stop overloading economy and the public sector as the driving forces of our economy, and to focus on an expanding private sector, on emerging industries and on an expanding service sector. Meanwhile, we will continue to work to create a more efficient and highly productive agriculture sector.

Public investment is essential to invert this situation, namely in the initial stages, so as to enable other areas to develop, particularly our private sector, from national to local level.

With a sustainable and diversified non-petroleum economy, the vision of the Strategic Development Plan is that by 2030 Timor-Leste will go from a low income country to a medium-high income country.

The developed world is facing one of its most serious economic crises, while supporting wars in various parts of the globe. Meanwhile we are seeing emergent economies consolidate themselves and increasing in potential. It is said that this is the century of Asia, and Timor-Leste can profit from this since we are also part of this region. Joining ASEAN provides us with great market potential, in addition to already having good economic relations with giants such as China, Japan and Indonesia.

The main petroleum field is Bayu Undan, which will continue to generate revenues up until 2025. An additional field, Kitan, will soon start generating revenues for the country as well. Conservative estimates put the full revenues from Bayu Undan and Kitan, by 2025, at 22 billion dollars. The Greater Sunrise field and other potential discoveries will increase revenues substantially within the two decades.

What does our Country need the most? Does it not need to develop its human capital and its infrastructure, so as to boost the economy? Or will our people be content to live in misery while we keep our money in the banks of other countries?

We are aware of the danger other countries faced because of the wrong use of petroleum revenues. As such, we remain committed to having full transparency in our petroleum income, so that everyone can see the financial returns, the movements of public funds and the return of petroleum fund investments.

Timor-Leste is the third Nation in the world and the first in Asia to sign and to be granted full compliance with the international transparency mechanisms, having adhered to the Extractive Industries Transparency Initiative.

We will be diversifying Petroleum Fund investments, with greater balance between bonds and equities, so as to safely protect and produce more wealth for the country.

In order to promote the initial start we placed the various funding instruments, from grants to borrowing, under private funding and the financial assistance by development partners.

I know that I have raised an issue that is seen as sensitive, that of public debts. We cannot continue to be ruled by the current budgeting practices for the public expenses of the State. That is simply unsustainable, since it is not adjusted to the country's level of development!

The 2002 National Development Plan already considered the difficulties of implementing the plan, with the document reading: *A plan that is forced into a budget is not a plan at all, but an 'allocation process'*, and ending with: *The planning process should not be budget-driven nor subordinated to international financial mandates.*

Thus we present the Public-Private Partnership mechanisms, including BOTs, as well as concessional loans as the more favourable public funding option to support infrastructure programs such as roads, bridges, seaports and airports.

Lastly, I can understand the existence of doubts regarding our implementation capability. Here I must list our strengths:
- the self-confidence, belief and determination of the Timorese in the pursuance of their goals, as we have proved to possess throughout our history
- the establishment of the systems created to enable ongoing control over programs, and their consequent execution
- the notion of the value of projects, based on their costs and their quality of execution
- the involvement of all citizens in the rebuilding of the Nation
- the revival of the spirit of determination and sacrifice towards a new participative, innovative and responsible nationalism

We, here all united, are the children of this dear People that we represent, in one way or the other. We are the children of this Country and our political and moral responsibility is to think about the future of this Nation.

The current situation of the Nation requires the leaders of this Country to assume their historical responsibilities, without hesitation, and to be brave in making decisions towards a brighter future for the People of Timor-Leste!

# First Graduation of the National Literacy Campaign: 'Yes I Can'

Meeting Hall of the Ministry of Education, Vila-Verde, Díli
23 November 2007

Your Excellency the Minister of Education
Your Excellency the Ambassador of Cuba
Your Excellency the Director of the National Centre of Non-Formal Education
Distinguished Guests
Dear Graduates,

First and foremost, I want to congratulate the group of students in attendance who today will receive the first graduation certificates of the National Literacy Campaign. These are approximately one thousand pioneers opening the way for the Country's development, which depends considerably upon literacy.

Fighting illiteracy, which affects almost half of the adult population in Timor-Leste, is considered a national priority, since it contributes to the reduction of poverty, to the improvement of the living situation of the population and to a substantial gain in terms of public health. It is also essential for promoting democratic values and civic rights and for exercising full citizenship.

'Yes, I can!' In addition to reading and writing, this includes having a more active and participative attitude in our communities. All of these students, aged 14 to 77, men and women, from every district in the Country, have conquered the learning challenge and can now use their knowledge to defend their ideas, to search for additional knowledge, to share information and to participate in democracy.

No matter how small their participation in vital areas for the Country, such as the environment, food, hygiene, health and other initiatives in terms of training for citizenship, they will be contributing to nation building. As such, the Government is committed to making this Campaign, which started in June

2007, an example of community development. We want to support and multiply the number of graduates, expanding the number of classes (presently 255) throughout the Country. I urge the Heads of Suco to promote this campaign at a community level, captivating children and youngsters outside of formal education, since the first step to learning to read and write may lead to entry in formal education and / or to the creation of tools that will be vital to their professional futures.

Still, the most stimulating thing about this Literacy Campaign using the Cuban method is that adults, the poor, the elderly and women are invited to learn. Since we know that illiteracy affects women even more than it does men, please allow me to say something about women, one of the fundamental targets of the Literacy Campaign: educated women have more confidence and contribute more directly to the fight against some of the plights of our society, such as maternal and child mortality. Furthermore, the acquisition of new tools resulting from literacy makes it easier for women to enter active — economic, social and political — life and reduces gender inequalities, as befits a modern and fairer society.

This initiative by the Government of Timor-Leste would not have been possible without the bilateral cooperation of Cuba, through the application of the 'Yo Sí Puedo' method. Cuba has the lowest illiteracy rate and the highest education rate in Latin America and has been contributing to eradicate illiteracy throughout the world, which is caused by lack of access to culture, science and education. In this context, the Cuban Government, sharing its resources and experience in this area, sent 11 Cuban advisors and trainers to Timor-Leste, who provided training to Timorese teachers. Presently there is one coordinator in each district and one sub-coordinator in each sub-district, who are responsible for teaching the Timorese population to read and write.

I would like to seize this opportunity to thank Cuba for their support of this fundamental social development area. Along with the assistance provided in the area of health, this has been another proof of the Cuban people's friendship and solidarity towards our Country. The charitable and friendly people of Cuba have our gratitude and our admiration for the human capital they develop throughout the world. This Government investment will continue up to 2012 and consists of three stages, so as to expand on the knowledge acquired in the first stage. Students who now possess this basic knowledge may continue to study and reach a third stage of knowledge consolidation, which may lead them to enter formal education.

It is an honour for me to symbolically present the certificates to the first Graduates of the National Literacy Campaign. I congratulate you all and I sincerely hope that you will continue to learn and to acquire greater intervention capacity in all areas, thereby implementing peace and local democracy.

Yes, I can read and write. Yes, I can be part of the Country's development.

# Awarding of the Order of Vanuatu First Class Medal for Achievement of the Highest Service to Vanuatu and Humanity at Large

Port Vila, Vanuatu
12 September 2011

> Excellency, Mr. Iolu Johnson Abbil Kaniapnin, President of the Republic
> Excellency, Hon. Meltek Sato Kilman Livtuvanu, Prime Minister
> Excellency, Hon. Dunstan Hilton, Speaker of Parliament
> Dear Members of the Government and Parliament
> Representatives of the Diplomatic Corps
> Excellencies, Ladies and Gentlemen,

It is truly a great privilege to be here tonight at this reception hosted by the Honourable Prime Minister of the Republic of Vanuatu, with the presence of the President of the Republic and Speaker of Parliament.

On my arrival here on Saturday, I was deeply honoured to be received by the traditional chiefs and leaders and the veterans of the Vanuatu Liberation movement in a moving ceremony enriched in culture and history. I wish to take this opportunity to thank the Vanuatu Government for the warm hospitality that they have shown to me and my delegation. It has been truly a wonderful visit so far.

Before I begin, I wish to acknowledge and pay tribute to all the great veterans of the Liberation Movement, in particular: The Late Chief Tinabuamat; The Late Moli Jimmy Stevens, Leader of the Nagriamel Movement; The Late Dr. Fr. Walter Lini, the first Prime Minister of Vanuatu; The Late Aiden Arugogona; Mr. Peter Taurakoto; Ambassador Donald Kalpokas; Fr. John Bani, first President of the National Party; Barak Sope, Secretary-General of the Movement; Kalkot Mataskelekele; The Late John Naupa; The Late Rev. Fred Timakata, Prominent Chief and Church Leader in the Movement; Ati George Sokomanu, Host of the Liberation Movement; and Hilda Lini, my sister, and the Coordinator of the

Women's Wing of the Movement, for their contribution not only to Vanuatu but to the causes of freedom around the world, including Timor-Leste.

We are both island nations in the Asia-Pacific. While Vanuatu may consist of many, many more islands than Timor-Leste, we share much in common. Importantly, we share common values. These include a respect for human rights, political solidarity, self-determination and democracy.

Ladies and Gentlemen,

We have just come from the Pacific Islands Forum in Auckland. This Forum was a great opportunity for the nations of the Pacific to affirm our collective spirit and our friendship as well as to learn from each other. As small, developing nations, we also face great challenges. We must continue to pursue development, the building of strong economies to provide jobs and opportunity, and the improvement in the health, education and welfare of our people. We must do this in an international environment that makes our task more difficult. We must face many threats, including from transnational crime, climate change and international conflict. And we are not immune to the turmoil in the world economy and the effect it has on our nations, including on the price of food, on the value of our exports and on our access to affordable capital.

In Timor-Leste, this reminds us of our vulnerability and of our fragility. Despite our fragility, we are engaging in the process of State building and peace building. The process of State building is one that Vanuatu has already undertaken. And we can learn from you. We can also learn from fragile States around the globe. This is why Timor-Leste, together with 16 other nations that represent 350 million people, have formed the g7+ group of fragile and conflict — affected nations.

This group, which consists of Liberia, Democratic Republic of Congo, Haiti, Afghanistan, Guinea-Bissau, Solomon Islands, Papua New Guinea, Central African Republic, Nepal, Ghana, Ivory Coast, Somalia, South Sudan, Burundi, Chad, Ethiopia, Sierra Leone and Timor-Leste (as the Chair), allows us to speak with one voice. And it provides an opportunity for our countries to re-acquire ownership of the development program and promote genuine aid effectiveness. It allows us to ensure that international aid does not weaken our self-determination. Our membership in the g7+ group is one of Timor-Leste's flagship contributions to the community of nations. It is our way of showing solidarity with the people and nations of the world that are trying to emerge from conflict and achieve peace and stability. With our participation in the g7+ we have learnt from your nation. Just as Vanuatu supported our people in the struggle for independence, we want to help other nations in their peace building and State building endeavours.

Ladies and Gentlemen,

During our struggle for independence, there were times of darkness. While our motto was 'to resist is to win', people throughout our nation, from our tropical beaches to our mountain ranges, came under sustained attack. They suffered greatly. At these times, our struggle seemed more hopeless, because we appeared to be forsaken by much of the international community. At these times, when we could count on few friends, Vanuatu stood with us. The good people of Vanuatu supported our struggle in the international community — and to their cost. We will never, never forget this.

While I am so pleased to be able to thank you for your historical support for our independence, this support is but an example of the values of your nation. As a nation, Vanuatu should be proud of its principles. These principles include support for self-determination, justice and human rights, compassion for the vulnerable and solidarity with the oppressed. In this way, Vanuatu makes a profound contribution to peace and humanity in our region.

Excellencies, Ladies and Gentlemen,

It is a great honour to receive the Order of Vanuatu, First Class Medal.

I accept, on behalf of the courageous people of Timor-Leste, this award with profound appreciation, but also with humility. It was the Timorese people who never gave up in their struggle, and who suffered greatly to achieve freedom, to achieve liberation and to achieve independence. This award provides international recognition to the exceptional bravery and great sacrifices of the Timorese people.

Yesterday, during Mass at the Cathedral, Bishop Jean Bosco Baremes spoke about forgiveness, and this award acknowledges the willingness of our people to forgive and their desire for reconciliation. This desire is what has driven our relationship with the Republic of Indonesia. On 20th August this year, we held a special demobilisation ceremony for our veterans (former guerrillas) and I cannot forget to mention that my dear sister, Hilda Lini, was present to witness this unique event. At this ceremony, the ex-Commander of the Indonesian Armed Forces and later the Vice President of the Republic of Indonesia, retired General Tri Sutrisno, together with the Indonesian Defence Minister and official generals, all paid homage to the Timorese veterans. Their presence at this poignant moment in our history was a concrete sign of just how far our reconciliation process has come.

Excellencies, Ladies and Gentlemen,

On behalf of Timor-Leste, I thank the people of Vanuatu for their support of our cause and for their recognition of our struggle. For, in truth, this award is for them too. I say again: at the darkest and most difficult of times, when we were alone and could count on few friends, Vanuatu stood with us. This unfailing support was evident again when, in 2000 and in the years following, you sent your police officers to help us restore peace. We know this came at your own cost and we are truly humbled by this. This is genuine solidarity! I know you are proud of this and we are deeply moved by your generosity! Timor-Leste will never forget this support and this is my message here today. We thank Vanuatu for the support that helped to make our dream of freedom come true.

Ladies and Gentlemen,

I would also like to take this opportunity to commend Vanuatu for conferring these awards. In doing so, Vanuatu looks beyond its beautiful islands to make a contribution to the community of nations, and to humanity. In a world of growing materialism, these awards remind us of our better side. They remind us that real achievement should be measured by the contribution we make to our fellow brothers and sisters. And so, Vanuatu should be commended for recognising international contributions to humanity. Next January, my President of the Republic and a very good and dear friend of Vanuatu, His Excellency, Dr. José Ramos-Horta, will come here to confer a posthumous award to the late Dr. Fr. Walter Lini. The award will be the highest order of the Democratic Republic of Timor-Leste, the Order of Merit *Laran Luak* (Big Heart) and will be given in honour and recognition of Dr. Fr. Walter Lini's tireless contribution to the freedom movement of Vanuatu and to the cause of humanity worldwide.

Ladies and Gentlemen,

I would like to end by saying a few words in Bislama: *Tank yu tumas. Mo papa God bai i blesem yufela evriwan!*

# Petroleum Fund Management Seminar

Convention Centre, Mercado Lama, Díli
10 May 2010

>Members of the National Parliament
>Members of Government
>Martin Skancke, Head of Asset Management, Department of Finance, Norway
>Peter Ryan-Kane, Head of Portfolio Advisory, Towers Watson, Hong Kong
>Tim Mitchell, General Manager Corporate Strategy, New Zealand Superannuation Fund
>Kevin Bailey, Honorary Consul General for Timor-Leste in Melbourne
>Alex Joia, Senior Asset Management Specialist, Bank for International Settlements
>Members of Non-Government Organisations,
>Ladies and Gentlemen,

First, I would like to thank the Lahame Group for that excellent cultural performance. The performance was a great reminder for us all that the wealth of our nation lies not only in the investments of our Petroleum Fund, but in our People and in our culture.

Ladies and gentlemen, it is with great pleasure that I am here today, in our new convention centre, to open this Seminar on an issue central to the future of our nation: the management of our Petroleum Fund. Revenue from the Petroleum Fund has underpinned Timor-Leste's social and economic progress. It is the primary revenue source for our State budget, providing funds to invest in our county's development. If managed properly and transparently, the Fund will continue to play a central role in the future of our nation. It will allow us, as a sovereign nation, to use our own resources to improve our infrastructure, invest in health and education and grow our economy so that we can build our country and provide a brighter future for our children.

>Ladies and Gentlemen,

As you know, I have been travelling throughout our country, speaking directly to many thousands of people, to discuss our Strategic Development Plan. When National Consultations finish, I will have spoken to Timorese from every sub-district in our country; from the enclave of Oecusse through to Lospalos in the east, from our north coast across our beautiful mountains to the coast on our south. During this journey, I am speaking with the People about their dreams and their aspirations for their country. This includes, of course, discussing the management and expenditure of our petroleum funds. But, as I have just mentioned, we must not forget that the true wealth of our nation is not the money we have in an investment fund. The true wealth of our country is the dignity, the determination and the strength of our People. And it is our People, working together, that will secure the future of our nation.

In this mission to develop our nation we are, however, fortunate. We are fortunate because of our oil and gas resources. But we must make sure our revenue from these resources is invested and managed well. Up until now, we have adopted a prudent and simple investment strategy for the Petroleum Fund. This has served us well. We now have a Petroleum Fund balance of US$5.9 billion. To give a sense of how important the Petroleum Fund is to Timor-Leste, the Fund's balance is ten times our non-oil Gross Domestic Product.

Ladies and Gentlemen,

When the Fund was established in 2005, we decided to take this conservative approach to avoid exposure to risk and volatility. The decision was also based on limited institutional capacity and prioritization. This, in hindsight, was a very wise fiscal approach. This allowed us to gradually develop our management and investment strategy, while increasing our institutional capacity. For most of this period, therefore, the Fund has been invested only in US Government bonds.

While the Petroleum Fund has served our immediate needs, the returns can and should be maximized with a diversification strategy in line with global best practice that is applicable to our conditions in 2010. Our law currently mandates 90 per cent in US Treasury bonds and allows for 10 per cent in other investment areas. I am happy to say the Government has already commenced a prudent diversification strategy, which is in line with the current laws. Approximately, five per cent is now managed with the Bank of International settlement and the completion of the remaining five per cent is being finalized, which means that we have pursued all avenues within the scope of the law to maximise returns.

We view this as a positive step in the successful management of the nation's wealth and a mark that we are coming to a new stage in our development.

So now is the time! Now is the time to review, analyse, seek the best advice available and reassess as a nation how to move forward. We have demonstrated our ability to manage the economy, increase expenditure through more robust budgets and navigate global financial conditions. In 2008 and 2009, we successfully managed the Timorese economy during the Global Financial Crisis (GFC), achieving some of the highest growth rates in the world. While other developing countries struggled under global conditions, Timor-Leste managed to expand the economy. And, so now it is important to recognize we must put equal attention into expanding the investment strategy of our Petroleum Fund for the best possible long-term outcomes and to meet the growing demands of our emerging economy.

The purpose of this Seminar is to start a national dialogue on the best way to manage our nation's shared wealth. This wealth belongs to the People, and the People must determine our approach to managing it. This will require a process of discussion and education, so that we can move towards making important decisions on how to invest our wealth. Everyone needs to be a part of this process — the National Parliament, members of Government, the heads of our organs of sovereignty, civil society, academia, media and the all Timorese People.

This seminar is part of this process. It will increase understanding of international financial markets and investment strategies. We have gathered very experienced and professional international experts to present to us on a range of issues concerning management of our Fund. We will ensure that Timor-Leste has the necessary expertise and advice to invest in the world's financial markets successfully for maximum benefits. Today is an important part of that journey.

It is our responsibility to make decisions about our future. We must decide what our investment objectives are, and then we must agree on an investment strategy to achieve these objectives. We must ensure that our investment strategy is sustainable; not only during periods when it gives us a good return, but also in periods of difficulty for international financial markets.

Ladies and Gentlemen,

So far, while we all agree our investment strategy has served the needs of our young nation, we should also agree that a successful investment strategy in the past is not necessarily a good strategy for the future. As we have seen recently, the international financial market changes, and there is a need for us to review our strategy taking account of these changes. A review of our investment strategy has also been provided in the Petroleum Fund Law from the beginning. The Law, approved in 2005, provides for a review of the investment strategy after five years — reassessment was important to take into account the size of the Petroleum Fund and the level of institutional capacity.

This review process has already begun. Last year, the Ministry of Finance engaged a highly skilled global investment consultant company, Towers Watson, to provide advice, research and analysis. Some of you would have attended the seminar on 6 March for Members of Parliament and civil society where this work was discussed. And Peter Ryan-Kane from Towers Watson will also present to this seminar.

The investment decisions for the Petroleum Fund are important and will have an impact on how much we can spend to develop our nation. That is why we are looking very carefully into these issues, and that we are seeking a comprehensive dialogue. And through this process, we hope to be able to increase our total returns over the long investment horizon that we enjoy.

Ladies and Gentlemen,

I have spoken about the need to invest our Petroleum Fund for the needs of our People, to provide decent houses with electricity and water, schools for our children and health clinics for our sick, and provide productive and core infrastructure for the economic development of our nation. We cannot rely on our petroleum resources. We must build our economy and our nation to provide a sustainable future for our People. But, this seminar is not one to discuss the expenditure of the Petroleum Fund; it is to discuss the management, investment objectives and investment strategies of the Fund. I urge you to approach this seminar with an open mind and to contribute to our national dialogue on how we invest the wealth from our petroleum resources.

I would like to thank Norway for providing advice and assistance on the development of our petroleum sector for many years, and for co-organising and sponsoring this important seminar. And I would also like to thank our distinguished guests and international experts who will be speaking at this important event. This seminar is an important step in our national dialogue on how we decide to manage our Petroleum Fund. Let us all work together for the long-term benefit of our Country.

# First Consultative Meeting on Monitoring Implementation of the Principles for Good International Engagement in Fragile States

Ministry of Foreign Affairs, Díli
2 March 2009

> Your Excellency the President of the Republic
> Your Excellencies the Representatives of the Diplomatic Corps
> Your Excellencies the Representatives of International Organisations
> Your Excellencies the Representatives of Civil Society
> Ladies and Gentlemen,

First and foremost, I would like to thank the World Bank for supporting the organisation of this meeting, as well as our Minister of Finance for her tenacity and energy in promoting and participating in this agenda to make assistance to national development more effective.

The history of Timor-Leste is characterised by a series of challenges. After the challenge of fighting for Independence, we had the challenge of building a young democracy, to establish a State based on the Rule of Law, similar to other States in the Community of Nations. For this, we had to create our democratic institutions from scratch. The lack of basic infrastructure and human resources has been a constant challenge throughout this endeavour, along with the consequences of a period of war that was too long and too painful for our People. This recent history shapes our culture and the way in which every Timorese acts. And it is also felt in our economy, where slow economic growth and low incomes made Timor-Leste one of the poorest countries in Southeast Asia. These factors present serious risks for national stability, as we have seen every two years with the crises or, rather, challenges that we have faced.

Consequently our youth is, first of all, our fragility!

The true challenge has only just begun. Independence has enabled our People to aspire to a better life. In the Vision 2020 — Our National Vision — over forty thousand Timorese stated what they wanted to see achieved by 2020. In short, this was freedom from poverty, hunger, sickness and a lack of education. This also means believing in a Developed Nation that is just in its application of the law, that manages our economy and finances with efficiency and transparency, and where our public and private institutions, our civil society and our leaders, are fully accountable before the People. These expectations guide the actions of our Government.

This year, Timor-Leste celebrates the 10 anniversary of our decision to become a Democratic and Sovereign State, as shown by Popular Consultation. Ten years ago, we were not able — in fact, we were not free — to decide what we wanted for our own Country. What this Government wants for Timor-Leste is to make this $10^{th}$ year the closing of a chapter where Timor-Leste is regarded as an unstable or post-conflict country, which is akin to being a country that cannot meet the expectations of its People. This is why it is time to say: Goodbye Conflict; Welcome Development!

In order for this to happen, we need responsible political leadership and quality public participation in decision-making processes. These two aspects, together with the generous assistance of the International Community, enable a dynamic balance between the expectations of the People and the capacity of the State to meet those expectations.

Ladies and Gentlemen,

We are aware that International Assistance for Development is not enough by itself, no matter how coherent and coordinated its mechanisms may be. The reforms that the Government of Timor-Leste has been designing and implementing are the key to making sustainable and real development happen, and to enable technical assistance projects in our country to be more effective. Therefore, knowing that the integrated problems of poverty, unemployment, hunger and social injustice lead to general discontent among the People, jeopardising national security and stability, as well as knowing that insecurity and instability prevent us from combating poverty, the development of strategic structural reforms is the first step to build the pillars that will support the development and the strengthening of the State.

Although they were another painful shock to our People, the events of last February 11 constituted a last warning regarding the need to change and the crucial importance of revising our national policies. Therefore we reorganised and, in a more coordinated manner, sought the right model for Timor-Leste, gathering the consensus of the Timorese and respecting the steps and timing necessary given our reality. Fortunately the results are there to be seen!

When you leave this building at the end of the day, what you will see by the beach, on the street named Rua dos Coqueiros, what could only have been a mirage just one year ago: the movement of commerce, people taking walks after a day's work and children playing on the beach. This is the result of the resolution of national security problems and the introduction of a deep reform in the sector of defence and security, along with other fundamental measures in the fields of social justice and administrative, legislative and financial reforms. This is also the result of the increase in public sector investment, which has been funding new construction, improvements in public services and public transfer programs. These policies have increased the purchasing power of the People and, indirectly, also benefited the private sector.

Your Excellency the President of the Republic
Ladies and Gentlemen,

There is still much to be done, particularly improving public service delivery, but at least we are taking firm steps in the right direction. The Government has decided that 2009 will be the year to make vital decisions concerning the development of infrastructure. This decision was made not only because it is clear the country lacks infrastructure that would provide better living conditions to every Timorese, but also because it has been proved time and time again that infrastructure is necessary for the development of all other sectors, as well as being an important generator of employment. The path ahead of us requires even greater coordination. The fact we are meeting here today is a clear demonstration that we intend to do better, with courage and determination, and that for this we will need to monitor our actions, as many lives will depend upon them.

One instrument we are drafting to enable better monitoring is a National Development Strategic Plan, which incorporates our key priorities, and which will make a real difference to our country. In a word, one that is achievable. We know by experience, both our own and internationally, that a plan is only useful if it is not improvised and if it can be implemented. Timor-Leste has seen many plans and studies that have not brought added value to the process of escaping a situation of conflict. This is why we are so committed to learning from this past. Further, although we can no longer help those who have perished as a result of the dramatic events in our history, there is much we can still do for those who live in the hope of a better future, since this future depends, in many respects, on government action.

A recent report by the World Bank has shown that 500,000 Timorese live below the poverty line. Half of these people are children, who suffer from hunger and malnourishment. These figures are disturbing. We must bear in mind that what we are discussing here, during these two days, is the identification of indicators that will monitor our actions, as these actions are vital to make a change in the lives of these 500,000 Timorese.

I urge all of you to be aware of this fact: the outcomes of the work by all participants here mean hope for nearly half the Timorese population!

Ladies and Gentlemen,

The alignment of wills, the implementation and monitoring of development plans and the maintenance of peace and security through joint and coordinated efforts, taking into account the three fundamental elements of Defence, Diplomacy and Development, may determine the success of Timor-Leste. Knowing of the engagement that international partners have dedicated to our young country, I underline that our success is also your success. Through the Government's programs and strategies, complemented by the programs of bilateral and multilateral donors, including the United Nations, which reflect the generous assistance provided by the international community, and through better accountability, coordination and monitoring mechanisms, let us make this 10th anniversary of our freedom a landmark to herald in a new stage, the stage of sustainable development. Let us work together so that the reminders of fragility in our country do not mean that we remain a fragile State.

# Closing Remarks for the Second Consultative Conference on Principles for Good International Engagement in Fragile States and Situations

Health Sciences Institute in Comoro, Díli
18 August 2009

> Excellencies
> Honourable Delegates
> Ladies and Gentlemen,

At the end of these two days of reflection and discussion, we can conclude that, despite some divergence of opinions and our different experiences, we are all in agreement that the main conclusions regarding fragile States are the following:

**First** — Every Nation is unique and that there is a combination of geographic, cultural, historical, ethnic and institutional factors that causes States to be fragile, thus requiring specific, case by case approaches to nation building. The measures to be adopted in Timor-Leste must be different from the ones to be applied in Afghanistan, in the Central African Republic, in the Democratic Republic of Congo, in Sierra Leone or in Haiti.

**Second** — Regardless of the concepts and definitions used, there are common factors to all these countries: recent or latent situations of conflict and widespread poverty. And they require a set of solutions to overcome these enormous challenges.

**Third** — The International Community may play a vital role in overcoming the fragile situation of some States, but its actions should be conducted and led by the States themselves and by the People of those States, hence the need for these consultative meetings and for International Dialogue, so that the international community may 'help to help us' in the best possible way.

**Fourth** — This alignment of wills has already been determined. The meetings before this one, and those to take place in the future, show that the International

Community is committed to promoting a constructive involvement between the national and international shareholders in countries facing problems that we call 'fragility'. The adoption of 10 structuring principles to achieve this goal leads us to believe that, in a long-term perspective, international intervention will contribute towards the sustainable development of our Nations and our Peoples.

Ladies and Gentlemen,

Timor-Leste is a blessed Country, for in 10 years of freedom and seven years of State building, we have made remarkable progress with the support of the International Community.

There is still much to be done to reduce poverty in our Nation, to make sure that past conflicts are not rekindled and to eliminate regional imbalances. Furthermore, despite the international assistance, we are aware that this progress would not have been possible without the steadfast will of the nation's leaders, our civil society and our People, which have demanded reforms to improve governance, and to ensure national security and stability, as well as institutional development.

This leads me to believe that the support of the International Community will be of no avail unless there is, in the first place, a spirit of national unity and cohesion, of agreed vision regarding the future, achieved through the active participation of all national actors. Therefore, I say again that, more than ever, we need political maturity and a collective vision concerning our future, so that we can achieve development and wellbeing for all.

Strong political institutions and a strong State (and here I mean all State Institutions, not only the executive) are the keys for the development of the nation. Only in this way will it be possible for the populations to trust their Institutions and to feel motivated to take part in the development process, eschewing internal conflicts and assuming a role of accountability and cooperation.

Undoubtedly Timor-Leste needs to find again the spirit of national cohesion — namely by its political actors — so as to achieve the common goal of stability and development; the same spirit we have already seen in our history through the rare, if not unique, history of our liberation.

The State — and once again I mean all Bodies of Sovereignty and not just the Government — has been implementing vital reforms in the country, in a spirit of solidarity and cooperation of which we can all be proud. This was how we solved the recent 2008 crisis, and this is how we have been striving to overcome the difficult problems our young nation faces: including corruption, social injustices and insecurity.

Honourable Guests,

The experience conveyed to us by our dear friend, Armand Kasumbu, from the Democratic Republic of Congo made us reflect, with some sadness, on how State building is such a broad concept, requiring deep change both nationally and within the international context.

What is happening in the Democratic Republic of Congo? In addition to the ethnic issues, can the natural resource wealth of some countries also be their curse? I ask why the intervention of the international community, which has been so successful in some countries, cannot even reduce the suffering of the people in others. I will go even further and ask you this, from a historical and social context standpoint: are all countries ready to immediately adopt the democratic values upheld by the more developed countries?

Democracy is not always a prerequisite for economic achievement. Take, for instance, the cases of China, Korea, Malaysia, Singapore, Indonesia, Thailand and even Chile. These are all examples of economic successes where the national values have diverged from the espoused standards of democracy. In the case of the Democratic Republic of Congo, I was left contemplating whether the country was ready to embrace democratic representation in line with the standards of the modern world. Perhaps a longer transition period to allow for national unity, deeper participation by the various ethnic groups, and the development of a common vision for the country, may have resulted in a smoother path to peace and State development.

Please note that I am not saying that democracy and its values, which we in Timor-Leste defend and cherish, are not essential for nations to develop in a constructive manner and to promote the fundamental rights of citizens, equality of opportunity, and the imperatives of justice and economic growth. What I am saying is that often the timing is important, and that urgency in calling elections to appoint representatives may result in pockets of social and political exclusion, as some feel alienated from central decision making and removed from the rewards of progress.

Let us consider the case of the first elections in Afghanistan and Iraq, which took place only a short time ago. Regrettably, to an extent these elections failed to meet the expectations of the people in improving the living conditions and circumstances in those countries — and they have not yet resulted in the achievement of peace and stability. For a family that does not have enough food to eat, lives in precarious conditions and has no access to health care, democracy can be a distant and abstract concept. And it is often through economic growth, social justice and the alleviation of poverty that democracy can best be consolidated. The international community may wish to consider the merits of longer transition periods, in order to enable processes to be established that ensure full democratic participation and avoid exclusion — that is, 'democratic exclusion'.

Comparing our brother country of the Democratic Republic of Congo with Timor-Leste, it seems to me that our task was clearly less demanding, since we only have a million people living in a nation of around 15,000 square kilometres — although we, too, are both the victims and the beneficiaries of our gift of natural resources. Democratic consolidation has achieving substantial results for us, although, even in our small country, many groups feel alienated and lacking in direct representation. While the Democratic Republic of Congo is a country where most are poor, natural resources of diamonds and oil abound, which has aroused the interest of industrialized countries. However, as the Democratic Republic of Congo lacks infrastructure to exploit its own resources, it is other countries that, to a large degree, are benefiting from its natural wealth.

Another example to consider, in order to understand such dilemmas, is that of Guinea-Bissau. This country has around the same population as Timor-Leste, as well as a similar history and a language in common. It has been overcoming one serious institutional crisis after another. But what is the root of the problem? We know that ethnic issues, in particular the presence of tribal groups within the Armed Forces, as well as the increasing use of the country as an international drug trafficking hub, have constrained the process of transition towards national stability and development. But to what extent is the International Community concerned about this State?

The recently elected President of Guinea-Bissau spoke a short time ago of the urgent need to strengthen national unity to enable economic growth and social development. Can the International Community make a greater contribution towards this goal?

I would also like to mention another case: Afghanistan. Afghanistan is located in an important geo-strategic area, as well as being the largest opium producer in the world. This country has seen successive military operations as well as international aid for its reconstruction. And yet, the international response has been insufficient to meet the basic requirements of the people. Is the internal political instability the sole cause of their poverty? Knowing the external issues involved, is it not possible to do better?

Ladies and Gentlemen,

The purpose of this process of consultation is to determine what we can do better — we, the fragile States and our Development Partners — to improve the living conditions of our people. Promoting an atmosphere of peace, security and trust is fundamental to providing an environment that allows economic, social and political development. Good governance is also essential so that our Development Partners have confidence to invest in areas that involve high costs, such as infrastructure, education and the development of human resources, but which also provide the greatest benefit to developing countries.

Timor-Leste is committed to reforms that not only promote economic growth, but that produce results that show how grateful we are to the countries that have been supporting Timor-Leste from day one. We can and we want to be an international example of what an effective intervention by the International Community can do in terms of putting a nation on the path to sustainable development. And this is why we are taking part in these consultations and sharing our experiences with such earnest and good will.

Participation by civil society is, therefore, essential, as is improving communication with our People, through listening and responding to their aspirations. In poor countries, however, these actions must be considered, and they must contemplate the immediate requirements of those in great need, even if it results in later controversies about 'buying peace'. The millions of dollars entering our country from the Development Partners, or the use of our natural resources to fund long-term projects, is for nothing if we do not manage to effectively reduce poverty.

We do not want a partial approach to the problem; but, rather, we see it as a whole. We want to proceed with dignity and respect, adopting a common goal, changing our mentality — not just within Timor-Leste but also through placing our achievements on the international agenda, and, if possible, supporting and contributing to the development of other countries in difficult situations. The participation in this important International Dialogue helps us to see more clearly the road we have walked and the road that is still ahead of us, by sharing our experiences and knowledge with our friends from more stable and developed situations than us, and friends that are in similar or worse situations than us. Most of all, this participation highlights the importance of our accountability as a Nation-State in the International Community.

Ladies and Gentlemen,

In conclusion, I would like to stress the extreme importance of the draft report we have discussed here, and I urge all of you to convey your comments to the Ministry of Finance's Coordination Office, in order to complete the report for publication by the OECD. In this way, we can be united in promoting the long-term development of the States that are considered fragile. We are confident that this consultation process will yield positive results, and that, in the end, which, as Ms Bella Bird said, should be in 2011, not only the countries I have mentioned today but also Burundi, Nepal, Liberia, Sudan and others, will benefit from the merit of this work, so that we all can leave behind the hardships of poverty and conflict, and join efforts to achieve the millennium goals.

I thank all those who contributed to making this event a success, and especially to those of you who came from afar to make your important contribution, strengthening the spirit of this consultative conference and ultimately working together in order to create a better world.

I would like to end by quoting an African proverb that many of you must know:

The best time to plant a tree is twenty years ago. The second-best time is now!

# National Dialogue on Truth, Justice and Reconciliation: Formal and Informal Justice

Opportunities to Strengthen Peace, Reconciliation and Prosperity in Timor-Leste; National and International Perspectives

21 October 2010
Conference Hall, Ministry of Foreign Affairs, Díli

> Excellencies
> Ladies and Gentlemen,

Over these last four years, we have been meeting and debating on the issue of formal and informal justice, reconciliation and peace. And the Reverend Bishop Gunnar has been tireless in his endeavors to bring us together to jointly reflect on these issues.

The first meetings were held in Hotel Timor, from where we could see tens of thousands of IDPs, as we could across other areas in Díli. The meetings continued in this hall at the Ministry of Foreign Affairs where we are today.

We are now living in a climate of stability. Instability and violence do not arise simply from problems of formal justice. They also result from a lack of social justice.

Last month we followed the events taking place in nearly all of the capital cities of Europe — 'the day of action', which was filled with demonstrations and violence. There were two days in Paris and yesterday also in Jakarta. All this that is happening in the world should make us avoid looking at the issue of peace and stability from only one angle.

As we are all responsible for the process of consolidating peace and democracy in our country, I cannot on this occasion forget to remind us all of the need for greater clarity of ideas so that they can guide our actions with certainty and consistency. The whole process surrounding Maternus Bere, of which I am solely responsible, could be an appropriate case for reflection in forums of this nature. This may help the conclusions drawn from this conference in terms of validity and objectivity, and help us respond to situations that we will face in the future.

I hereby declare that I am and will continue to encourage a Timorese, who lives in West Timor, to submit himself to justice — one dual citizen that is responsible for more than half a thousand people who are anxious to return to their homeland. He is on the list of those accused of crimes against humanity. He consciously made the decision that he could not continue living with the burden of guilt: 1) of being responsible for dozens of people who want to return, and 2) of having been involved in the violence of 1999. Thus, he prefers to live at peace with himself! Bringing these people back and serving his sentence.

Excellencies

Ladies and Gentlemen,

This is a case of honesty and courage and I will continue to assist him both morally and psychologically.

I invite you all to think that, while we brandish the sword of justice, there exist humble people who know how to sacrifice their personal interests in favour of the interests of hundreds of innocent people.

# Sixtieth Anniversary of the People's Republic of China

New Embassy of the People's Republic of China, Díli
29 September 2009

> Your Excellency, Ambassador Mr Fu Yuancong
> Honourable Mrs Yuancong
> Distinguished Guests
> Dear Chinese Friends,

It is an honour and great privilege for me to stand before you today to say a few words on this special occasion when we celebrate the sixtieth birthday of the Foundation of the New China. The changes that have been taking place in China are absolutely remarkable, and one cannot be unmoved by what China represents to the Asian region and to the entire world.

For us, the Timorese, who live in a small and young nation with only a million people, it is incredible to look towards the giant nation of China, the most populous in the world, and observe its great progress and achievements, particularly in lifting many millions of people out of poverty and growing one of the largest and strongest economies in the world. The path travelled by the People's Republic of China, therefore, provides an important reference to Timor-Leste as well as to the world. China's strength and superior economic management in responding to the global financial crisis is pulling the world out of recession. And China's global investments and its cooperation and support of development in the poorest of countries is making a unique and invaluable contribution to humanity. Timor-Leste, along with the world, benefits greatly from China's positive engagement with countries across the globe. The contribution of China that results from its policies of promoting peace and development make it, at the dawn of this century that has barely began, a force for good.

In coming decades, as China moves towards becoming the largest economy in the world, its growing prosperity and commitment to development will both guide and teach us all. China's domestic accomplishments in promoting unity and its pursuit of economic growth for the benefit of its People is matched by its contribution to international diplomacy and development.

More and more, China's successes are world successes. The benefits of China's progress and reforms, which have fuelled their economy's development, are not limited to their own Country or even to the Asian region — they cross continents and oceans, bringing hope to countries that need it the most, including, importantly, African countries undergoing reconstruction. China's direct investment in infrastructure projects, as well as other critical sectors, is evident throughout Africa, including Ethiopia, Sudan, Nigeria, Ghana, Tanzania, Zambia, the Democratic Republic of Congo, Uganda, the Central African Republic and Angola, just to mention some examples from a long list, and it reflects China's commitment to promoting peace, cooperation and development in post-conflict and developing countries. In addition to the transfer of skills and medical assistance, as well as often peacekeeping that these engagements provide, these public and private investments in productive economic sectors lead invariably to increased opportunities and the improvement in living standards of the populations of Africa. China has, through various partnerships with many nations, provided food to the starving, education to children, health to the sick and major infrastructure to support the development of the private sector and promote economic growth.

Ladies and Gentlemen,

China has spared no effort in Timor-Leste as well, hence the ties of friendship that we have been strengthening. It would also do well to remember that the People's Republic of China was the first Country to accredit its Embassy in Díli, and that it provided us financial, institutional, technical and training assistance, as well as support in the construction of infrastructure and the development of our agricultural sector. In view of all this contribution, we seek to continue to learn from and alongside China, as well as seek new strategic partnerships together. I thank the Government of the People´s Republic of China for their ongoing and generous support and I am very pleased to be here in this new Embassy in Díli. It is a significant occasion in the relationship between our two countries and symbolises the depth and strength of our friendship.

By serving as a reference to small and poor countries such as Timor-Leste, and in captivating our interest and gaining our admiration, China also becomes a recipient of the hopes of the countries in reconstruction. Clearly we wish to continue strengthening the friendship and cooperation between our two Peoples and in the coming days of 16, 17 and 18 of October, I will be in Sichuan, to participate in the Western China International Economy and Trade Fair, and I will have the opportunity to have a working meeting with the Premier, His Excellency Wen Jiabao.

Ladies and Gentlemen,

At this time of celebration in China, I must praise the vision and leadership of His Excellency President Hu Jintao. The Government of Timor-Leste shares his international vision, that all peoples in the world enjoy the same development opportunities and that, by working together, we can overcome challenges and promote peace and development for all humanity.

I would like to conclude by extending my heartfelt congratulations to the Chinese citizens living in Timor-Leste, in China and throughout the world for the amazing sixty years they have had since the Foundation of the People's Republic of China.

Gong-xi nin, wo quin-ai de Zhong-guo peng-you men! (Congratulations, my dear Chinese friends!)

# Inaugural Session of the Bali Democracy Forum

Building and Consolidating Democracy: a Strategic Agenda for Asia

Nusa Dua, Bali
10-11 December 2008

>Your Excellency President of the Republic of Indonesia
>Your Excellency Minister of Foreign Affairs of Indonesia
>Your Excellencies Heads of State and Government
>Distinguished Members of Delegations
>Ladies and Gentlemen,

First, please allow me to thank the Government of Indonesia and, in particular, our host, His Excellency, Dr Susilo Bambang Yudhoyono, for the warm welcome we have received and for this forum's excellent organisation. I would also like to express my profound appreciation to be able to take part in this important initiative. This Democracy Forum is at this moment more than timely to the Asian region; it is also a strategic opportunity in respect to the new international circumstances that we face.

Today's globalised world pays little heed to individual and regional borders, transforming internal problems into problems common to all countries. And, today, we live in a situation of multi-dimensional threats, which include those posed by the recent economic and financial crisis, as well as the food and energy crisis. The impact of these threats on poor and vulnerable countries, such as Timor-Leste, is still unpredictable.

Terrorism has of course also emerged as a significant threat of our time, becoming a scourge against the values of the rule of law, democracy and freedom — the cornerstone of our societies — and affecting the international order. A recent example were the terrible attacks in Mumbai, which deserve more from us than merely expressions of solidarity and condolences to the victims' families and to the Government and the People of India. It is also crucial that we fight against this unexpected enemy and that we create a common regional and international cooperation platform, in order to protect innocent victims. This terrorist act represents an attack on the largest democracy in the world and shows how much this system, historical and based on the noblest ideals of humankind, can be vulnerable against the arrogance of man.

The Asian continent, including Timor-Leste, has been the stage of recent internal disputes resulting from ethnic and religious tensions or caused by political, military, social and cultural factors, showing how vulnerable States can be when anti-democratic feelings persist within them; when men pursue individual interests against the collective interests of a People. The fight against terrorism and internal disputes, which devastate democratic aspirations and deteriorate economical, social and humanitarian conditions, as well as the architecture of regional security, is both a moral imperative and an essential condition for development.

Ladies and Gentlemen,

Timor-Leste, the youngest democracy and one of the poorest countries in South-East Asia, cannot be isolated from its regional partners, but must instead seek strong partnerships to overcome today's challenges, the challenges of a globalised world. The people of Timor-Leste have earned their place in the history of democracy, through their selfless fight for national sovereignty and independence, based on the popular will and in the respect for the dignity of the human person. Last year the People once again gave evidence of their collective democratic awareness, when, in the most unlikely of times, after a crisis that shook our Institutions deeply and caused great human and material losses, the People elected first the President of the Republic and then their representatives in the National Parliament.

Still, consolidating a Democracy is no easy task. It is not enough to call ourselves the Democratic Republic of Timor-Leste, to have political parties and to promote free and regular elections; we must also work hard to give meaning and a practical effect to this ideal, so that it may be embedded in our Institutions and in the daily life of our People. The true challenge has only just begun. Freedom, in democracy, has a broader meaning than acting without oppression. Releasing people from poverty, hunger, sickness and ignorance is not achieved overnight, and it takes more than simply setting rules that regulate individual and collective rights and duties.

The Timorese People have trusted in democracy, and now expect this to also represent good government, economic progress and justice, and this is more than merely equal political rights. Our People seek an effective State, with democratic and stable political institutions, able to unite the Timorese and respond to the plurality of their interests. We have adopted as immediate priorities the consolidation of national security and stability, together with social justice measures for the poorest and most vulnerable, as well as urgent State management reforms. We have been studying the public sector reform in Indonesia, and my Government is also determined to create an effective, independent and corruption-free civil service, relying on collaboration by all Sovereign Bodies so that the transformation of the public sector leads to a governance of transparency, accountability and efficiency in the management of public finance and in the delivery of essential services to communities.

After achieving national Peace and implementing new administrative, financial, legal and institutional systems, we are now ready to start our economic development policy. Timor-Leste is a country blessed with natural resources that, if used wisely, may free the Timorese from poverty. To achieve this, our medium term strategic agenda seeks to:

- develop national infrastructure;
- develop human capital; and
- develop agriculture and rural areas.

This economic growth policy will enable the creation of employment, increase revenue, reduce dependence on essential commodities from abroad and, of course, gradually improve the living conditions of the population. These are vital factors for supporting the strengthening of the democratic system. We know that, without peace and social and economic stability, without responding to the needs of our People and satisfying their social aspirations, it is difficult to consolidate democratic values and principles.

Your Excellencies,

This is not an agenda, political and economic, exclusive to Timor-Leste, but a strategic agenda common to all countries in Asia. Strengthening the quality of democracies is strengthening the States. It demands commitment and the spirit of institutional cooperation of all organs of sovereignty and the active participation of civil society in the decisions that affect all citizens. The challenges faced by the young democracy of Timor-Leste, which every second year has found itself regressing and in conflict situations, culminating with the attacks against the Head of State and Head of the Government on February 11 this year, showed us the fragility of the process of consolidating democracy and obligated us to review our national policies.

This fragility is not unique to my country. The experience of other Asian States also shows that democracy can be easily subjugated to acts of violence and repression. We must, with solidarity between our nations, reinforce our mechanisms of dialogue and our mutual support to walk the path of building and consolidating democracy in Asia. We represent here different cultures, different political options and different states of economic and social development. However, this diversity provides an excellent opportunity to learn lessons, share best practises and, especially, explore approaches to overcoming common challenges, in consideration of democratic principles and values.

We cannot borrow success formulas from other countries, but we can create innovating regional cooperation partnerships, learning from our various experiences and assuming with responsibility a commitment of regional development. Democracy is first and foremost an issue of responsibility!

We must strengthen our regional alliances based on shared and lasting responsibilities, and we assume right from this moment the commitment to contribute to this goal. Bringing democracy to the forefront and promoting a dialogue that leads to new partnerships and cooperation mechanisms means believing that the destiny of humankind is to achieve peace and sustainable development.

In concluding, I would like to express final words of appreciation to our closest neighbour, Indonesia, which provides a remarkable example of a transition process from autocratic governance towards a pluralistic democracy and an open and tolerant society. The democratic vision and the leadership of their President have enabled the Indonesian people to enjoy a climate of peace, freedom and development, promoting 'unity in diversity'. It is not by chance that this forum is being held here, and it is also not by chance that Timor-Leste immediately agreed to take part in this meeting, which seeks to promote a true democratic culture in our region. This is the spirit of young democracies, and our common destiny.

# Bali Democracy Forum IV — Enhancing Democratic Participation in a Changing World: Responding to Democratic Voices

Nusa Dua, Bali
8 December 2011

> Your Excellency the President of the Republic of Indonesia,
>     Dr Susilo Bambang Yudhoyono
> Your Excellency, the Co-Chair, the Prime Minister of the People's Republic
>     of Bangladesh, Sheikh Hasina Wajed
> Your Excellencies the Heads of State and Government
> Distinguished Participants
> Ladies and Gentlemen,

I must again give praise, Mr President, for the persistence and dedication that you have shown to this noble cause. Those of us who, for the last four years, have witnessed the growing participation and the increasing intensity and depth of discussions at the annual Bali Democracy Forum, must congratulate its organisers, the Institute for Peace and Democracy.

It is a great honour for me to be once again side by side with my dear friend, the President of Indonesia, Dr Susilo Bambang Yudhoyono, and to be able to contribute to a future of democracy, freedom and dignity in our region. As the world's third largest democracy and with a huge emerging economy, Indonesia's pragmatic outlook and national vision is becoming an important international reference. Timor-Leste is inspired by this neighbour's growth and its promotion of a successful democracy. The history of Timor-Leste will be forever connected with that of Indonesia. The victory of democracy and of the democratic voices of our people, have helped shape not only our nations, but also our region of South East Asia.

It was in 1999 that the democratic voices finally started to be heard. The Indonesian people and the Timorese people began together a new chapter;

when they voted for democracy, they voted for respect for human rights, they voted for freedom and they voted for social and economic development.

Today's times give us confidence in important initiatives such as this Forum. As I said at the Third BDF, it is these meetings that stimulate reflection, encourage dialogue — and lead to change. The year of 2011 will be recorded in history, written in many languages and with different narratives.

Ladies and Gentlemen,

Every day we see crowds of people agitating with feverish passion and enthusiasm for the profound changes taking place in the world. We see other groups, however, expressing their despair with a world facing enormous challenges and we feel suffocated by these emotions and feelings. There is something wrong in all of this.

We see victories achieved through the might of weapons, we see the despair of hunger, we see post-election violence, we see veiled threats at the polls, we see fear in the faces of people living with the presence of foreign troops, we see repression of peaceful demonstrators by police in democratic countries, we see world leaders powerless to find a solution for our economic and environmental problems, we see leaders from developing countries holding absolute power, we see intransigency in postures that dignify no one. And no one is pleased with this imbalance of values. There is something wrong in all of this.

It turns out that, after all, the world is not changing. The world is saturated with problems that world leaders have always avoided rather than tackled. It is people who are trying to change the world, while leaders refuse to heed their demands.

World leaders believe they represent the views of their people when they proclaim so-called 'national interest' as if they were representing the real national interests of the people. In this way, the leaders of many countries believe that their own interests are also the interests of the people they rule, if not oppress. World problems are systemic, after all. Most of humanity remains illiterate, barefoot, ignorant of their rights, homeless and living in misery.

Universal standards, criteria and human rights are introduced as ends in themselves, as if selling cheap products from the civilized world, and those who do not purchase them are shunned as not being part of the group of well behaved children, as measured by indicators set by experts who live in skyscrapers and work for CEOs.

Elections are proclaimed as ends in themselves; and then we watch an Italian model of non-elected government composed of technocrats, and another government simply tailored with a Greek suit, which offend common standards and sensitivities that would, if occurring in a developing country, be considered unpalatable and raise human rights hackles everywhere from Brussels to Geneva, from the capitals of democracy to the Security Council in New York. We are witnessing an orchestra playing without a conductor, as no one is able to pick up the baton. And the problem is not political or economic or even social. This is a problem of the system. There is something wrong in all of this, and no one wants to take the blame.

We are at a particular conjuncture where it is much easier to make small repairs than to promote long-term solutions. It is much easier to demand from others who are weaker and poorer than to demand from one's self. The result of this is an accumulation of contradictions and problems that are becoming unsolvable, and this affects everyone. In every summit of the powerful, solutions are always 'too little' and, in the end, we all reach the conclusion that it is all 'too late'. And this is making people truly exasperated! And, in their speeches, they bring the same tone of doubt, of distrust, of rivalry — with a mix of politics, economics and ideology, of human rights and supremacy, of trade and security, of intelligence and defence, all in a desperate search for justifications to impose upon others.

The mentality of the Cold War will continue to be the main obstacle in this Millennium.

Ladies and Gentlemen

But let us talk of ourselves, because we need to take care of ourselves. Allow me to say a few words on the interaction of the concept of 'democratic participation'. I will divide this in two levels, as the Institute for Peace and Democracy has done so well.

One of the fundamental problems of developing countries is the State building process. This process is vital for the establishment of a multi-party constitutional system, with properly defined checks and balances, with clear medium and long-term plans that, with well prepared human resources, are guaranteed to be implemented, and with all the necessary conditions to enable effective performance delivery. Only a gradual but efficient implementation of a well-designed plan can inspire trust in society and give governance credibility.

The State must legislate to ensure the transparency of its acts and the accountability of public accounts, which can be viewed by all. This is the only way for citizens to have confidence in the future of the Nation. Technology provides the means for the State to assist society in the monitoring of government at all times, through the use of internet-based transparency portals which include procurement, revenue, State budget execution and project implementation websites. This is the way in which we can ensure good governance.

On the other hand, there is a need to balance the demands of society with the responses by the State. This is the challenge of leadership in setting action plans and the challenge between understanding the totality of the needs of the country and the demands of its parts, so that there can be consensual acceptance of the annual programs of government according to national and sector priorities. Civil society must have an overall understanding of the problems of the country and of the effort made by the State if it is to make a constructive contribution and a critical interpretation of the acts undertaken by leaders and undertake a mediating role instead of a disruptive one that would distort democracy.

The challenge ahead of us is how to change the mentality of our societies, which are fond of copying models from highly industrialized countries and supposed role models of democracy. In changing mentalities in our societies, it is important to clarify that duties and rights go hand in hand. Citizenship is a coin with two sides: rights and duties. In young democracies, it is common for people to focus on rights and to forget that they also have the duty to do something positive for the country, without demanding extra benefits from the State. I believe that the substance of democratic participation by the State and by society is as follows:

- Collective responsibilities towards the Nation, in terms of commitments and duties;
- National Reconciliation, in the search for truth, tolerance and peace;
- A critical society under a constructive ideal, in the collective search for solutions and defending national identity;
- Safeguarding national interests, without gross chauvinism or deceitful alienations.

In young democracies, people in society tend to consider themselves 'independent', that is, operating 'outside the State', in the sense that they are more activists than they are citizens, or better yet, that they are the citizens of the international organisations that pay them so handsomely, and defend them so well, rather than citizens defending their own country.

We also have the opposite phenomenon, where false nationalism feeds a feeling of unbridled aversion to that which is foreign, sometimes for no valid reason at all, merely to cover up the lack of a mature national perspective in regard to the social and economic development of the country. In short, through such attitudes, they attempt to cover up the lack of political development.

Ladies and Gentlemen

These are the lessons we are taking from the world's 50 Least Developed Countries and from the g7+ group that fragile nations established, and which represents over 350 million people who live in a situation of political, social and economic fragility.

The true challenge is in our hands, in each of our countries, in each of our societies, in each of our peoples. Most of all, the challenge is in the hands of the country leaders, which can make their countries either stronger or weaker. We need to be the agents of our own processes. A process is only genuine and able to produce positive results, in the medium and long term, if it is promoted mainly by internal factors. Whenever a process is led from outside it invariably suffers uncontrollable convulsions and distortions, causing much more damage than gain.

Across the world there are 1.5 billion people living in States that are fragile and affected by conflicts. Over 70 per cent of these fragile States have been enduring conflict since 1989. Thirty per cent of International Aid (ODA) is provided towards fragile States, and yet they are very far from meeting the MDG targets for 2015.

Consequently, Mr President, while Indonesia is leading, with courage and conviction, the concept of relationship between 'democracy and development', Timor-Leste is leading the relationship between 'Peace building' and 'State building'.

As I have announced at this Forum previously, Timor-Leste co-chaired the First International Dialogue on 'Peace building and State building', which took place in Díli, in 2010, as well as the second Dialogue, which was held in Monrovia, Liberia, in 2011.

Along with this International Dialogue, the g7+ group is also a space for fragile States (a term not appreciated by some) to share experiences and be heard as one voice by the international community, in a collective attempt to build States, build Democracies and build Peace. Timor-Leste is proud of its leadership and establishment of the g7+ as a permanent forum. For a small and young Nation, being able to participate in the consolidation of this group and to give voice to States that, by themselves, would be voiceless, is also giving expression to democracy.

We started as a group of 7 countries that, when coming together to discuss issues related to Good International Engagement in Fragile States and Situations, found that, despite coming from different contexts and continents and having different languages and cultures, we had the same types of challenges. Currently, we represent 19 countries, after the recent admissions of Equatorial Guinea and Togo, which discuss amongst ourselves and with international donors improving the principles for good international engagement in regard to development assistance.

Recently I had the opportunity to visit Juba, on the occasion of the g7+ Inter-Ministerial Retreat. When we arrived, the Southern Sudanese were reflecting on their first 100 days as an independent State, happy to be able to so soon host an international event that would also discuss their State building challenges.

Let us have no illusions — for countries that have to deal with poverty, instability and violent conflicts, taking charge of their own development is no easy task. The people who suffer yearn for democracy because they believe it will mitigate their suffering. The benefits of democracy, however, take time to be reaped. The democratic formulas of the West do not always work when carbon copied to other countries. And furthermore, the democratic experience of developed countries is not always appropriate to fragile States. These are countries traumatised by war and devastated by poverty, often instigated by interests of economic supremacy.

Additionally, international aid has always followed unacceptably strict criteria and 'one size fits all' standards. Democratic values are universal; however, the specific circumstances of each country and the manner in which those values are assimilated are individual. It is necessary to consider the historical, social and cultural context of each country before attempting to implement a development program, without ever losing sight of human dignity. For poor countries, aid is often a matter of survival — lives depend on that aid!

Still, the debate on international aid is almost as old as the debate on democracy. International aid and lessons of democracy from developed countries go hand in hand almost every time, but, nevertheless, thousands of people remain in poverty. Sometimes, if not most times, when a large volume of aid comes close to the population of a country, it becomes poorer than before the arrival of that aid. Poor countries are accused of corruption and blamed for international failures. However, do rich countries have effective mechanisms of transparency and accountability for the failure of international aid?

It will be difficult to meet the Millennium Development Goals for 2015. Donor countries feel frustrated and I believe that their taxpayers question the amounts channelled into international aid when, during this time of global economic crisis, those very taxpayers are enduring hardship.

These are all the issues that should be discussed within the scope of democracy. For all this I say: fighting poverty, hunger, disease and ignorance is promoting democracy! And I will add: promoting peace and promoting a more active and understanding international diplomacy is investing in the democratic process at a global level. Here I would like to commend the US Secretary of Defense, Luis Panetta, when he urges Israel to break its auto-isolationism and to sit at the table with its neighbours to talk for the good of humanity! It is high time for us all to honour universal values with the same commitment!

Your Excellencies

Ladies and Gentlemen,

Last week, at the opening session of the Fourth International Forum on International Aid Effectiveness, held in Busan, South Korea, the Secretary General of the United Nations said that international aid is not charity but rather an intelligent investment in security and prosperity. I agree. And, as a result of the Juba Inter-Ministerial Retreat, the g7+ presented, in Busan, its New Deal for Engagement in Fragile States. Thirty-four countries and international agencies immediately endorsed this New Deal.

This is an important landmark in the relationship between fragile States and partner organisations. This is an honest attempt to understand better the challenges inherent in post-conflict and fragile countries when pursuing development goals. Therefore, in order to achieve the MDGs, Fragile States will have a period of transition through the PSGs (Peacebuilding and Statebuilding Goals).

The New Deal gives new hope in terms of achieving the MDGs. With the New Deal there is a new focus on sustainable development for these fragile countries, under their ownership and with confidence in new commitments to achieve greater transparency, internal capacity and management to enable better international aid outcomes.

This is also democracy — in the true sense of the word — in action.

As Timor-Leste is Chair of the g7+, I will be distributing copies of the New Deal for all countries in attendance. I would also like to seize this opportunity to urge you all to give us your support in September 2012, when we will be taking the five PSGs to the General Assembly of the United Nations. These five PSGs are:

- Legitimate Politics
- Security
- Justice
- Economic Foundations
- Revenue and Services

Your Excellency Mr President
Your Excellencies
Ladies and Gentlemen

The world in which we live is seriously threatened. Signs are emerging of the eminent threat of climate change. From the fires in Australia, to the floods in Thailand and the rising sea levels threatening the very existence of some Pacific islands, nature is trying to warn humanity that it needs to take urgent measures. Natural disasters are testing the world´s people, as we saw with the earthquake and tsunami in Japan, the earthquake in Christchurch, New Zealand, and the very recent ones in Turkey. Unfortunately, for all that has not been done following Kyoto, Copenhagen and Cancun, it seems that Durban is without hope, as noted by the UN Secretary-General yesterday.

Furthermore, the serious threats of terrorism, illegal immigration in frightening numbers, trafficking of persons, drugs and weapons, the global economic crisis, the search for limited food and energy resources, the proliferation of nuclear weapons — among other threats — can lead to conflict and to global insecurity. Now, more than ever, we need strategic cooperation, dialogue and alliances to undertake intervention. These alliances should not and cannot be constrained by the strategic interests of the major powers. Instead, they must serve the fundamental interests of humanity. We need new alliances to make peace and not old alliances to wage war. We need a new political and economic world order in which conflicts and discord are replaced with dialogue; in which democracy is used to give voice to the weak and the vulnerable; and in which assistance and solidarity are used correctly to mitigate people's suffering.

This is the message that must be conveyed to the world's nations, particularly the poorer and weaker ones, so that they can have faith in democracy.

# Redefining Future Relations between Indonesia and Timor-Leste

Indonesian Council on World Affairs, Jakarta
1 May 2008

Excellencies
Ladies and Gentlemen,

It is always an honour to address you all, particularly in this Council that gathers members from the most varied sectors of Indonesian society, and which has already received illustrious international figures for debates on issues with global importance within a truly democratic and universal context. I therefore salute the members and patrons of the Indonesian Council on World Affairs for the excellent work they have been doing.

The subject 'Redefining Future Relations between Indonesia and Timor-Leste' holds an exceptional emotion for me. The mutual sympathy and friendship that unites both our countries did not begin yesterday, and I believe they will not fade in the future, since they are part of the history of our two Republics. Thus, I will speak to you with an open heart, as one does among old friends. The common origins and the way in which the more painful memories of our past have been overcome, through a process of mutual reconciliation, allows us to foresee that our relations, by being strengthened, can contribute in the future for the consolidation of our two young democracies.

In 1999, the people of Indonesia and the people of Timor-Leste added a new chapter to the history of democracy in Southeast Asia. Against all scepticisms, our peoples voted for democracy and the principles of a State under the Democratic Rule of Law, with Indonesia abandoning irreversibly its legacy of autocratic governance, and with Timor-Leste starting the path towards national sovereignty and independence. Here, I must congratulate His Excellency the President of the Republic Susilo Bambang Yudhoyono for his democratic vision for the Indonesia Nation. Under his leadership, the Indonesian people have known the opportunities provided by a climate of peace and stability, and they have enjoyed the ideal of freedom.

Timor-Leste, as a young democracy, also aspires to be distinguished by a culture of tolerance and, like its neighbour, promote 'unity in diversity', nurturing a true democratic culture.

As founding member of ASEAN and as an emergent democracy, Indonesia has been playing a leading role in terms of change and leadership, which are vital for the region of Southeast Asia where Timor-Leste is also inserted. Your country, within a very specific context of respect for customs and traditions, has been distinguishing itself by way of significant changes that enabled the development of the economy and the promotion of peace and national stability. These progresses, accompanied by Timor-Leste with great enthusiasm, become even more remarkable since we are talking about a country with an ethnical, historical, cultural and language diversity that cannot be neglected, thereby proving that diversity can indeed be a factor of development and union.

Timor-Leste has been extending and consolidating cooperation relations with several countries in the world, with special attention to the regional context. The membership in ASEAN is a priority for the Timorese State, since we consider that it is extremely important to belong to this family and to extract the implicit advantages that derive from here: security, stability, economic development and regional cooperation. What is more, the fact that we will be full members of ASEAN is also a way for us to have a more active participation in the collective regional development effort. I cannot miss this opportunity to salute the Indonesia Government for the creative and responsible way in which it has conducted the Aceh stabilization process (I consider it to be a triumph of Peace), a fruit of the commitment by the Indonesian leaders and civil society, in nurturing reconciliation and democracy in the Country. This victory would not have been possible without the participation of all Indonesian people, which keeps on surprising us with demonstrations of courage and compassion, as well as with the way in which they have overcome the natural disasters that have hit them.

I would also like to say a few words condemning vehemently the terrorist attacks that have killed hundreds of Indonesian citizens, mostly Muslims. These attacks represent an attempt to destroy the traditions of cultural tolerance and freedom, and the damaging connotation that is often made between Islam and terrorism must also be fought against effectively. Indeed, we can see in the entire world the fundamental contribution that the Muslim community has made to the development of humankind itself, co-existing healthily with other religions and sharing its knowledge and wisdom in an open and constructive manner. Indonesia, the Country with the largest Muslim community in the world, has been a singular example of this reality. Timor-Leste has a small but dynamic Muslim community, the rights of which are acknowledged in our Constitution. Our Government has been giving all necessary support for this community to develop itself and to have an active participation in the development of the Country.

The dialogue between cultures and civilizations requires strong and demanding internal agendas, in what regards the respect for difference and the inclusion of everyone in society, regardless of beliefs, religions and cultures, especially today when we must carry on opening paths towards dialogue and hope through all the existing tensions. This dialogue must take place within a framework of universal values and principles, respecting the individual assurances and liberties. Thus, I must highlight the efforts made by the Indonesian Government and by His Excellency the President of the Republic Yudhoyono, which, within the scope of ASEAN, have been defending the fundamental rights of the people of Burma. The dramatic situation lived in Burma is being accompanied by us with great concern and disappointment. These people have been the victims of policies that have laid waste to their democratic aspirations and that have deteriorated the economic, social and humanitarian situations in a country too close to us. It is impossible for us to contain our indignation. We truly hope that a solution can be found urgently for Burma, a solution that includes the leader of the opposition and the Nobel Peace Prize winner Ms Aung Suu Kyi, returning freedom and the full use of democracy to their people.

The common features that united Timor-Leste and Indonesia are too many for us to think of a future that does not involve the strengthening of our ties: we have a common historic past; we have common borders; we have Timorese citizens living in Indonesia and Indonesian citizens living in Timor-Leste, completely integrated. The Indonesian language has been declared a working language by our Constitution, and we also have determinant cultural features that make us feel closer to each other. In addition to this, we face similar challenges: to build a sound democracy; to consolidate transparent and accountable institutions; to enhance the rule of law; to strengthen the judicial system; and to enable a free and independent media contributing to the accountability of the leaders towards their people.

In view of all this, our future relations must be built around a strong partnership that promotes peace and security, as well as new opportunities of prosperity, freedom, justice, tolerance and democracy for our neighbouring and friendly countries. The development of the creation of the Truth and Friendship Commission, which represented a unique reconciliation model, is evidence of how this is possible. We were pushed forward by the strong will to move on and by the determination to turn the pages of the past, through joint efforts, as the solution of old problems will contribute to promote our bilateral relations. This innovating way to bring our two peoples together in an uncommon approach in the search for truth and in the promotion of friendship, instead of starting legal cases, contributes for them to be even more united, within the conviction that we all suffered because of a regime.

The final report of the TFC will be ready within the present year, as a result of the acknowledged commitment by the commissioners from both countries, and its recommendations will be implemented as much as possible. Let our recent history state that, despite the concerns underlying the creation of this Commission, the Republic of Indonesia and the Republic of Timor-Leste spared no effort to develop relations of stability, friendship and mutual advantages between the two countries and peoples, making reconciliation indeed a reality.

The IV Constitutional Government of Timor-Leste entered office about eight months ago and assumed the responsibility for the definition and implementation of reforming policies in a country that, in addition to being democratically young, was also in a particularly weakened condition as a result of the 2006 crisis. The 2006 political crisis, which shook the foundations of our State and submitted our People to unforeseeable suffering and anguish, left behind a heavy legacy with painful consequences, of which the assassination attempts of February 11 is a dramatic example. However, those who tried to attack the sovereignty of the State could not achieve their goals, as once again the institutions of our Country, despite their little temporal experience, were able to face this new trial with firmness and determination.

The State of Timor-Leste chose to declare martial law in order to prevent greater public disturbances, as well as to undertake the necessary investigation and operational diligences to capture the suspects of the crimes, while at the same time ensuring the population a social climate of public normality and tranquillity. These measures allowed a significant evolution in the internal security situation of the Country, with most of those involved in the attacks having already surrendered themselves to justice. Only a small group remains to be captured, a group that is already restricted to an area of the Country.

This evolution results in part from the creation of a Joint Command between the Armed Forces and the National Police, which have demonstrated that they are able to operate in a coordinated, efficient and effective manner. If we can take positive aspects from difficult periods, we should highlight the reapproximation of these two institutions, proving that, when confronted with common objectives, they can work well and in a duly articulated manner, thereby disrupting the doubts cast in 2006 saying that these forces would never see eye to eye in the pursue of the consolidation objectives of a State under the Democratic Rule of Law.

It is with satisfaction that I announce that at this time the exceptional measures suspending the rights and assurances of the citizens have been lifted, and that the country has returned to normal, with the exception of the region of Ermera, where the rebel group yet to surrender to justice is located. Our Government is also committed to the urgent resolution of the problems that condition economic growth in our country, such as the problem of the thousands of internally displaced persons. We are aware that peace and stability cannot be achieved without returning dignity and justice to these sectors of the population who deserve the protection of the State and the material and spiritual well being to make use of the freedom earned with so great a sacrifice.

Efficient governance is essential to strengthen the confidence of the People in the Government. The protection of Human Rights, Justice and the Rule of Law, together with the assurance of security and stability to the people, are the main obligations of the State. In this sense we are faced with huge challenges, which need to be overcome urgently. We have been accompanying the Public Sector Reform in Indonesia, and my Government as well has chosen 2008 as the year for Administrative Reform. The Government is committed to create an efficient, independent and free from corruption civil service, relying on the collaboration from other Sovereignty Bodies, so that the transformation in the public sector may lead to a governance of transparency, accountability and efficiency in the management of public finance.

For the immediate fight against poverty, we are implementing a proactive economic policy for mobilizing foreign investment and attracting investors. We believe this is the more immediate way to create employment at the same time as we transform the national business climate, namely in what concerns the inherent administrative procedures. In addition to this, we are reviewing the investment laws and other essential laws, such as the one on law property, and captivating foreign investment, while undertaking tax reform and reducing taxes in the non-oil sector, in order to increase private investment. It is here that I would like to see an increase in the investment and economic cooperation between Timor-Leste and Indonesia. We want more Indonesian companies to invest in Timor-Leste, and we want Timorese and Indonesian businesspersons to have a closer relationship.

The truth is that around 70-80 per cent of our external trade is with Indonesia, and therefore we have to develop mechanisms making these commercial relations easier and appealing to the Indonesian private sector. The strengthening of the economic and commercial ties between our two countries is also an investment in our very security. Together with the establishment of new dynamics of cooperation in the area of defence, mostly in the border areas, this will be fundamental for the future dialogue between our Nations.

I must also thank Indonesia for closing the land border posts so as to prevent our bilateral relations from being affected during the most critical periods we have experienced in the recent past. The threats to internal stability within the global world of today are shared with concern by us all. The subversive actions against national identity and cohesion, the acts of terrorism, guerrilla war and force by movements with political goals contrary to the constitutional order (as we have witnessed with the attacks of February 11), and of course organized crime such as drug trafficking and others, are threats that we must fight together, as neighbouring countries. The strengthening of our diplomatic relations makes the entire country benefit from stability, rather than just the border area, thus promoting development and fighting the threats that have an increasingly more global nature.

I would like to conclude by saying that the bilateral meetings we have had have been rather productive. I can highlight the signing of various agreements in fundamental areas for the development of Timor-Leste. In addition to these bilateral and also trilateral agreements including Australia, the United States,

Brazil and Germany, I must also state my appreciation for the contribution that Indonesia has made towards the development of the institutional capacity of my country, providing technical cooperation and assistance in areas so diverse as health, forestry, transports, telecommunications, power and diplomacy, among others. With Timor-Leste being a country that consists mostly of young people faced with the drama of unemployment and social integration, the scholarships and facilities attributed to our university students are very much appreciated by us.

Lastly, it is with great satisfaction that we receive the creation of an Indonesian Cultural Centre in Díli, in response to the request by His Excellency the President of the Republic, Dr Ramos-Horta, as a way to promote an even closer cultural cooperation between Indonesia and Timor-Leste. Despite the setbacks that have conditioned the sustainable development of our country, I consider that Timor-Leste has great potential to succeed and to be a reason of pride for all those who have supported us and believed in us. The common agenda of added cooperation defining the relations between Indonesia and Timor-Leste is promising! For the future I propose that we explore even further that which brings us close. Let us reinvent new partnerships, formulating serious cooperation proposals, as a way to defend the freedom of our brother countries. Our common history is made by our two peoples. Let us create the conditions for the friendship and solidarity among them to grow stronger and stronger!

# Opening Ceremony of the 10th Western China International Economy and Trade Fair: Second Western China Forum on International Cooperation

Chengdu, Sichuan Province
16 October 2009

> Your Excellency, Governor of Sichuan Provincial People's Government
> Your Excellencies, Heads of Government
> Distinguished Members of Delegations
> Ladies and Gentlemen,

Firstly, I would like to thank you for the warm welcome we have received from the People's Government of the Sichuan Province and the Organising Committee of the Western China International Economy and Trade Fair. I would also like to express my profound appreciation for the opportunity to take part in this important event and to congratulate the forum's excellent organisation.

The Western China Forum on International Cooperation is an important initiative for the Asian region. It is a strategic opportunity to face international challenges at a time when cooperation that crosses continents and oceans could strengthen our common goal of development.

Ladies and Gentlemen,

It is a great honour and privilege to be here in this vibrant city of Chengdu and see the substantial achievements of Sichuan's post-quake reconstructions. In just a little over one year, the path travelled by the Province of Sichuan in the post-disaster provides an important lesson to Timor-Leste. You have faced the obstacles of reconstruction by committing to fast-tracking social and economic development, and you have achieved.

The Government of Timor-Leste, like the Province of Sichuan, has experienced similar shocks, calamities, loss of human life and material destruction. We express, in a very modest way, our solidarity. Our People know well the suffering and the struggles of basic survival. Now that we are here, we can better understand China's strengths in responding to difficult challenges. It is through excellence in both political and economic management. The changes that have taken place in China over the past 60 years are remarkable, and one can only be inspired by what China represents to both the Asian region and the international community.

Ladies and Gentlemen,

Timor-Leste, one of the youngest and the poorest countries in South-East Asia, cannot be isolated from its regional partners. We must instead seek strong partnerships to overcome today's challenges, the challenges of a globalised world. It is these shared experiences that contribute to our common values that help define who we are as a nation, and what binds nations together in unity for common goals. The people of Timor-Leste have earned their place in history, through their selfless fight for national sovereignty and independence, based on the popular will and the vision for their own humanity. We have overcome the experiences of foreign occupation, which is now replaced with hope inspired by the blessings of independence — but sadly that hope, for many of our people, is dampened by extreme poverty. The needs of our People are great. However, Timor-Leste is a country blessed with natural resources that, if used wisely, may free the Timorese from poverty.

As we celebrate 10 years of self-determination, we can cast our eyes over a growing economy and emerging businesses, people safely walking our streets with improved health and access to education, all of which are adding to the great hopes for our new Nation. Development is a word that Timor-Leste embraces as the foundations of both peace building and nation building.

We are prepared to learn, which is why we join our neighbors and friends here today — to explore how we can fully participate in the global platform of investment, promotion, trade and economic cooperation. We are seeking opportunities to develop our economy, to create jobs, increase revenue, develop crucial productive sectors and, of course, above all, establish the viable conditions to rise from the depths of poverty.

Your Excellencies,

This is not a political or economic agenda exclusive to Timor-Leste, but a strategic agenda common to all countries represented here today. We must, with solidarity between nations, reinforce our mechanisms of dialogue and mutual cooperation to walk the path of consolidating economic growth.

At this forum, we represent different cultures, different political ideologies and different states of economic and social development. However, this diversity affords us the opportunities to share best practises in economic management, explore new avenues in trade and investment and, above all, exchange ideas to overcome common challenges in regional and international development.

Excellencies,

I would like to express some words of appreciation to China, a great friend to Timor-Leste, at this time of celebrations to the Chinese People for the astonishing 60 years they have had since the Foundation of the People's Republic of China.

China is a remarkable example of growing prosperity. China's domestic accomplishments in promoting unity and its pursuit of economic growth for the benefit of its people is matched only by its contribution to international diplomacy and development. China's success should be considered the world's success. The benefits of China's progress and reforms have not only fuelled their own development and economy but have had far-reaching benefits to the Asian region, and had a profound impact on the global economy. This brings great hope to developing nations like Timor-Leste.

It should also be recognised that China has, through various partnerships with many nations, provided social welfare: Food to the starving, education to children, health to the sick and they have made vital contributions to economic developments by providing major infrastructures, supporting private sector development and public sector growth.

In Timor-Leste, we also want to create better conditions for the People of our Nation by building vital infrastructure, reforming Government institutions and establishing the foundations for sustainable development. Our participation in this forum provides us the opportunity to learn from your experience, your history in creating a peaceful and prosperous nation.

Last but not least, on behalf of my Government and my people, I would like to express my gratitude to the people of China and the People's Republic of China for their ongoing support and contributions to Timor-Leste, and, in a particular way, the doctors, men and women from Chengdu who are in Timor-Leste combating the disease in my country.

# Inauguration of the United Nations Educational, Scientific and Cultural Organizations' Timor-Leste National Commission — Cultural Performance and Reception

Ministry of Foreign Affairs, Díli
23 April 2009

> Your Excellency, Dr Atul Khare, Special Representative of the Secretary-General for Timor-Leste
> Dr Hubert Gijzen, Director of UNESCO Jakarta and Regional Bureau of Science for Asia and Pacific and Representative to Timor-Leste
> Ms. Eloisa Ramirez, Assistant Director Philippines UNESCO National Commission
> Her Excellency, Kirsty Sword Gusmão, Goodwill Ambassador for Education
> Excellencies
> Distinguished Guests
> Ladies and Gentlemen,

It is a great pleasure to host this Cultural Performance and Reception to celebrate the inauguration of UNESCO's National Commission in Timor-Leste. The goals of UNESCO reflect the goals of our nation, and so the inauguration today of the UNESCO National Commission in Timor-Leste is a significant event in the development of our country. And it is one we will celebrate tonight with performances that will highlight the importance of our cultural heritage to our people.

Tonight I will only speak briefly so that we can enjoy the cultural performances that we have all come to see. I would, however, like to say a few words about the importance of UNESCO and the National Commission in Timor-Leste.

Ladies and Gentlemen,

I have a strong personal connection to UNESCO after the organisation awarded me with the UNESCO Felix Houphouet Boigny Peace Prize in 2003. This was a great honour and receiving the award conferred, in my view, a moral obligation to establish the Xanana Gusmão Foundation to contribute, at least in a modest way, to the intellectual and professional development of Timorese girls and boys who demonstrated merit and ability, many of whom lack the support and resources needed to develop their potential.

UNESCO promotes international co-operation among the nations of the world in the areas of education, science, culture and communication. In this task, it works to promote dialogue based on respect for the values and the dignity of each culture. Its goal is ultimately to bring peace to the minds of the people of the world. While UNESCO has ambitious goals, they are nevertheless goals shared with Timor-Leste as part of the international community. A process of dialogue based on respect and the dignity of the individual has been a foundation for the progress of our nation. The history of our country has been one of struggle as well as loss and, through dialogue and respect, we have been able to work together towards a better future for our people. And, in working towards this future, we are focused on providing education to our children, promoting our cultural heritage and alleviating poverty.

When in Paris, I asked the Director-General of UNESCO, Koichiro Matsuura, to assist us with the preservation of our cultural heritage that we were at risk of losing. However, I was told that UNESCO was not in a position to help protect 'intangible' cultural heritage, as opposed to material objects, and that there were no international conventions that would provide the foundation for this kind of assistance. Following these discussions, I invited the Director-General to visit Timor-Leste, which he did in July 2003, and on this occasion I again reinforced the request that I will again make today.

This focus will help us achieve one of our country's key priorities — the development of human capital. It is only through improving the human resource and capital base of our people that we can achieve our development goals. In working in this way to improve our human capital we will also address intolerance and promote humanitarian values, which will contribute to the achievement of lasting peace in our country.

Ladies and Gentlemen,

The inauguration today of the UNESCO National Commission in Timor-Leste is a significant event for our country. The National Commission that Timor-Leste has set up will operate as a cooperating body with UNESCO. The members of the Commission represent civil society, religious denominations, Government and the National Parliament. And we will also be linking UNESCO to Government Ministries that have responsibilities for education, science and culture in order to reinforce Government action in these areas. In this way, we will ensure that there is wide ranging and effective communication between governmental as well as non-governmental bodies with the work of UNESCO, to allow us to work together to further our shared goals.

Ladies and Gentlemen,

An important role for the National Commission will be promoting and enhancing our culture and our heritage. In our post-conflict nation, our shared culture is central to the progress of reconciliation and development. Our culture is fundamental to our national identify and the strengthening of our unity and our national cohesion. And it is important that this culture is both safeguarded and celebrated. Our cultural heritage is rich and deep and provides us with great opportunities. I urge the National Commission to grasp these opportunities for the future of our people and of our nation.

Tonight we have the opportunity to witness an important aspect of our uniquely Timorese culture, our traditional song and dance. Song and dance has an important position in Timorese society and in the shared experience and history of our communities. It plays a central role in our expressions of meaning as well as in our healing and, of course, in our celebrations. And we take pride in the musical expressions of our people, including, importantly, that of our young people.

In this respect, I would like to mention today that we have been approached by the Dean of the Australian Institute of Music, Dr Raffaele Marcellino, who is proposing a project to preserve Timor-Leste's extraordinary musical and linguistic heritage. The Australian Institute of Music is seeking to work with the Government of Timor-Leste to establish a National Sound and Music Archive. In addition to this, I have had discussions with representatives of the Government of Austria who are also committed to assisting us with preserving and enhancing our musical culture.

This willingness to support us in our goal, from UNESCO, the Australian Institute of Music and the Government of Austria, provides the National Commission with a great opportunity that I urge it to grasp to help preserve our cultural heritage. As well as the music and dance performances tonight, I would also encourage you all to attend the other events and activities during the Cultural Festival. These events will showcase our cultural heritage, expressing our shared values and the richness of our people.

Ladies and Gentlemen,

It is a great pleasure to host this Cultural Performance and Reception to celebrate the inauguration of UNESCO's National Commission in Timor-Leste. I urge UNESCO and the National Commission in Timor-Leste to work together to promote our shared values, develop our human capital and nurture a culture of tolerance, dignity and peace. I now ask you to relax and enjoy the cultural performances, which reflect the heart and the soul of our homeland.

# Goodbye Conflict, Welcome Development — the Timor-Leste Experience

Johns Hopkins University, Washington, DC
24 February 2011

> Your Excellencies
> Ladies and Gentlemen,

First and foremost, allow me to say how happy I am to be here today at the prestigious Johns Hopkins University to share with you a reflection on the Timorese experience in its transition from conflict to development. It is a great honour for me to address such a distinguished audience, knowing of your keen interest to know a little more about the Timorese process and our goals for the future. I would like to thank you for coming here today, and to acknowledge the Southeast Asian Studies program at SAIS and Asia Society Washington, DC, for organising this event and our Embassy for its support.

Since we began our struggle for self-determination and freedom, the pages of our History have been filled with massacres and hardships; but also with heroic deeds, victories and successes achieved by our People seeking to attain their right to Independence. To talk about Timor-Leste is to talk about perseverance, hope, determination and courage. For more recent times, it is also to talk about advances and setbacks, errors and lessons learned, conflicts and recovery. It is to talk about enormous challenges!

In sharing our experience, in terms of transition and change, I do so with an open mind, without trying to impose any type of model or political lesson. Indeed, as an LDC (Least Developed Country), our story is similar to that of many other countries throughout the world, with similar backgrounds and difficulties, and we know that we are not the only ones undergoing continuous Peace building and State building efforts after emerging from a situation of long conflict. I said that because there is no success formula that can be transferred from one country to the other, if we think that it will accelerate the transition towards development. On the contrary, it is necessary to respect the specific circumstances and timings of the reality of every country.

Every program, project or political decision must be objectively adapted to the cultural, social and economic context of each society. They must correspond to the needs and aspirations of the People, and be accepted by them. Ignoring these facts is often the reason why international assistance to LDCs undergoing transition always fails.

Ladies and Gentlemen,

Allow me to start by talking about ourselves as People. Allow me to talk about what we were, what we are and what we want to be. Timor-Leste is half of a small island, with the other half belonging to Indonesia. As such, we are located between two giants, Indonesia and Australia. In addition to its ethnical, cultural and linguistic diversity, Timor-Leste underwent centuries of administration by foreign countries, in an endless, conflicting co-existence, starting with the Portuguese colonial domination, which caused several struggles for independence, promoted by the various Timorese kingdoms. The last one was in 1912, and next year, 2012, will mark its 100 anniversary. While still recovering from that war, we were occupied by the Japanese from 1941 to 1945. Although this occupation was short-lived, it covered the entire territory and caused great suffering to the Timorese, with dozens of thousands of deaths.

In 1963, as a result of the Cold War era, it was thought and may have been decided that the integration of Timor-Leste to Indonesia would be the best solution for World Peace. And, so, it came to pass that in the fatal year of 1975 we started a new war. But this war would not have lasted 24 years, if other countries had not supplied weapons, tanks, aircraft and training to the Indonesian military in order to improve their fighting skills and therefore annihilate the resistance of the small Timorese guerrilla army.

As such, we can say that our past, for centuries, in terms of conflict, was not one of conflicts between Timorese kingdoms or ethnicities. Instead, the war was between the Timorese and all those who came from the other side of the sea, the foreigners. Evidently, having endured and fought alone for over two long decades, without any external military support, the Timorese people were scarred and developed a contesting nature that can propel them, easily, from peaceful demands into violent acts, without thinking about the consequences of their actions. To make matters worse, the violence and the physical destruction that followed the Referendum in 1999 deepened the already frail psychological and political situation, and worsened the already miserable living situation of the people. On the brink of independence, the People of Timor-Leste struggled to even survive.

Still, the People of Timor-Leste made another display of their great spirit by telling their Indonesian brothers and sisters that it was just our common past in fighting for freedom, and assuming a commitment to cooperate in solidarity and live in fraternity. The People of Timor-Leste also began an arduous period of State building.

Your Excellencies
Ladies and Gentlemen,

With the arrival of the United Nations mission and, together with the international community, we began to build from scratch the foundations for our democratic institutions.

When, on 20 May 2002, we became the masters of our fate as a State that was finally independent and sovereign, the expectations were that we Timorese might decide the future of our Nation. Naturally we believed that this future in freedom was promising. But I would like to remind that there were some factors that seriously threatened this ideal, namely:

- Lack of prepared and qualified human capital;
- Lack of political experience in democratic governance, a system that was completely new to our society;
- Lack of basic infrastructure and other essential equipment; and, most importantly
- Lack of financial resources of the Country itself.

Nevertheless, our people began with dignity to strive for a new life and for the better living conditions that they dreamed about. This led to a demanding society, both individually and in terms of social groups, which expected immediate results, as if they would be the simple and logical outcome of emancipation. Unfortunately, democracy does not triumph easily in a Country that is mostly poor and psychologically traumatised.

For a family that starves both in times of war and of peace, that lives in precarious conditions and lacks access to health or education, democracy is a concept too erudite and abstract to be well absorbed. Concepts such as tolerance, mutual respect, dialogue and even justice cannot be assimilated in a day as a direct consequence of the rights and duties inherent in freedom.

The truth is that there are no shortcuts for consolidating democracy and development. It is necessary to walk a long and arduous path, in order to change the mindset of our society and to transform the so-called democratic values into realities that every citizen can feel. And is this not what we call Development? Yes, I know, it's only one of the aspects, but an important one! This is why eight years of Independence are not enough to build a strong State, much less a developed society. It is natural that our young and fragile Nation had to contend with the resurgence of a few conflicts during this period.

The first social disturbance took place immediately after the euphoria of the celebrations of 20 May 2002. Then, we had further disturbances every two years, as if Timor-Leste was condemned to a vicious cycle of violence. In 2006, we had a serious political crisis that caused an atmosphere of insecurity in the Country, and various other problems that eventually led to confrontations between the Police and the Military, resulting in hundreds of thousands of internally displaced people and countless damage to the State.

From these crises, we learned our first major lesson: we urgently needed to learn to deal with the fragility of our State, which resided in the inability to address the root causes of problems, resulting in a trend to avoid problems rather than seeking proper solutions. We also needed to grow politically, that is, to impose a political will within State institutions to cooperate among themselves in the search for solutions, rather than focusing on the political dimensions of every situation and, in doing so, losing the judgement required to handle and solve crises.

Your Excellencies

Ladies and Gentlemen,

Today, leading a five-party Coalition Government that, when it came to office in August 2007, vowed to effectively introduce the necessary changes, we have achieved remarkable progress through a principle that is as simple as it is essential: to govern in dialogue! We focused our efforts on establishing peace and stability, as well as solving the most critical problems of the Country, knowing that, without addressing the problem of stability and internal security, any development effort would be wasted. It was through permanent dialogue and genuine cooperation between all Bodies of Sovereignty and Civil Society, together with the introduction of social justice measures, comprehensive reforms and public investment, that we managed to break the vicious cycle of conflict. In the end, we reorganized and, in a more coordinated manner, looked for the way that was right for Timor-Leste. We succeeded in:

- solving the problem of the 150,000 IDPs in two years, while we were told it would take decades to resolve, like the experiences brought from several countries;
- reforming core institutions for national security and stability, namely the Police and the Military, which began a new stage of cooperation and solidarity and, in doing so, they started to regain the trust of the people.
- starting a bold program to acknowledge our national heroes, the National Liberation Combatants, who were living in extreme poverty.
- introducing other social justice measures, namely, the payment of pensions to the elderly, the disabled, widows and orphans who sacrificed so much so that Timor-Leste could be independent, and supporting other vulnerable groups, such as women, children and youths, who make strong contributions to the stability and development of the Country.

From these initiatives, with their direct impact on the lives of the population, there was greater participation and confidence by all Timorese People towards the resolution of conflict and the consolidation of National Unity and Stability. This awareness resulted in the adoption of a new motto for our Nation, adopted in 2009, on the 10th anniversary of the Referendum: 'Goodbye Conflict, Welcome Development'.

Today, we are prepared to greet this new decade, from 2011 to 2020, with optimism, and to lay the foundations for bold national development. And what is it that gives us the confidence to face this next challenge without fear? It is being free from the instability and conflict that has for so long diverted our energies from building the country — wasting time as well as human and financial resources which are so much needed to be invested in the productive sectors of the country. On the contrary we are now implementing institutional and structural reforms that are vital for development and economic growth.

We have started the reform in the defence and security sector, by improving training programs to ensure their professionalism, competence, ethics and discipline. We have professionalised the public sector and introduced State management reform, to enable better service delivery to the people, including in our rural areas. On the other hand, we have been working to promote transparency and good governance, with the creation of the Civil Service Commission, the Anti-Corruption Commission and Public Finance Management reform, which will soon provide data on State expenditure, in real time, and available for public viewing through our website.

We also started building the capacity of our private sector, which was practically embryonic, promoting criteria for competence, professional honesty and technical capability, in regard to the cost-effectiveness of projects. We believe that our private sector should become a true partner of the Government in this vital period of Country building.

Together with national stability and the reform of our tax system, to provide attractive rates for national and foreign investors, our Country also offers great investment potential in nearly every sector. Business opportunities are on the rise and one needs only to look at commerce, industry, construction and tourism to see that they are growing and that our economy is emerging. The current situation in Timor-Leste speaks for itself. Even with the serious world financial crisis, Timor-Leste had two-digit economic growth rates for the past three years. In 2009 we had an economic growth rate of 13 per cent — this was not only the highest growth rate in the region, but also one of the ten highest in the entire world. This growth resulted in a nine per cent decrease of poverty, enabling around 96,000 people to escape from a situation of extreme poverty. The 2010 United Nations Human Development Index had Timor-Leste move up 14 positions, while the Millennium Development Indicators were met in regard to child mortality rates and other health indicators. We managed to create strong and dynamic growth, able to fight unemployment not only in the Country's capital but also in the countryside, by way of funding a decentralised private sector building fund.

In addition, Timor-Leste also became only the third country in the world to be granted full compliance with the Extractive Industries Transparency Initiative. The Revenue Watch Institute and Transparency International ranked Timor-Leste in 2010 as being in the group of the countries with the most transparency in regard to revenue.

Your Excellencies

Ladies and Gentlemen,

We have a Country blessed with great natural wealth and our Petroleum Fund currently stands at approximately 7.2 billion dollars. This amount is expected to increase to more than $20 billion over the next ten years. And this revenue is from the Bayu Undan field only!

As a result of our experience in the long Liberation Struggle, we are accustomed to meeting great challenges. This means that, today, the people of Timor-Leste are determined to achieve sustainable growth and to free themselves from misery. And so, after thoroughly reviewing our needs, we are currently drafting the Strategic Development Plan, which will include a lengthy public investment program for developing our human capital and the infrastructure required for sustaining a strong and growing economy.

What does Timor-Leste want to be in 20 years? Undoubtedly, it wants to be a country focused on the hydrocarbon industry, a country with dynamic urban centres and consolidation of rural areas to ensure that basic services reach every citizen. For this to be possible, we must, first and foremost, accelerate the extension, diversification and modernisation of agriculture. In the meantime, we will need to focus on a new paradigm of production and productive employment opportunities through the enhancement of industry and tourism, social service delivery and human capital development. If the needs of the country require fast and sustainable economic growth, we need to invest in basic infrastructure to be able to diversify the economy. We cannot and we do not want to be eternally and excessively dependent on oil revenues. But, Ladies and Gentlemen, we need to use oil revenues to develop the Nation. As a development strategy, we want to make good use of our natural wealth and we want to be the legitimate part of their exploitation.

As such, Timor-Leste is strongly committed to building a petroleum industrial base, which includes the construction of a pipeline from the Greater Sunrise field to Timor-Leste's onshore. We have been discussing these development plans with the Australian company, Woodside, and we believe that a pipeline from Greater Sunrise to Timor-Leste is the only way to transform these sovereign resources into a benefit for Timor-Leste. We have been conducting technical and feasibility studies with international companies and, in addition to being feasible, the Timor-Leste option represents an equitable distribution of benefit for Australia and Timor-Leste, and for their respective people. This is why it is an imperative for our joint development. In view of this, we will start to develop the Southern Coast of our country, establishing a Supply Base, a Refinery and an LNG plant, as well as necessary infrastructure such as port, airport and roads.

We Timorese are ready for this tough battle towards development! And we know that we will achieve our dreams, because our People have always responded when our Homeland calls on them to act! And, what is important is that the current state of the Nation requires that all Leaders of the Country assume their historic responsibility and to be courageous in making decisions towards a brighter future for the People of Timor-Leste!

Before I conclude, I would like to state that Timor-Leste is fortunate to be part of a region of the world that drives todays global economy. Our closest neighbours, Australia and Indonesia, are both regional economic powerhouses: Australian growth is fuelled by China and its demand for resources and Indonesia is becoming a remarkable success story.

We are integrating our economy in our East Asian region, which includes Japan, China and South Korea, as well as the major economies of ASEAN, Singapore, Thailand, Malaysia, Philippines and Vietnam. We are currently formalising our membership application for ASEAN to be made during the Indonesian presidency of this regional forum. We believe that having Timor-Leste join ASEAN during the Indonesian presidency is of great symbolic value, not only for Timor-Leste and Indonesia, but also for all the members of this Association.

Timor-Leste also had the honour of being invited to preside over the g7+ group, which enables fragile and affected-by-conflict countries to gather and to speak with a common voice, making use of the wisdom and shared experiences of a group representing 350 million people, from seventeen member countries in Africa, Asia, the Caribbean and the Pacific.

This invitation happened as a result of Timor-Leste hosting, in April 2010, in Díli, the International Dialogue on Peacebuilding and Statebuilding, which was chaired by Timor-Leste and the United Kingdom, with the participation of the LDCs from the g7+. The general goal of the g7+ is to awaken leaders and peoples so that they may reacquire ownership of their processes, viewed within a long-term perspective, without losing sight of the characteristics of each country and their priorities, and without forgetting to focus also on the need for a better control and adjustment over outside help, requiring greater transparency by donors and beneficiaries, so that the real impact of that support can be seen in the development of the countries.

As a Nation, we have received the generous assistance of the International Community; which we hope to be able to reciprocate in a genuine manner and within the same spirit of solidarity by sharing experiences, both sweet and bitter, with other fragile countries throughout the world.

Ladies and Gentlemen,

Finally, and in conclusion, I must mention that one of the key aspects that enabled our Country to move away from conflict, hopefully forever, was the fact that our leaders and our People accepted in a consensual manner that there was a deep need in our society to practice Forgiveness and Reconciliation. In view of the complexity of our history, there is no better way to progress as a Nation than to cultivate forgiveness and social harmony within our society. As Prime Minister of the young Timorese Nation, I am proud and moved to acknowledge the nobility and dignity of our People who, despite decades of suffering and living in Poverty, remain steadfast and hopeful, working tirelessly in order to develop the Nation.

In conclusion, Ladies and Gentlemen, there is no development without democracy. But there is also no democracy without development. Democracy is not an end; it is a process that makes people hold on to the commitment of values and principles of humanity. Thus, democracy cannot be imposed. Societies and peoples will always have the exact moment to defend the values that constitute their individual and collective fundamental rights. It has happened in the past, and it is happening in the present.

There are no models of democracy or of development. The values are what we have in common and each country and its people are the ones who will know the path to take!

# Closing Session of the Díli International Dialogue: Peacebuilding and Statebuilding

Díli
10 April 2010

> Your Excellencies
> Ladies and Gentlemen,

This is a historic day for Timor-Leste.

We have been writing the pages of Timor-Leste's history since we began our struggle for self-determination and for freedom. We have recorded stories of massacres and heroic deeds, tales of hardship, suffering and conflict, but also tales of victory and achievement — and it is these chronicles that tell of how our People gained the right to Independence. These are pages of history written with blood, but also with hope, courage and pride. These pages recount advances and setbacks, errors and lessons learned, conflict and recovery. And, today, ladies and gentlemen, we have joined our history with that of other countries with a common past, and we have realised that we are not alone in our Peacebuilding and Statebuilding endeavours. We have joined together with a common voice with nations that have similar histories and situations of fragility, as well as with partner countries committed to assisting us in our great challenges. In the words of Minister Kamitatu, we have moved from a monologue to dialogue.

Hosting the International Dialogue on Peacebuilding and Statebuilding, which will forever be marked by the Díli Declaration, gives our country great pride and emotion. I thank you all, ladies and gentlemen, for the honour we received in being chosen to host this first formal meeting.

> Your Excellencies
> Ladies and Gentlemen,

I have personally been inspired, moved and also encouraged by the contributions made at this dialogue. I am also humbled.

It can be easy to breathe a sigh of relief when you begin to show signs of progress, when you achieve a level of apparent stability, because, in times of peace, we can forget the hardships of conflict. This may be a reason for the resurgence of conflicts, with the human condition encouraging us to erase from our memory the difficult times of suffering and to move on quickly towards progress. This can cause us to miss some important steps. In seeking to move ahead, we risk overlooking the roots of our problems. In seeking to hasten the healing process of deep wounds that have not yet had time to properly heal, we start to believe that reconciliation can be possible in a mere five or six years. That is why I am pleased with the common agreement, by both fragile States and development partners, on the need for a long-term approach to Peacebuilding and Statebuilding. And this agreement has been properly reflected in the Díli Declaration.

Ladies and Gentlemen,

We understand from the statements made at this Dialogue, that the deep complexity of issues that constrain conflict or post-conflict countries means that it becomes impossible to deal with all problems at once. And we have also learnt that failure to acknowledge the true time it takes to resolve our difficulties may be fatal and lead to resurgence of conflict. On the other hand, if donor countries cease providing ongoing assistance at the first signs of improvement in stability and economic and social progress, this leaves a void in the processes and programs that have been started, ultimately leading to their failure.

It is absolutely necessary to respect the time frame and context of each society. This is our true challenge, as there are no two identical cultures or circumstances. Nevertheless, each and every society, and each and every People, value Peace as precious. Humans, both individually and collectively, desire Peace. It is critical to us all. Regrettably, as many of us know, starting conflict is so much easier than resolving it. It is easier to make war than to make Peace.

War focuses all our energy and all our effort on a single goal: to destroy the enemy. But Peace requires consensus building and reconciliation. It requires bringing together the aspirations of many to develop a common long-term vision — and then to implement it. Peace requires sacrifices in putting the interests of the whole ahead of the interests of the individual. It requires patience, forgiveness and trust, and most of all, compassionate and strong leadership. Perhaps it is for these reasons that there are so few exceptional individuals that the world acknowledges as pioneers of Peace. But, as President Ramos - Horta said so eloquently to this Dialogue, Peacebuilding also requires leaders connected to their People. And, ladies and gentlemen, even being the most worldly of Presidents, Ramos-Horta is first and foremost close to our People, and to their fears and to their dreams and aspirations.

Ladies and Gentlemen,

Like some here, I can speak from personal experience that it is more difficult to lead in times of peace than in times of war. I have been there. I lived many years convinced that I would never have to endure difficulties as hard as when I led my People during struggle. But, when I was given the challenge to become the First President of a nation traumatised by war, I realised that the greater struggle would be to build Peace, and subsequently the nation.

To join an entire People who have been scarred from conflict in the struggle for Peace is more difficult than to achieve unity in times of conflict. As we know, there are so many legitimate expectations from People who have fought for so many years for the ideals of freedom, equality and development that we can say that achieving true peace also means freeing People from poverty.

Ladies and Gentlemen,

This is also the challenge of Statebuilding, a process that is inter-related with the building of peace. As two sides of the same coin, it is important that emergency international support does not withdraw when peace appears to have been reached, and that we understand that Peacebuilding is consolidated when Statebuilding is strong. And so, we must ask, how do you empower people who have never known what power is? How do you build a democratic State with the participation of all when People have never known what it means to be free from misery, hunger, ignorance and disease? In our poor societies, people still kill each other for survival, for simple access to water, food, land, schools and health care. It is, therefore, perhaps easier for us to understand why people also kill for access to political power and control over national decision making, especially in countries with valuable natural resources.

One aim of this Dialogue is to find better solutions and to share best practices to address these problems. And if, in this Dialogue, we do not resolve all the problems affecting fragile States, at least we will have taken one more step in this direction of concrete actions.

As we have discussed, Statebuilding means a transition not just for countries, but also for their People. It can mean transforming militias or guerrilla fighters into soldiers of conventional forces; youths without childhoods of joy and education into responsible adults; hardened resistance activists into professional journalists; and leaders of a struggle into mature political office holders. And many cases presented at this Dialogue demonstrate that we cannot underestimate the challenges, especially when the edifices of the pillars of the State hide its inherent weakness.

An example that saddens us deeply in Timor-Leste is Guinea-Bissau. This country's achievement of independence inspired our People in their struggle. The turmoil in this country upsets us greatly and we feel solidarity for our brothers and sisters in this African nation. Guinea-Bissau has received huge quantities of international assistance in comparison to the size of its national economy and yet it continues to struggle. And so, we can conclude that this assistance must not have been appropriate to the circumstances.

Ladies and Gentlemen

This is why all g7+ countries have emphasised the importance of understanding the need of each country to have a transitional period of their own time and at their own pace. As Ms Bella Bird wisely commented to this Dialogue, the transition from fragility to resilience requires a balanced and flexible approach. This balance requires fragile nations and donors to be nimble enough to respond to emerging situations that may threaten recovery, while continuing to address the ongoing root causes of conflict.

Life is a process of building knowledge, of learning from experiences, and following our dreams and our visions. The life lived by citizens in fragile countries is far from easy — not only is it a constant struggle for survival, but it can be a challenge to come to terms with new concepts and values.

The road towards democracy and development knows no shortcuts. One must walk the hard road to transform mentalities and achieve social inclusion. That is why the g7+ countries have asked our friends, the development partners, to walk in our shoes and be aware of our conditions and our needs. We can then better walk together towards our shared goal of spreading peace and prosperity. And with our achievements the hopes and visions of donor countries can be fulfilled.

I draw hope and confidence from the Díli Declaration. The development partners and fragile States have recognised that we can both do things better while reinforcing our common shared goal. We are encouraged by the proposal to develop an action plan and by the determination to take immediate steps to address issues of concern in the delivery of development assistance. The Díli Declaration has committed strong support to the g7+ institutional grouping as a permanent forum to bring together fragile States in a spirit of solidarity and friendship and allow for better preparation in the international discussions with the development partners. And I would like to thank Australia for offering today to provide the funding to support this body and I hope that other countries will join with them in this effort.

I am also very pleased that, following the inspiring leadership Mr Kamitatu, that our own Minister Emilia Pires will take over as co-chair of the International Dialogue. It is not only a matter of pride for Timor-Leste but also a symbol of the responsibility we wish to bring to this process.

This Dialogue is part of an ongoing process and I am pleased that the Díli Declaration will guide and inform the international community in its future work. And, ladies and gentlemen, I hope that the suggestion made today, that Díli become a centre for international and United Nations conferences, becomes a reality.

Ladies and Gentlemen,

We must all learn from the lessons of our past and remain vigilant and determined in our mission to prevent political violence and conflict. Walking together gives us strength in this mission. Walking together, fragile States and their development partners can minimise the suffering that results from conflict and extreme poverty. Let us all work together to bring hope and confidence and develop a long-term vision for Peacebuilding and Statebuilding in our fragile nations. Hopefully, we can make sure that no more tears of conflict fall on the snow of Nepal's majestic Himalayas; that no more blood covers the sparkling diamonds of Sierra Leone; that the soul of the people of the DRC reflects the richness of their lands; that the People of Southern Sudan achieve self-realisation; that 'bridges' of peace can be built between the islands of the archipelago of the Solomon Islands; and that all our fragile nations can achieve peace and development.

# Opening of the International Investment Conference

Convention Centre, Díli
21 October 2010

> Excellencies
> Members of Government
> Distinguished Guests
> Ladies and Gentlemen,

It is a great pleasure to be here to open this International Investment Conference. The holding of this Conference is a reflection of both the expanding investment opportunities in our economy and the increasing optimism in our future. And it reflects the Government's commitment to growing our economy and building our nation. With this optimism, our strong economic growth and the Government's plan for our future, Timor-Leste offers great investment prospects.

> Ladies and Gentlemen,

We now enjoy an economy that is booming with unprecedented levels of growth and economic activity. This success is evident in more than our positive economic statistics. It is clear to us as we walk our busy streets with their new shops, restaurants and businesses. It is clear as we witness the building boom across Díli and in our other regional centres. And, most important, it is clear from the sense of belief in the future and the optimism of our People.

We have come a long way in the last few years, but, we still have much to do and great potential to realise. And so, today, I ask you to imagine what we can achieve working together over the coming years. We are already experiencing some of the highest rates of economic growth in the world. And, into the future, Timor-Leste will benefit from being located in Asia, the powerhouse of the global economy and will greatly benefit in the future when Timor-Leste becomes ASEAN's 11th member. As the world economy struggles, our Asian and Pacific neighbours, including Indonesia, Singapore, China, South Korea,

Japan and Australia are growing strongly and we are well positioned to join them in this great Asian growth story.

Ladies and Gentlemen

The Government understands the central importance of private sector investment for the future of the country. For Timor-Leste to develop a sustainable economy, it will need a well-developed private sector that provides jobs and opportunities, builds infrastructure and creates wealth for our People. That is why the Government strongly supports and commends the establishment of Timor-Leste's Chamber of Commerce and Industry.

A well-developed private sector and strong economic growth is also essential to alleviate poverty. The experience of China shows us that economic growth is the best way to lift of people out of poverty. That is why the Government is dedicated to working with investors to create a modern and diversified economy with high quality infrastructure. We are committed to developing a sustainable economy that is self-sufficient in food, that expands the tax base, and the supports that provision of quality health care and education to our People.

Ladies and Gentlemen,

The Government's steadfast commitment to transforming our nation will take shape with the Strategic Development Plan. The implementation of the Strategic Development Plan will provide a long-term economic vision for Timor-Leste. It will allow our country to realise its potential as a modern economy with quality infrastructure including roads, ports, power and telecommunications. And it will provide many investment opportunities across all sectors of the economy, from mega-projects to micro-businesses. With innovation, creative business thinking and hard work, there is great scope for successful investment in Timor-Leste.

To achieve the vision of the Strategic Development Plan, the government will also need to work in partnership with the private sector, creating more opportunities for both national and international investors. I do not want investors to sit on the sidelines and then, in five years' time, or 10 years' time, hear them say with regret that they missed Timor-Leste's growth phase. That chance to invest is now.

We, of course, know that Timor-Leste presents investment challenges. We know that we can improve our systems and our processes to provide a better business environment. The Government is working to address these challenges. At this conference, we will be discussing many issues that are critical for investors, including tax policy, land law, business registration and investment law. I hope, at the conclusion of this conference, we have explored ideas and developed approaches to address our challenges. And, importantly, I hope we also acknowledge our fundamental strengths and decide on ways to promote them. These strengths include our taxation system, with Timor-Leste being one of the lowest-taxed economies in the world. And we have a stable macro-economic environment, with consistency in monetary and fiscal policy. But our greatest strength is our People.

The Timorese People are resilient, determined and resourceful. Our People's commitment to building our nation was proved during the struggle for independence. It is this determination that we will now apply to building a strong and sustainable economy, to build our nation and lift our People from poverty.

I wish you the best for this conference and hope that it will contribute to the development of clear strategies and policy approaches to improve our investment environment. I urge you to be part of the Timor-Leste's economic success story and join with us to build our Nation. And, most of all, I ask that we all work together for a better Timor-Leste and for a brighter future of hope and opportunity for our People.

# Address to the Rio Branco Institute: Lecture for Young Diplomats on the Creation of the Timorese State

Brasília
2 March 2011

> Your Excellencies
> Ladies and Gentlemen,

First and foremost, I would like to highlight the great pleasure it gives me to be once again in this wonderful Country that is Brazil, particularly at this prestigious Rio Branco Institute, so that I may share with such a distinguished audience a reflection on the Timorese experience in creating the Timorese State and subsequently in transitioning from conflict to development.

I would like to give a special salute to the young diplomacy students in attendance here today, with whom I have the utmost pleasure in exchanging ideas and experiences on a subject that is as dear to Timor-Leste as the creation of our young State.

Timor-Leste is, without the shadow of a doubt, one of the finest examples of the importance of diplomacy. It is through diplomacy that many countries come together to debate and overcome the problems we face today. It is also through diplomacy that important negotiations are held, which may lead certain countries to peace or to war. In the case of Timor-Leste, the strong determination and courage of our People, allied with the perseverant action by young Timorese in the diplomatic front in various parts of the world, led to the end of a long period of war and to the achievement of our Independence.

Here I must mention our President of the Republic and Nobel Peace Prize Winner, Dr José Ramos-Horta, one of the most remarkable Timorese diplomats, who, along with other young Timorese, spent years using words rather than guns, language and education rather than intimidation and persecution, and talent for debating ideas rather than physical confrontation, in order to fight for the Timorese cause at world level. His efforts contributed very significantly to the international recognition of de Timor-Leste as a free and independent Nation.

Ladies and Gentlemen,

As you know, the pages of our History, since we started our struggle for self-determination and freedom, are filled with massacres and hardships, but also heroic deeds, victories and achievements by our People in gaining their right to Independence. Looking back, to talk about Timor-Leste is to talk of perseverance and hope, determination and courage. More recently, it is also to talk of advances and setbacks, errors and lessons learned, conflicts and recovery. It is to talk about enormous challenges!

As such, when I convey our experience in building the Timorese State, I do it with an open mind and without trying to impose any sort of model or political lesson. Indeed, since we are an LDC (Least Developed Country), we have joined our history to that of other countries in the world with common pasts and / or difficulties, and we know that we are not the only ones undertaking these Peace building and State building efforts after a long period of conflict.

There are no success formulas that can be transported from one country to the other to make development faster. On the contrary, it is necessary to respect the circumstances and timings of each country. Each programme, project or political decision must be adapted to the cultural, social and economic context of each society. It must correspond to the needs and aspirations of the people, and be accepted by them. Ignoring these facts is often why international assistance to least development countries in transition periods fails, regardless of all the goodwill and commitment by the donor countries.

Ladies and Gentlemen,

Allow me to start by talking about ourselves as a People. Allow me to talk about what we used to be, what we are and what we want to be. Timor-Leste is half an island, shared with Indonesia, and, as such, is located between two giants, Indonesia and Australia. In addition to its ethnic, cultural and linguistic diversity, Timor-Leste spent centuries being administrated by foreign countries, where coexistence was difficult. This started with the Portuguese colonial administration, which caused violent struggles for independence promoted by the various Timorese kingdoms.

Not yet recovered from this, we had to endure the Japanese occupation from 1941 to 1945. Although short-lived, it covered the entire territory and caused great suffering to the Timorese people, with thousands of people being killed. Subsequently, in 1963, during the Cold War period, some thought and probably decided that the integration of Timor-Leste in Indonesia was the best solution for world peace. And so it was.

In the fatidic year of 1975, we started a new struggle. But this struggle would not have lasted 24 years if other countries had not supplied weapons, tanks, aircraft and training to Indonesian officers, in order to improve their fighting prowess and to annihilate the resistance of the small Timorese guerrilla army. Therefore, we were also the victims of a new world order that demanded the fall of communist regimes. Victims from these global events or merely from our own fate, the truth is that Timor-Leste spent the better part of its past fighting almost exclusively against foreigners, rather than Timorese. As such, having endured and fought alone for over two long decades, without any external military support, the Timorese people were irremediably scarred and developed a contesting nature that can propel them from peace into violence easily, without thinking about the consequences of their actions.

The violence and physical destruction that followed the 1999 Referendum worsened even more the already frail psychological and political situation and the already miserable living conditions of the populations. Still, the People of Timor-Leste gave another display of their greatness of spirit, by forgiving their Indonesian brethren and assuming a commitment to cooperate in a fraternal and solidary manner. The People of Timor-Leste also began an arduous period of State building.

Your Excellencies, Ladies and Gentlemen,

With the arrival of the United Nations mission and together with the international community, we began to build from scratch the foundations for our democratic institutions, that is, building our State. When, on 20 May 2002, we became the masters of our fate, as a State that was finally independent and sovereign, the expectations were that we Timorese might decide the future of our Nation. Naturally we believed that this future in freedom was promising. Once again, international diplomacy sped up processes and united the International Community around Timor-Leste, as partners committed to this ideal of building the world's youngest Nation. The UN stayed in the Country, working towards peacekeeping, economic cooperation, institutional capacity-building and the propagation of values, such as justice and the protection of human rights.

Although this international contribution to the creation of the Timorese State was priceless, it was not sufficient by itself. Although we had myriad opportunities ahead of us, there were also some factors that seriously threatened the achievement of our goals, namely:

- Lack of prepared and qualified human capital;
- Lack of political experience in democratic governance, a system that was completely new to society;
- Lack of basic infrastructures and other essential equipment; and, most importantly,
- Lack of financial resources by the Country itself.

Nevertheless, the Timorese people began with dignity to strive for a new life and for the better living situation they dreamed about. This led to a demanding society, both individually and in terms of social groups, which expected immediate results as if they were simply the logical outcome of emancipation. Unfortunately, democracy does not triumph easily in a Country that is mostly poor and psychologically traumatised. For a family that starves both in times of war and of peace, that lives in precarious conditions and lacks access to health or education, democracy is a concept that is too erudite and abstract to be acquired. Concepts like tolerance, mutual respect, dialogue and even justice cannot be assimilated in a day, as direct consequence of the rights and duties inherent to freedom.

The truth is that there are no shortcuts for consolidating democracy and development. It is necessary to walk a long and arduous path in order to change the mindset of our society and to transform the so-called democratic values into realities that every citizen can feel. This is why eight years of Independence are not enough to build a strong State, much less a developed society. It is natural that our young and fragile Nation had to contend with the resurgence of a few conflicts during this period.

The first social disturbance took place immediately after the euphoria of the celebrations of 20 May 2002. Then we had new disturbances every two years, as if Timor-Leste was condemned to a vicious cycle of violence. In 2006, we had a serious political crisis that caused an atmosphere of insecurity in the Country, and various other problems that eventually led to confrontations between the Police and the Military, resulting in hundreds of thousands of internally displaced people and countless damages to the State.

From these crises we learned our first major lesson: we urgently needed to learn to deal with the frailty of our State, which resided in the inability to address the root causes of problems, resulting in a trend to bypass problems instead of finding proper solutions. We also needed to grow politically, that is, to impose a political will within State institutions to cooperate among themselves in the search for solutions, rather than giving political aspects to every situation and thus losing the levelheadedness required to handle and solve crises.

Today, leading a five-party Coalition Government that, when it was entered into office in August 2007, vowed to effectively change the Country, we have achieved remarkable progresses through a principle that is as simple as it is essential: to govern in dialogue! We focused our efforts into establishing peace and stability, as well as into solving the most critical problems of the Country, knowing that, without handling the problem of stability and internal security, any development effort would be wasted. It was through permanent dialogue and genuine cooperation between all Sovereignty Bodies and Civil Society, together with the implementation of social justice measures and strong reforms and public investment, that we managed to break the vicious cycle of conflicts. In short, we regrouped and, in a more coordinated manner, looked for the model that was right for Timor-Leste. We succeeded in:

- solving the problem of the 150,000 Internally Displaced Persons in two years, when the International Community said it would take decades to solve.
- reforming core institutions for national security and stability, namely the Police and the Military, which started a new stage of cooperation and solidarity, consequently regaining the trust of the populations.
- starting a bold program to acknowledge our national heroes, the National Liberation Combatants, who were living in extreme poverty.
- starting other social justice measures, namely the payment of pensions to the elderly, the disabled, widows and orphans who sacrificed so that Timor-Leste could be independent, and supporting other vulnerable groups such as women, children and youths, who make strong contributions to the stability and development of a Country.

From these initiatives, with direct impact on the lives of the populations, we felt greater participation and confidence by all Timorese People towards the resolution of conflicts and the consolidation of National Unity and Stability. This awareness resulting in a new motto for our Nation, adopted in 2009, on the 10th anniversary of the Referendum: 'Goodbye Conflict, Welcome Development'.

Today, we are prepared to greet this new decade, from 2011 to 2020, with optimism, and to lay the foundations for bold national development. Following the political and social stability we have achieved, that is, without the instability and conflict episodes that diverted the energies required for building the Country, we are not wasting the time, human resources or financial means needed for investing in the production sectors of the Country. On the contrary, we are implementing institutional and structural reforms that are vital for development and economic growth.

We have started to reform the defence and security sector, ensuring the professionalism, competence, ethics and training of our Forces. We have professionalised the public sector and introduced the State management reform, thus enabling better service delivery to the populations, including rural areas. On the other hand, we have been trying to promote transparency and good governance, namely through the creation of the Civil Service Commission, the Anti-Corruption Commission and the Public Finance Management reform, which will soon have data on State expenditures available in real time for public consultation by way of a website.

We also started building the capacity of our private sector, which was practically inexistent, promoting criteria of competence, professional honesty and technical capacity in terms of the cost-efficiency of projects. We believe that the private sector should become a true partner of the Government in this vital period of Country building.

Together with national stability and the reform of the tax system of the Nation, with very attractive rates for national and foreign investors, our Country also offers great investment potential in nearly every sector. Business opportunities are on the rise and one needs only to look at commerce, industry, construction and tourism to see that they are growing and that our economy is emerging.

The present situation of Timor-Leste speaks for itself. Even during the serious world financial crisis, Timor-Leste has had two-digit economic growth rates for the past three years. In 2009 we had an economic growth rate of 13 per cent — this was not only the highest growth rate in the region, but also one of the ten highest in the entire world in 2008 and 2009. This growth resulted in a 9 per cent decrease of poverty, enabling around 96,000 people to move away from a situation of extreme poverty. The 2010 United Nations Human Development Index had Timor-Leste move up 14 places, while the Millennium Development Indicators were met in what concerns child mortality rates and other health indicators. We managed to create a progressive growth dynamic, able to fight unemployment not only in the Country's capital but also in the countryside, by way of decentralised private sector operation mechanisms and the creation of local employment. And, of course, we continue to have the trust of friendly countries like Brazil that have contributed so much to this process of change and transition.

The Brazilian cooperation has been essential for the development of key areas such as education, health and justice in our Country. We will always be grateful to our Brazilian brothers and sisters for the solidary manner in which they have been going to Timor-Leste, befriending our People and contributing to build our Country right from the very start!

We have a Country blessed with great natural wealth and we have approximately 7.2 billion dollars in our Petroleum Fund. We expect this figure to increase to over 20 billion dollars within the next ten. And these revenues come from a single oil and gas field, Bayu Undan!

Having grown accustomed to enormous challenges during our lengthy Liberation Struggle, today, the people of Timor-Leste are determined to achieve sustainable growth and to free the populations from misery. Thus, and after thoroughly reviewing our needs, we are currently drafting the Strategic Development Plan, which will include a lengthy public investment programme for developing our human capital and the infrastructure required for sustaining a strong and growing economy. Like Brazil, with which we have so much to learn, we want to grow and to develop. Brazil, with its high level of industrialisation and a diversified economy, is becoming a rapidly developing economic powerhouse and a role model for Timor-Leste.

What does Timor-Leste want to be in 20 years? Undoubtedly, it wants to be a country focused on the hydrocarbon industry, a country with an urban expression that is well distributed throughout the territory, and with rural urbanisation that enables the populations to live in communities, where basic service delivery reaches every citizen. For this to be possible, we must first and foremost accelerate the extension, diversification and modernisation of agriculture. Subsequently, we will need to focus on a new paradigm of production and productive employment opportunities through the enhancement of industry and tourism, social service delivery and human capital development. If the needs of the country recommend fast and sustainable economic growth, we need to invest in basic infrastructures to diversify the economy. We cannot and we do not want to be exclusively dependent upon oil revenues invested in a Petroleum Fund.

Ladies and Gentlemen,

Before I conclude, I would like to state that Timor-Leste is fortunate to be part of a region of the world that includes the driving force of global economy today. As you are aware, our closest neighbours, Australia and Indonesia, are great economic powerhouses. While Australia is growing, driven mainly by China and its need for resources, Indonesia is becoming a remarkable case of success.

We are also taking our due position in our region, which includes Japan, China and South Korea, as well as other great ASEAN economies like Singapore, Thailand, Malaysia, the Philippines and Vietnam. We are presently formalising our membership in ASEAN, during the Indonesian presidency of this regional forum. I believe that having Timor-Leste join ASEAN during the Indonesian presidency will have great symbolism not only for Timor-Leste and Indonesia, but also for all the members of this regional association.

We are also fortunate and proud to be part of CPLP, with which we share historic, cultural and linguistic ties, as well as a solid friendship. This puts us in the European agenda, thanks to the privileged relationship between this Community and Portugal, and provides us with unique cooperation and development opportunities.

Timor-Leste also had the honour of being invited to preside over the g7+ group, which enables countries that are fragile and affected by conflicts to gather and to speak with a single voice, making use of the wisdom and shared experiences of a group representing 350 million people, from 17 member countries in Africa, Asia, the Caribbean and the Pacific. This invitation happened as a result of Timor-Leste hosting, in Díli, the International Dialogue, in April 2010, under the motto 'Peacebuilding and Statebuilding', which was presided by Timor-Leste and the United Kingdom and had the participation of LDCs from the g7+. The general goal of the g7+ is raising the awareness by leaders and populations so that they may reacquire ownership of their processes, as well as in what concerns the need for a better control over outside help, requiring greater transparency by donors and beneficiaries, so that the real impact of that support can be seen in the development of the countries.

As a Nation, we have received the generous assistance from the International Community; presently we hope to be able to reciprocate in a genuine manner and within the same spirit of solidarity by sharing experiences, both sweet and sour, with other fragile countries throughout the world.

Ladies and Gentlemen,

Finally, and in conclusion, I must mention that one of the key aspects that enabled our Country to step away from conflict, hopefully for good, was the fact that our leaders and our People accepted in a consensual manner that there is a deep need in our society to practise Forgiveness and Reconciliation. In view of the complexity of our history, there is no better way to progress as a Nation than to cultivate forgiveness and social harmony within our society. As the Prime Minister of the young Timorese Nation, I am proud and moved to acknowledge the nobility and dignity of our People, who, despite decades of suffering and living in Poverty, remain steadfast and hopeful, working tirelessly in order to develop the Nation.

In conclusion, Ladies and Gentlemen, there is no development without democracy, but there is also no democracy without development. Democracy is not an end in itself, but rather a process that enables peoples to maintain their commitment to the values and principles of humanity. As such, democracy cannot be forced upon anyone. Societies and peoples will always have the proper time for learning to defend the values that constitute the core of their individual and collective rights. It happened before and it is happening now.

There are no democracy models; there are no development models. Values are common, but it is up to each country and its people to know the path they must take! These are the values that we hope the young Timorese diplomats will assimilate in the training process of the Timorese State, so that they may defend the cause of world peace in the international stage with the same determination and firmness that young men and women in the past defended the cause of Timor-Leste.

# Official Opening of the International Conference on Community-based Ecotourism

Díli
24 August 2009

> Excellencies,
> Members of Government
> Members of the National Parliament
> Guest Speakers
> Representatives from NGOs and International Agencies
> Members of the Press
> Ladies and Gentlemen,

It is with great pleasure that I welcome you all to this International Conference on Community-based Ecotourism, in particular those of you who came from afar to participate in this event.

Right now, I would like to congratulate the Minister of Tourism, Trade and Industry for this excellent initiative of organizing a Conference dedicated to a theme that is so important for the young Nation of Timor-Leste. This conference is part of within the official program of the celebrations of the 10th Anniversary of the Popular Consultation, and those who know Timor-Leste will surely understand just how important this subject is, precisely at a time when we are celebrating a date that means so much to every Timorese citizen.

> Ladies and Gentlemen,

Please allow me to be so bold as to speak about my Country, to say it is undoubtedly a magical place, with a unique history and culture, which carries a mystical soul enshrined within the perfect combination of the best that nature has to give us. Our tropical forests, our sumptuous mountains that descend unto our paradise-like beaches, the depth of our seas, which conserve the wealth of our corals and maritime fauna — these were the elements that nurtured our People during the terrible times of the resistance. We can even say that our

People's perseverance was fed by the strength of the nature that this half-island possesses and where, despite the suffering, the forced departure of our children, parents and siblings, and almost even our dreams, the sun never stopped shining and the great beauty of our landscape never let us lose heart. Because of all of this, to preserve our Mother Nature and to develop ecotourism are priorities for the Government of Timor-Leste.

Ladies and Gentlemen,

By celebrating the 10th anniversary of the Timorese People's remarkable display of courage in voting for its right to National Independence, we wish to mark a new stage in the history of Timor-Leste, in which we remove from the conflicts of the past and finally live in an atmosphere of peace and stability. We are ready to move firmly towards national development and the reduction of poverty.

Tourism is one of the main sectors that can ensure the economic development of the country, having already contributed around 11 per cent of the overall GDP. It is expected that tourism trips will increase to 1.6 billion by 2020. As I have said already, our Country has enormous tourism potential. In cultural and historical terms, we have unexplored natural landscapes and incredible biodiversity. For all this, tourism is undoubtedly a priority sector for national development, affecting other sectors, such as agricultural, rural and infrastructure development, and which must be thought over and planned with due care, to ensure the preservation of nature and to contribute towards the sustainable development of the population.

Accordingly, ecotourism projects to be developed in our Country must seek to preserve our natural and cultural legacy, promote equality and the reduction of poverty in local communities, and to preserve the ancestral traditions of the Timorese people, namely in local music, dance, cooking and handicraft. Tourism is an important factor for the economic growth, not just because of the revenues and employment it generates, but also because of all the other infrastructures associated with it, namely, restaurants, hotels, leisure and entertainment equipment, and small and medium businesses. However, tourism development must be balanced. We must capitalize the unexplored areas of Timor-Leste and work in close cooperation with local communities to ensure that the Timorese people are both partners and beneficiaries in this process. In this task it is essential to involve our more remote communities. We need to realize the dreams of all Timorese citizens, involving them directly in this great project of national development, with confidence that the Timorese are among the most skilled people in the world in what regards transforming basic resources into major achievements, and consequently that we can realize our dream of development without any type of exclusion.

We want to develop tourism in Timor-Leste, but we want the right tourism for our Nation. We want to be hosts to tourists that respect and value that which are the most precious things to us, the Timorese People: our land, our nature, our culture. In this way it will be possible to provide Timorese citizens with better opportunities to improve their lives. We can give you some examples of successful community intervention in the sector of tourism, namely:

- Project 'Tua Koin Eco-Aldeia' in Ataúro has had a rather positive impact in the management of marine resources, contributing to increase the income of the local community;
- Valusere Cooperative in Tutuala showed an increase of US$2500-4000 per month, in terms of revenue increase in its last quarter review. Furthermore, it achieved significant improvements in terms of the living conditions of fishermen, by improving fishing activities, transportation services and local guides;
- Also in this region, the community members had benefitted through the creation of the First National Park Nino Konis Santana. And I would also like to use this opportunity to compliment the work done by Haburas Foundation and its Portuguese partner, CIDAC;
- The Com community has managed to increase community revenues by developing support activities to tourists and increasing the sales of handicraft products;
- The Maubisse community has established housing facilities and other services, with support from the Ministry of Tourism, Trade and Industry.

These are small examples of projects we want to multiply in order to benefit local populations, taking into consideration that it has been proven that community initiatives for developing tourism have been having positive effects in terms of the living conditions of the communities.

I would like you to use the next two days to reflect on this: we can achieve sustainable development if we work together towards developing community-based tourism in Timor-Leste. During this process, we may also have to experiment with errors and failures, until we find the right model for Timor-Leste. It is here that we rely on the collaboration from our friends in attendance who have come from Spain, Portugal, France, Indonesia and Australia so that we may share experiences, and review and draft strategies seeking to develop the tourism sector, in particular, community-based ecotourism.

There are no perfect and instantaneous formulas that we can import and apply to our Country, but I am confident that we already share the same basic principles that are vital for developing ecotourism in Timor-Leste:

- Respect for nature
- Respect for rural communities
- The direct involvement of our communities in this process, and
- The preservation of our natural, historical and cultural heritage.

# Opening Session of the G7+ Meeting

Díli
8 April 2010

> Your Excellencies
> Ladies and Gentlemen,

It is a great pleasure for me to be here today at the start of this meeting, which we call g7+. First and foremost, I would like to thank you all for being here in Díli. I trust that throughout this meeting we will be able to better understand each of our realities.

One of the main principles of this meeting is to share experiences, obstacles and challenges faced in each of our States. We are considered fragile States, but nevertheless we are determined to provide better responses to the needs of our Peoples.

Our group consists of seven countries: Afghanistan, Central African Republic, Democratic Republic of Congo, Haiti, Ivory Coast, Sierra Leone and Timor-Leste. No other group of countries could be more different, yet at the same time more similar. We are different in relation to geography, culture, religion, history and even politics and ideology. But at the same time, we are similar because we are post-conflict or latent conflict countries, where generalized poverty is sadly still a reality. Still, we take strength in knowing that we are not alone, that it is up to us and no one else to act in the defence of our peoples and to decide the manner in which the International Community may be more constructive and better directed to our real needs. Therefore, I would like to suggest everyone engage in an open and trusting dialogue, forging a new alliance and a common agenda, based on the fact that we are a group of countries that is facing various types of difficulties but that we are also the ones most interested in helping ourselves.

Unfortunately not all countries from the group of seven are represented here today, however we are very pleased to have a 'plus' that brings value to this meeting. The presence of Burundi, Chad, Southern Sudan, Nepal and the

Solomon Islands for the first time in our country makes us believe that this is truly a forum of great expectations.

Timor-Leste is truly committed to assuming its rights and duties as a Member of the International Community, using our collective experience as a nation and people to support other nations involved in democratic consolidation and nation-building processes. We do not want the 'Third High Level Forum in Accra' to be just another goodwill initiative where the 'Principles for Good International Involvement in Fragile States and Situations' are just that: principles! We want today's meeting, which we may call the first 'Fragile State Forum' to continue, to expand and even to become institutionalized, so that we can improve the coordination of international assistance from Development Partners.

Still, as I have said before, as members of the community of nations, we have both rights and duties, and one of the latter is contributing so that the assistance provided by our Development Partners is used in an effective and responsible manner. I believe we have this moral obligation towards the taxpayers from the donor countries. Therefore, Ladies and Gentlemen, we have a series of topics in our common development agenda that needs discussing, so that the ten structuring principles agreed upon in Accra may be implemented with coherence and responsibility. This is what I ask of you at this meeting. We need to coordinate consultation mechanisms and synergies, as well as to share experiences, successes and failures, so that we can definitively move away from situations of conflict and adversity that are inherent to our societies, particularly poverty.

Yesterday, at the Timor-Leste and Development Partners Meeting in which some of you were present, I had the opportunity to speak about the Timorese context and our obstacles and challenges. I described our past, our present and what we want for our future. Today, I would like to state that Timor-Leste is, in a way, fortunate to be part of the region of the world that is presently the driving force of global economy. Taking into consideration the context of the current international financial crisis, this is something that is very encouraging for us to boost our own economic growth.

Some countries from the vast African continent have also recently experienced high levels of growth. Considering that most countries assembled here come from Africa, we have one more reason to learn from each other, seeking better practices and setting better policies to achieve economic growth and sustainable development in our countries.

I would suggest that we explore the lessons each one of us has acquired, and the best ways for us to:

- manage our international relations and our relations with our development partners;
- raise the awareness of the developed countries, the G8, regarding our concerns and needs, to ensure our own development and the achievement of our dreams, the dreams of our Peoples;
- convey that we have our own objectives, benchmarks and milestones, so that we can achieve progress aligned to our societies according to our own intrinsic realities;
- make the most of our natural wealth and reduce exploitation by third parties;
- show that our sovereignty is a cause for national pride and identity.

Furthermore, through this Forum we may convey a message to the international community saying that, although we are fragile States, we are not alone and vulnerable. Instead, we are strengthened by common ideals and goals.

Timor-Leste is still a rather young State, one of the youngest in the entire world. Nevertheless, with only eight years of State building and consolidating, we want to strengthen our political and institutional maturity. This maturity includes acknowledging that the responsibility for our national development is, in the first place, ours! The message we want to convey to the world, which I believe many of you share, is that we are able to guide our own destinies, to set our own paths. We are not merely relying on international generosity and dependent on our Development Partners to ensure our future and the future of our children.

# Address to the Pacific Islands Forum, 2011

Auckland, New Zealand
7 September 2011

Your Excellencies
Ladies and Gentlemen,

It is a great pleasure to be here with you, celebrating the 40th Anniversary of the Pacific Islands Forum. While Timor-Leste always ensures we have high-level representation at the Pacific Islands Forum, this is my first opportunity to address this Forum and it is a great honour. I would like to thank the host nation, New Zealand, and its Prime Minister, John Key. When Prime Minister Key invited me to attend this Forum, I was very pleased to accept as this is also an opportunity to watch the Rugby World Cup!

I would also like to take this opportunity to express our solidarity with the people of New Zealand, and, in particular. Christchurch, after the terrible earthquakes they suffered a year ago and more recently. Our hearts and our thoughts have been with the people who have endured such great pain and grief. While the tragic events remind us all of our common humanity, we also know well the strength and the fortitude of New Zealanders, and trust that this will ensure a future of promise and returned confidence.

As you are all aware, Timor-Leste has observer status at the Pacific Islands Forum. Our country wishes to step up our engagement with the Pacific Islands Forum and strengthen our relationships with its member nations. Some of them contributed to put an end to the violence and destruction that followed the Referendum in 1999.

Our country, shares much in common with our Pacific Island friends. 2012 will be a special year for us. In March, we will have Presidential elections followed by Parliamentary elections in June.

We will celebrate our 10th anniversary on 20 May; on 30 August, we will celebrate the 100th anniversary of the last great rebellion against Portuguese colonial rule and on 28 November, we will mark 500 years since the arrival of the first Portuguese sailors and traders. We would be honoured if leaders of the Pacific Island nations would join us in Díli for these celebrations.

As you can see, we are a new nation. As a new nation, there is much we can learn from the experiences of Pacific Island countries. We share not only common values but also common challenges and opportunities. We can learn from your experiences in tackling some of our shared issues, from your approaches to development and from your success stories. In what is proving to be a rapidly changing world, Timor-Leste wants to work together in partnership so that we can all achieve better results for our people.

Ladies and Gentlemen,

We are witnessing an historic shift in the structure of the global economy. While this is creating volatility and uncertainty, it also promises great hope. We may be small island States, but we are not immune from these major political and economic structural changes. These global changes mean we are now in the 'Asia-Pacific century'. We are seeing global economic and strategic weight shift to our region. And the Asia-Pacific has been, and will continue to be, the powerhouse of global economic growth.

According to experts, we will see the financial centres of the world slowly move from New York to Shanghai, from London to Mumbai. The world's largest economies will be in our region, including China, Japan, India and Indonesia, and they will continue to grow and provide our nations with great promise.

Together we can make sure we seize these opportunities. We can learn from each other on how to benefit from the huge numbers of new Asian tourists. We can learn from each other on how to build our industries, our fisheries, our agriculture and our markets to feed the demand from the great emerging economies. We cannot stand apart from these global changes, even if we wanted to.

Therefore, I agree with you: we must convert our potential into prosperity! Thus, as a small half-island nation, Timor-Leste would rather not navigate this new world alone. Instead, we want to set off to engage with this new world not with a single boat, but as part of a fleet of nations. This will allow us all to realise the promise of the Asia-Pacific century with greater strength and with confidence.

The rapid changes we are witnessing around the world will also bring with them great challenges. These challenges could range from rising food prices to transnational crime and illegal fishing, from climate change to international conflict at sea. The truth is that we do not know all the challenges ahead, but we do know that we cannot tackle them alone.

Today, we are already witnessing bad governments fall in the Middle East and Northern Africa. We have also seen spontaneous riots in the centre of London; and mass protests in the south of Europe, as once great nations struggle to pay their debts. This reminds us all of our own fragility. And in Timor-Leste we know well what it means to be fragile, to experience conflict. Timor-Leste is engaging in a process of State building and peace building and we know how important peace and security is to economic and social development. And we are not the only country to experience fragility.

To share our experiences and learn from other countries, 17 nations from around the globe that represent 350 million people have joined together to form the g7+ group of fragile and conflict-affected nations. The g7+ group allows us to speak with one voice and explore new possibilities for solidarity and action in fragile States. This new international grouping affirms the view that a leader who only knows one country knows no country. And it presents an opportunity for our nations to re-acquire ownership of the development program and to ensure that it does not weaken our self-determination.

I am pleased to say we are joined in the g7+ group by our good friends, the Solomon Islands. Together we are working to influence the global dialogue on aid, development and State building. I urge you all to follow the progress of the g7+ as we tackle issues that will be shared by many of you here today, as we are all preparing to participate in the Fourth High Level Forum on Aid Effectiveness in Busan, in December.

Ladies and Gentlemen,

Timor-Leste has performed well in recent years. We have enjoyed an extended period of peace and stability with the help of the United Nations and the International Stabilisation Force (ISF) from New Zealand and Australia, which will leave Timor-Leste, following our parliamentary elections next year. We are grateful to them and to all our development partners. And Timor-Leste is experiencing some of the highest levels of economic growth in the world. Despite this, many of our people continue to live in extreme poverty and struggle every day, and we continue to try our best to achieve the Millennium Development Goals.

There is much we have to do to build our nation, eradicate extreme poverty and provide a good quality of education, health and life for all our people. Timor-Leste has a long-term plan to achieve these goals: our Strategic Development Plan 2011-2030. In strengthening our relationships with the South Pacific Island nations, we can learn new ways to implement our plans. We know we have much in common.

After this Forum I will travel to Vanuatu to visit a country that has been a long time friend of our people. Vanuatu has supported us during difficult times and we feel great solidarity and friendship for this fellow island nation. Timor-Leste looks forward to also strengthening our relationship with all the islands of the Pacific.

The Pacific Island Forum provides a great opportunity for us to work together and shape our promising future based on our shared values and common interests. Timor-Leste looks forward to contributing to our regional prosperity and working in partnership with you all in the years ahead. It has been great pleasure to address the Pacific Islands Forum.

# Reception Hosted Jointly by the Embassies of Timor-Leste and Indonesia

Indonesian Embassy, Washington, DC
23 February 2011

> Excellencies
> Distinguished Guests
> Ladies and Gentlemen,

It is a great pleasure to be here at this reception, which is jointly hosted by the Embassies of Timor-Leste and Indonesia. I would like to start by thanking the Indonesian Embassy for hosting this reception with us. Indonesia offered this impressive Embassy to us as a venue because our Embassy would not have been able to accommodate you all. But, offering to co-host this event at the Indonesian Embassy means a lot more to us than a friendly gesture from a close neighbour.

For us, having Indonesia host this event is a symbol of the profound affinity and solidarity between our nations. It is a display not only of how far our People have come, and the priority Timor-Leste has given to our relationship with Indonesia, but the genuine sense of affection and friendship that we share. We are here in a friend's house.

I would also like to say a few words about my friend, Ambassador Dino Patijalal. Ambassador Dino Patijalal is a man of compassion and of character. He was, of course, a senior adviser to the Indonesian President, Susilo Bambang Yudhoyono, and I can understand well why the President would want such an accomplished person to represent his country in the United States.

I would also like to convey my respect and admiration for President Susilo Bambang Yudhoyono. Under his leadership, the largest Muslim country in the world is taking steady steps towards consolidating democracy and to becoming one of the great emerging economies of the world.

Tonight, we are among good friends. As I look around the room I am reminded of the international community that has shown us such good will.

I am pleased that the Ambassadors of ASEAN are here this evening. Next month we will be making our formal application to join ASEAN. We will be making our application in a year in which Indonesia is the chair of this important regional body. We consider that taking this step at this time, during Indonesia's mandate, has profound meaning not only for our two nations, but for the countries of our region.

I am pleased to see people here from the American administration and I would like to take this opportunity to thank the United States for its welcome and hospitality during this visit. Friends from the CPLP group of nations are also here. Our Portuguese-speaking colleagues share bonds of culture, history and kinship that cross continents. It is a pleasure to come together here in Washington, D.C. It is also good to have so many representatives of the European Union, a grouping of nations that is so supportive of our development. I am also pleased to welcome our neighbours from the Asia Pacific community. The Asia Pacific is one of the most dynamic regions of the world and Timor-Leste is pleased to have countries, including China, Japan, South Korea, Australia and New Zealand, as our good friends. We all share concern, sympathy and solidarity with the people of New Zealand after the tragic earthquake that has brought such devastation and loss in Christchurch.

After this important visit to the United States, I will also be travelling to Cuba, where over 700 Timorese are studying medicine, as well as to Brazil, a country that has also supported us in so many ways.

And this evening I am also pleased to welcome many of the friends of Timor-Leste that have supported our People through difficult times and continue to support us in solidarity.

Ladies and Gentlemen,

I will briefly speak about why we have come to the United States. Yesterday, I addressed the United Nations Security Council and discussed the progress that we are making us a nation. I was pleased that our fellow CPLP nation, Brazil, is now chair of the Security Council.

I am very pleased to say that Timor-Leste has now experienced several years of peace and calm. There is a new great sense of confidence and promise on our streets and in our villages. People are reveling in this atmosphere of goodwill and safety, and Díli must now be one of the safest capital cities in the world. This stability and peace has also laid the foundation for a strong national economy. Timor-Leste is now one of the fastest growing economies in the world.

In July of this year, I will be launching Timor-Leste's Strategic Development Plan, which will signal the commencement of our multi-billion-dollar infrastructure program. On conclusion of this program, we believe Timor-Leste will have created the foundations of a diversified economy. The Strategic Development Plan will be built on three pillars: oil and gas; agriculture and fisheries; and tourism, in particular, eco-tourism. An oil industry will be established in the South Coast with a supply base, a refinery and an LNG plant. And we will also focus our investments in agriculture and fisheries and put a special focus on tourism, particularly eco-tourism, because of our Country's raw beauty.

With the achievement of peace and stability, we are now looking at how we can contribute to the international community.

Last year we were honoured to host the 'International Dialogue on Peace building and State building' in April. This event was possible thanks to the participation of the g7+, which is now chaired by Timor-Leste. The g7+ allows fragile and conflict-affected nations to come together in solidarity to speak with a common voice, learn from and share experiences and create new possibilities for peace and development. It now has seventeen member nations, covering 350 million people, and Timor-Leste is fully committed to this group in a spirit of commitment to the global community of nations.

Thank you for coming this evening and welcome. I hope you have a good night and I look forward to chatting to you throughout the evening. It is special for me, and for the delegation, to see representatives from nations from across the globe attend this reception. I would, of course, be pleased to have the opportunity to also welcome you one day to our beautiful nation of Timor -Leste.

# Timor-Leste's Transition from Conflict to Stability

Department of Development, Palace Street, London
7 March 2011

> Mr Mark Lowcock, Director, General Programmes
> Ms Bella Bird, Head of Governance and Social Development Department
> Ms Sue Lane, Head of Fragile States Team
> Ladies and Gentlemen,

It is a pleasure to be here and to speak to this Seminar on 'Timor-Leste's Transition from Conflict to Development' and to share with you some reflections on international situations. I would also like to thank the Department for International Development for hosting this event, and the United Kingdom Government and the Foreign and Commonwealth Office, for their support during my short visit to London.

While I am here to talk about Timor-Leste's transition, we are, of course, currently witness to rapid change in parts of the Arab world. While we watch with interest and concern as events unfold, we must be clear in condemning all violence against citizens. And we must all hope that the transition of these countries leads to a better life. For this to happen, if Timor-Leste's experience is any guide, people must move forward with empathy, good will and a commitment to peace, reconciliation and dialogue.

Timor-Leste's transition from conflict to development has been difficult. As with some other countries in South East Asia, our experience has involved terrible violence, loss and struggle. We do not forget the pain we have experienced, and, it has become part of who we are. But we also remember the great acts of courage and sacrifice and the extraordinary determination of our people to prevail. Our achievement of Independence was, however, just the start of our struggle. Now we face the ongoing challenge of peace building and state building.

While we have great hope and have made progress, we have also suffered setbacks and made mistakes. We have learned many lessons, lessons we are eager to share. We share our experiences, however, knowing that we are not the only country emerging from conflict, and that there is no one template or one model to achieve development. Each country has its own history, its own lived experience and its own culture and context. Any development program that does not try to recognise the individual complexity of local circumstances is sure to fail. And so, to be successful, development approaches must respond to the demands, needs and aspirations of people.

Please let me put the lessons we have learned in this context and talk about our experience.

Timor-Leste is half of a small island with just over one million people. With the other half being part of Indonesia, we are located between the two regional giants, Indonesia and Australia. Following the withdrawal of Portugal after over four centuries of colonial domination, we were invaded by Indonesia in 1975. This led to our 24-year war for independence, in which around 200,000 thousand Timorese died. On 30 August 1999, our people voted overwhelmingly for independence, but the violence and destruction that accompanied the vote was also incredibly traumatic. After over two long decades of brutality and fighting, the Timorese people were scarred. It was in this context that we embarked upon the arduous task of State building.

On 20 May 2002, following a period of United Nations administration, Timor-Leste became a sovereign and independent State. This was a time of great hope in which Timorese dreamed of a future full of promise. However, many challenges threatened to destroy this dream. We lacked infrastructure, human and financial resources and political experience in democratic governance. Coupled with the impact of trauma, poverty and historical division, the fragile nation of Timor-Leste began its history with a cycle of unrest and violence. This cycle included a crisis in 2006, which resulted in deaths and around 150,000 internally displaced people. The failure to address the causes of this crisis led, on 11 February 2008, to simultaneous attacks on both the President and myself.

From these crises we learnt that the path to development is difficult. We learnt that development is not a matter of taking some easy and universally applicable, steps, like following a recipe in a cookbook. And, most importantly, we learnt that we needed to directly address the root causes of our fragility.

To respond to our particular circumstances, we took steps that we considered necessary, while adhering to a simple yet essential principle: to govern in dialogue. We began by focusing our effort on securing peace and stability, for there can be no development without security. We worked to heal wounds, to change mentalities and to address deep social problems. These steps included:

1. solving the problem of our 150,000 internally displaced people through returning IDPs to their homes and closing the camps — we had to buy peace;
2. reforming the police and military forces, and building trust and cooperation between them;
3. introducing a new framework of public sector governance and public financial management, including the establishment of a Civil Service Commission and an Anti-Corruption Commission;
4. introducing social justice policies to provide pensions to the vulnerable, the disabled and the elderly;
5. acknowledging and supporting our national heroes, the National Liberation Combatants, many of whom were living in extreme poverty; and
6. supporting the emergence of a local private sector.

These steps increased the trust and confidence in the institutions of the State and created a foundation of security and stability, on which we could develop our nation.

During this time, as we were dealing with pressing demands, putting out fires and engaging in dialogue with our people, we experienced some tension with our international development partners. Our partners were asking us for medium- and long-term plans, so they could prepare their multi-year aid strategies. But during this time, we did not have the space or the luxury of developing a long-term plan. Events were also changing so rapidly, that we needed to be able to change course, when necessary, to ensure the survival of the State.

During these periods, to be effective, donor nations need to be flexible and to have the capacity to adjust to new and emerging priorities. This means, in circumstances of fragility, development programs need to be able to respond rapidly to urgent needs, and must avoid locking in financial resources to narrow modes of support or discreet policy areas.

Ladies and Gentlemen,

We have now enjoyed three years of peace and stability. There is a great sense of confidence and goodwill on our streets and in our villages, and Díli must now be one of the safest capital cities in the world. Our stability has also fuelled the emergence of a strong national economy. Timor-Leste now has one of the fastest growing economies in the world. Even with the global financial crisis, Timor-Leste has enjoyed a two-digit economic growth rate for the past three years. In 2009, our growth was 13 per cent, one of the ten highest in the entire world. Timor-Leste is now debt free, with US$7.4 billion dollars invested through our Petroleum Fund.

While our economic growth is a means by which we are reducing poverty, we know it is not the only answer. That is why we are focused on achieving the Millennium Development Goals and have developed programs to reach our people across our country, in our villages and in our towns. While we are still a poor country, with enormous challenges, we have made the transition from conflict and are embracing the path to the development.

The international community has been with us since the beginning, and Timor-Leste has been fortunate to have the support of generous development partners. We now want to do what we can to make a contribution to other nations of the world in this same spirit of solidarity and friendship. Timor-Leste has the honour of being invited to preside over the g7+ group, which enables countries that are fragile or affected by conflict to join together and speak with one voice. It allows us all to learn from the wisdom and shared experience of 17 nations from around the globe, that represents 350 million people.

The g7+ gives us a mechanism to use the space provided by the global development dialogue to explore new possibilities for solidarity and action in fragile States. It presents an opportunity for our countries to re-acquire ownership of the development program and to ensure that it does not weaken our self-determination. The g7+ will allow weaker countries, as well as the strong ones, to contribute to the creation of knowledge about development, and will enable us to hold the machinery of the development process to account for its failures while at the same time celebrating its successes. It will also provide a forum to seek to grasp the consequences and the lessons of China's rise, and of living in a world where the most significant poverty reduction project in human history has been largely independent of foreign aid and financial market globalisation.

The invitation to chair the g7+ resulted from Timor-Leste hosting, in April 2010, the 'International Dialogue on PeaceBuilding and StateBuilding'. This dialogue, which is co-chaired by Timor-Leste with our Minister of Finance, Emilia Pires, and the United Kingdom with Ms Bella Bird, has enormous potential to transform international development assistance relationships and improve outcomes for the world's most vulnerable people.

I would like to say one final point on development. I am aware that many are cynical about the possibility of countries of the third world achieving development. They dwell on the failures of international aid rather than its successes. In Timor-Leste, we are well placed to comment on the failure of development programs — we have lived through the experience and, in a profound way, felt the disappointment. But voicing these concerns is the easy way out. The more courageous path is to work hard, with optimism and hope, towards a better future. Giving up on alleviating extreme poverty and improving the health and education of our people, is not an option. Timor-Leste is fortunate to live in a region that is home to most of the world's development success stories, including China, India, Malaysia, Indonesia, Singapore, South Korea and Thailand. We can see clearly the promise of development.

I would like to thank the United Kingdom for its important role in supporting both the International Dialogue and the g7+, and for its commitment to fragile States. I look forward to continuing our work together, not only to make Timor-Leste one more development success story, but to improve the lives of the people of the world's least developed countries.

# Presentation of Timor-Leste's Draft Penal Code

Hotel Timor, Díli
16 October 2008

> Your Excellency the Representative of the Speaker of Parliament
> Your Excellency the Acting President of the Court of Appeal
> Distinguished Members of Parliament
> Distinguished Members of Government
> Representatives from Civil Society
> Members of the Press
> Ladies and Gentlemen,

I am very pleased to welcome all participants in this Public Presentation of the Draft Penal Code of Timor-Leste. I would like to say a few words on this initiative, which represents two fundamental aspects of the process for building our Democratic State under the Rule of Law.

Firstly, the Public Consultation fulfils one of the goals of this Government, by promoting popular participation in major decision-making processes, particularly in very important matters, as is the case of the Penal Code. We all know that Timor-Leste is a Country that is growing in every aspect, including the democratisation of ideas, the social assimilation of legally tolerated behaviours and attitudes and the exercise of Democracy as a process that is participated by all citizens, including the selection of the Justice model that the Timorese want to see employed by the Courts. Therefore, the drafting of a final Penal Code project gathering the support and input by all sectors of society is a step forward towards the promotion of a culturally more democratic and fair society, promoting the public debate of ideas, facilitating dialogue and the solutions of the more socially pressing problems and nurturing the sense of union in favour of the whole.

Secondly, the approval by Parliament of the Legislative Authorisation Law in terms of Penal Matter grants the Government the possibility, in relation to crimes, penalties and security measures, to create and strengthen the penal types, ensuring more and better safety to the community, the citizens and the State — this is indispensible for Courts to be able to carry out their action more efficiently, thereby consolidating National Independence and Sovereignty itself. Drafting a Penal Code is a demanding task that entails great responsibility. More than a challenge, the approval of a legal diploma:

- respecting the fundamental rights, liberties and guarantees of citizens;
- taking into account the social and cultural specificities of the Country; and
- making progress to replace the Indonesian normative legacy.
- is the achievement of a democratic exercise joining individual liberties and rights with living in community.

As such, the Penal Code reflects matters that represent an extremely important dimension in the lives of every Timorese, which is why it must be drafted very carefully. As I have said before, to ensure an efficient and successful implementation, we must take into consideration the suggestions made by national (and international) organisations. At the end of this process, all judiciary and social actors must feel that another vital step has been taken towards the development of the Country. Consequently this is a document that gathers several opinions and sensitivities, but also a document that obeys unconditionally the constitutional requirements, particularly in what concerns the respect for the dignity of the human person and the consolidation of the fundamental values accepted by the community, namely, absolute respect for the inviolability and dignity of human life.

Lastly, the draft presented to the public today has as main reference, the Universal Declaration of Human Rights, in full compliance with the international legal instruments to which Timor-Leste is bound.

It was with great personal satisfaction that I saw that the approved Legislative Authorisation Law clearly reflected the concerns displayed by society, such as:

- punishment of child and spousal abuse, i.e., domestic violence;
- sexual criminality;
- control over juridical assets concerning Peace and public tranquillity;
- criminalisation of behaviours that may breach religious values solidly rooted in the Timorese society;

- punishment of acts of bribery and corruption — this is imperative for this Government;
- incrimination of behaviours that are susceptible to jeopardising the Rule of Law and its Institutions;
- incrimination of fiscal fraud and smuggling; and, finally,
- sensitivity regarding the specific matter of young people, by way of penal treatment that is adequate to their reality and to their social reinsertion.

All that is left is for me to thank all those who participated in the effort to enable the achievement of yet another fundamental instrument for Justice in this Country, and to await the contributions that the Timorese society will, within the next few days, offer to the ongoing process, so that in the end everyone may think highly of the approved Penal Code.

# Launch of the Strategic Plan for the Justice Sector

Díli
16 April 2009

> Your Excellency the President of the Court of Appeal
> Your Excellency the Bishop of Baucau
> Your Excellency the Special Representative from the United Nations
> Your Excellencies the Ambassadors from Portugal, Australia, United States of America and Brazil
> Your Excellencies the Representatives from International Organisations
> Your Excellency the Prosecutor-General of the Republic
> Your Excellency the Provedor of Human Rights and Justice
> Your Excellencies the Minister of Justice and the Secretaries of State for Security and for the Promotion of Equality
> Ladies and Gentlemen,

It is with great pleasure that I take part in this session on 'Working together to strengthen Justice for the Timorese', and I would like to seize this opportunity to thank all those who will be debating the vital subject of Justice in Timor-Leste within the next two days.

Developing the sector of Justice is vital for consolidating a democratic governance structure in Timor-Leste. Two of the first obligations of the State are to promote the better operation of Justice Institutions and to provide better services to the populations in the area of Justice. Therefore, I congratulate this workshop for being one more step towards the strategic definition of a common vision for Justice in Timor-Leste. This, along with the proper operation by the institutions and with the assurance of national security and stability, will enable the sustainable development of the Country.

This Government believes that improving the Justice system in Timor-Leste is part of a broader process of State-reforming and economic and social development. If Justice is not prompt, efficient and universal, it contributes to breeding an atmosphere of impunity that weakens the democratic authority of the State. As such, I must highlight strategic planning capacity as an essential factor for developing any State sector, which in this specific case is the sector of Justice. Planning becomes even more essential when one seeks to expand Justice mechanisms and instruments to every citizen, particularly those who have greater difficulty in accessing the Justice system. Access to Justice is still not a reality for all Timorese, particularly in the more remote parts of the Country. Furthermore, our traditional justice sometimes operates in a discriminatory manner, for instance against women, which is why it is imperative to change this situation. A Country where Justice is not for everyone cannot be considered a fair Country.

In the sector of Justice, there is already a high level of integration and coordination in terms of multilateral and bilateral international assistance. The launching of the Strategic Plan for the Sector of Justice will enable the further consolidation of this harmony and cooperation among international partners towards the strategic goals set by the Timorese legal agents for the sector of Justice. The integrated Strategic Plan for the Sector of Justice seeks, in the medium term, to strengthen some of the achievements already made by our young Nation and to achieve new strategic goals, such as:

- Ensuring the independence and quality of the sovereign bodies and the respect for the fundamental principle of checks and balances;
- Training Timorese staff — this is a vital task that needs to be done in a sound and sustainable manner and will require international technical assistance, ensuring the more complex and skilled work during the training years;
- Developing Justice infrastructures and equipments throughout the territory;
- Decentralising Justice Services and the Justice System so as to ensure the fundamental rights of citizens and to enable human, social and economic development throughout the territory;
- Enhancing coordination between PNTL, the Ministry of Justice and the Office of the Prosecutor-General of the Republic in relation to supporting the development of Criminal Investigation. This is

essential for improving the operation of the Legal System and for ensuring the Fundamental Rights of citizens;
- Modernising and computerising Justice Services, particularly in the area of Registry and Notary services, where it is urgent to ensure more qualified technical support and better equipments, namely in the areas of Commercial Registry, Building Registry and Notary Services;
- Implementing an entire legislative package that will enable the attribution of the first property titles in Timor-Leste. This is a vital measure. The Ministry of Justice has been working hard to submit the draft Land Law to Parliament, while developing a vast package of legislation, regulation and administrative and financial measures that enable the full and efficient implementation of the Land Law.

These are challenges that require the commitment and involvement of all Timorese Institutions, not just when drafting the plan, but particularly when implementing it.

Before I conclude, I wish to thank the AusAID bilateral project, UNDP and the international advisors for their support to the drafting of a Strategic and Integrated Plan for the Sector of Justice. I am confident that the work done so far through the Ministry of Justice, the participation and commitment of all Justice Institutions and the ongoing support by our partners, through bilateral and multilateral cooperations, will enable us to achieve the more just cause that a Nation can aspire to: a Sector of Justice that is strong and efficient and that responds to the need of every Timorese citizen!

# Swearing-in of Ms Maria Natércia Gusmão as Judge of the Court of Appeal

Congress Centre, Díli
11 April 2011

> Your Excellency the President of the Republic,
> Your Excellency the Speaker of Parliament,
> Your Excellency the President of the Court of Appeal,
> Your Excellency the Prosecutor-General of the Republic,
> Your Excellency the Defender General,
> Your Excellency the Minister of Justice,
> Your Excellencies the Members of Parliament,
> Your Excellencies the Members of Government,
> Your Excellency the Bishop of Baucau,
> Your Excellency the Bishop of Díli,
> Your Excellency the Chief of Defence,
> Your Excellency the Commander-General of the PNTL,
> Your Excellency the Representative of the UN Secretary-General,
> Your Excellency the Judge Maria Natércia Gusmão,
> Your Excellencies Judges, Prosecutors and Defenders,
> Your Excellencies the Ambassadors and Representatives of the Diplomatic Corps,
> Illustrious Guests,

It was with great satisfaction and joy that I accepted to take part in this ceremony, which I believe to be historical for the Timorese magistracy.

Ms Maria Natércia Gusmão's swearing-in as Judge of the Court of Appeal represents a decisive step towards the affirmation of our magistrates, who at last see the fruition of the efforts they have made throughout the past few years in order to properly prepare for the tasks inherent to the career they have chosen.

Ms Maria Natércia Gusmão's election by Parliament, in conformity with the Constitution, has a very special meaning since it is the first time a Timorese citizen is part of the Country's most important Court. As you know, in addition to its duties as a last instance court, the Court of Appeal is presently also assuming the competences normally given to a Constitutional Court and to an Administrative Court. Furthermore, the first magistrate to rise up to the Court of Appeal is a woman, which once again proves the vital role that women have always played in our society. I would like to highlight in particular the dedication they have shown to State building, both during the struggle for the liberation of our Motherland and during this stage, where we grow as a sovereign Nation. Timorese women are examples of strength, persistence and devotion to the causes to which they are committed. It is in great part because of them that we can today live in freedom and be the masters of our fate. But we still have a difficult way to go before we can say that we are a fully sovereign state. For our dream to really come true, we need the holders of the sovereign bodies, the Presidency, the National Parliament, the Government and the Courts, to be exclusively made up by citizens of Timor-Leste.

As for the first three of these bodies, we have no doubt whatsoever that, nine years after gaining our independence, we Timorese are the only ones responsible for them. We are the ones who draft all policies related with the governance of the Nation. Only last 27 March, the responsibility for the Country's internal security changed from the United Nations Police to the National Police of Timor-Leste.

The next in line is the judicial power. Our judges, prosecutors and defenders, who have already been trained but still lack the numbers to fully staff Justice Administration, continue to require external support. This is achieved through the coming of colleagues from friendly CPLP countries. We acknowledge the importance of this support. Without it, our Courts would surely not be able to properly safeguard the rights of our People. We thank all international magistrates who have enabled the construction and consolidation of our judicial system. We have no doubt that they have done their best and that they have intensely shared their expertise with their Timorese colleagues, but the time has now come for us, gradually and rationally, to give our judges, prosecutors and defenders the opportunity to prove what they are worth.

Naturally we will continue to require the precious assistance of the international magistrates, but, in the near future, this assistance should be focused on direct advisory to the work to be developed by the Timorese magistrates, rather than doing the work for them. This is not a matter of sovereignty, although that is evidently a chief concern, but rather the fact that at some point one must practise what one has learned. While our magistrates continue having someone who does their work for them, while they are not the only ones responsible for Justice Administration, it will be very difficult for them to acquire all the knowledge they need for their profession. Mistakes are acceptable, since everyone makes them, not only during learning but also throughout one's career, no matter how well prepared one is. But when this happens, we must have the humility to accept the advice of those who are more experienced and who have come here with the only purpose of imparting what they know.

We are also aware that Timor-Leste, in order to be able to declare itself a Nation that is truly free and in which the People is never deprived of its Constitutional rights, requires exempt, independent, apolitical and non-partisan Justice. Judges and prosecutors do not serve one political party or the other. They cannot and should not behave according to interferences from outside the Courts, where the purpose is not to punish an offender but rather to seek political or any other type of profit through personal persecutions that breach the most elemental rights of the persons being targeted.

Political assessments are made by the People alone, when called upon to select its rulers through free and fair elections. Courts cannot aspire to replace the People regarding a power that belongs exclusively to it, such as controlling the exercise of political power. A judge is not a politician. A prosecutor is not a politician. A defender is not a politician. They can have their political ideologies, and it is only natural that they do, however they cannot disclose them to the public, much less let themselves be influenced by them when deciding on a certain case or during a trial.

It is not enough to be exempt and impartial. They must also appear exempt and impartial, so that they can merit the trust of all those who have to resort to Justice or who are compelled to do so. And in order to appear exempt and impartial, it is essential that they be completely cut off from any political activity, so that they are not subjected to any suspicion of favouritism or ungrounded persecution.

The only task of Courts is to administer Justice, treating everyone equally, regardless of political convictions, religious beliefs or social origin. This is what the People expect and require from its magistrates. Furthermore, only by meeting these conditions will we be truly able to say that we live in a State under the rule of law.

Judge Maria Natércia Gusmão,

On this day that is so symbolic for the Timorese magistracy, I wish to convey to you my utmost confidence, respect and admiration. I am certain, because I know you well, that you will always guide yourself by a sense of Justice, serving only the Country and the People. I have no doubt whatsoever that you will hold your office as Judge in the Court of Appeal with competence, dedication, exemption and the devotion befitting someone who has dedicated her life to the public cause and to the common good.

Your past speaks for you. Prior to becoming a magistrate you fought against the occupation, being part of the National Resistance of Timorese Students. As such, you have played an active role in our People's struggle for freedom and independence. I trust that you will meet with great success in the performance of the tasks you have now been given. I hope that you will become an example and a role model for all Timorese working in the area of Justice.

# Swearing-in of the Trainee Judges and the Trainee Public Defenders; III Training Course

Court of Appeal, Díli
10 May 2010

> Your Excellency the President of the Republic
> Your Excellency the Speaker of Parliament
> Your Excellency the President of the Court of Appeal
> Your Excellency the Public Defender
> Your Excellency the Assistant Special Representative of the United Nations Secretary General, Mr Finn Reske-Nielsen
> Illustrious Members of Parliament
> Illustrious Members of Government
> Illustrious Representatives of the Diplomatic Corps
> Illustrious Representatives of the International Agencies
> Illustrious Members of Non-Governmental Organisations
> Your Excellencies the trainee Judges and Public Defenders sworn in today
> Ladies and Gentlemen,

The act that brings us together here represents another landmark for Timor-Leste in a sector so elementary and important for national development as Justice.

First and foremost, I would like to congratulate the trainee Judges and Public Defenders who have attended this third training course and who have just been sworn in in their new tasks. Today, you are entering a new stage of your professional lives that, despite being demanding and requiring great responsibility, will certainly be a great cause for individual and collective pride. As Timorese citizens, and for the common good of the Timorese citizens, you are among the main actors in the building of one of the Country's most important Sovereignty Bodies — the Courts.

We all recognise that this is no simple task. Better yet, it is not a mission to take on lightly, considering the enormous challenges and even obstacles that you will face in the exercise of your duties. But this is also why your swearing-in represents progress in the training of Magistrates and other justice officers, something that is considered to be invaluable for the Country. The development of the sector of Justice is essential to consolidate a culture of fair and inclusive governance in Timor-Leste, with respect for the rules of democracy and human rights. As such, promoting the better operation of Justice Agencies and providing better services to the populations in the area of Justice are two of the first obligations of the State.

Ladies and Gentlemen,

The economic development process we want for the country is not limited to economic growth, although that is crucial. We also want access to other fundamental areas such as health, education and justice. And when we talk about justice, we talk about providing every Timorese citizen, regardless of social, professional or economic standing, gender or religion, the same rights and the same duties before the Law. This is the only way we can conciliate the ideals of development, freedom and security. To administer justice on behalf of the People means enabling our People to live with the dignity that they deserve. Magistrates and Public Defenders serve the interests of the Nation and the interests of the People, in the firm defence of the Democratic State under the Rule of Law set in the Constitution. As such, they will be acknowledged by the community as stalwarts of the fundamental rights of the People.

Dear Judges and Public Defenders,

By entering the Courts and the judicial institutions, you are making a commitment to the entire community, saying that you will promote Justice and defend the rights and the legitimate interests of the citizens. This starts with a responsible conduct and with working every day to make justice prompt and efficient. The Government is strongly committed to providing institutional support to this mission of yours. It is imperative to rekindle hope in a future for Timor-Leste ruled by peace and justice.

In our current context, it is urgent to motivate citizens to a culture of civic awareness and to the importance of Law and the respect for the Law. This is particularly true of our young, who will be the future of our Nation. Therefore, in addition to the recognition and stimulus you deserve for performing your mission, it is important to underline that you will be role models for our young. It is essential that young people understand how democracy, development and wellbeing are dependant on an effective justice, thereby instilling a culture of honesty and accountability not only in power bodies and officers of justice, but also in every citizen.

Dear Judges and Public Defenders sworn in today,

I wish you all good work and urge you to act every day with daring, courage and determination, so that we may develop a stronger and more efficient sector of Justice. The Timorese society is relying on your dedication and commitment. Our Nation, currently undergoing dynamic changes towards national development, requires great dedication from all of you.

# Message to the Nation

Following the events that took place today in Timor-Leste and that resulted in serious attacks against the lives of the President of the Republic and the Prime Minister, the Government of Timor-Leste urges all Timorese citizens to remain calm. In a time like this, it is absolutely necessary that every citizen cooperate to ensure public order and tranquillity.

Although a strongly armed group, led by Alfredo Reinado, has threatened the Country's security and stability, the group's goals have not been achieved. The President of the Republic, Dr. José Ramos-Horta, is free from danger after surgery in the Australian Armed Forces Hospital. His health is now stable. A vehicle belonging to the Prime Minister was hit, but no one was injured.

Nevertheless, taking into account that there was an attempt to overthrow the Democratic Rule of Law and that two holders of Sovereignty Bodies have been tragically threatened, it is now imperative to ensure that the State carries out its obligation of ensuring public order, safety and tranquillity, protecting persons and assets, preventing crime and contributing to assure the normal operation of the democratic institutions, the exercise of the fundamental rights and liberties of the citizens and the respect for democratic legality. Consequently, as the Head of Government and Minister of Defence and Security, and after hearing the representatives from the Parliamentary Benches, the Government of Timor-Leste has taken the initiative of requesting the Vice-Speaker of Parliament, which under section 84 of the Constitution is the interim Head of State, to declare martial law in order to deal with this situation of instability.

Under sections 25 and 115.2 (c) of the Constitution of the Democratic Republic of Timor-Leste, the Government has proposed:

- a) To declare martial law for an initial period of 48 hours;
- b) To declare martial law throughout the entire national territory;
- c) To suspend the right of free circulation, with curfew from 8:00 PM to 6:00 AM;
- d) To forbid assemblies and demonstrations during the period of martial law.

It is now up to the acting President of the Republic to activate the necessary mechanisms set in the Constitution, to consider the adequacy of this proposal and to make the decisions he considers to be more favourable to ensure the unity of the State and the regular operation of the democratic institutions, respecting the legally applicable principles.

For the time being, the Government of Timor-Leste urges all citizens not to take part in activities that may contribute to the atmosphere of instability and to collaborate with the authorities in order to restore law and order. Let us remain together to overcome this new challenge to our stability. Today, more than ever, we need to work together and with serenity so that we may leave this moment behind us!

# Extension of Martial Law in Seven Districts and Declaration of State of Emergency

## 20 March 2008

1. Following the attacks on 11 February 2008, martial law has been decreed in the entire territory, so as to ensure constitutional order and public safety and peace, thereby preserving the Democratic Rule of Law;
2. The martial law period extended for 42 days, during which significant progress has been achieved in order to:
   - Reduce the potential for disturbances that might affect the normal life of the populations;
   - Enable State Institutions to continue operating normally;
   - Ensure that the policing of activities and movements by the populations leads to a peaceful atmosphere.
3. This period has also enabled several actions:
   - Investigation of facts to carry out arrest warrants issued by the Public Prosecution;
   - Execution by the police of its internal security tasks, fully meeting its requirements in terms of general and special prevention;
   - The approval of a Council of Ministers' Resolution tasking the Chief of the Defence Force with the creation of a joint command integrating PNTL and F-FDTL, so as to carry out the security operations resulting from the declaration of martial law.
4. The cooperation developed between F-FDTL and PNTL, which formed a Joint Command Operational Structure for establishing a Force Articulation and Mission was an operational success. This is a great part of the reason why one can consider that major steps have been taken to restore normality in the Country. The creation of the Joint Command and the manner in which the HALIBUR joint operation was designed demonstrated that F-FDTL and PNTL, in coordination, operate

efficiently and are able to meet the highly demanding challenges currently posed to the Nation.

Distinguished Members of Parliament,

5. The reason why we first requested the declaration of martial law was based on the fact that:
   - there was an armed group at an unknown location;
   - there was a group of supporters of Alfredo Reinado and Leopoldino Exposto, being impossible to predict whether they would cause public order disturbances and compromise peace and tranquillity in the Country;
   - there was a threat against the democratic constitutional order resulting from founded information indicating that new attacks might take place on other holders of sovereignty bodies or on State institutions;
   - there was a popular basis of support for dissident groups that might seize the circumstances to avenge old issues, as has been done in a recent past, and to start a wave of violence, related or not, with the current events.

6. In short: the Government, during the initial period of martial law, was unaware of the exact circumstances of the problem, was unaware of the true shape of the threat — in a way it was working in the dark — and therefore the declaration of martial law was essential to enable the investigations and operations that led us to our present situation, where we know the suspects of the attacks and are more familiarised with eventual sympathisers of the rebel group that might promote disturbances and generate public disorder.

7. The characteristics and the size of the threat are now known. The armed group (the threat) is circumscribed, the population has been collaborating with the defence and security forces in order to stabilise the Country, the Petitioners have displayed great openness in collaborating in the State and almost all of them have concentrated in Díli, and relevant elements who took part in the attacks have presented themselves to justice!

8. The Country is presently in a completely different situation than the one we had a month ago. This makes us more confident that we

will be able to solve this threat in a permanent manner. As such, the Government requested His Excellency the President of the Republic to:

- Maintain martial law in the districts of Aileu, Ermera, Bobonaro, Covalima, Ainaro, Liquiçá and Manufahi, districts where the acts of force or insurrection may jeopardise the constitutional order due to the presence of a strongly armed group. For operational purposes, the security forces should be placed under the command of the Armed Forces subject to the F-FDTL / PNTL Joint Command;
- The declaration of a state of emergency in the remaining districts, as the threat is considered to be smaller there, although there is the possibility of cases of public disturbance caused by eventual support by marginal groups to the armed group, the presence of which has already been limited to the districts above. As such, only some restrictive measures will be applied, without the need to strengthen the powers of the civilian administrative authorities. Nevertheless, the Government may order the Armed Forces to conduct specific support missions should the situation become too difficult for PNTL to control alone;
- The district of Oecussi and the sub-district of Ataúro will not be covered by any exceptional regime, taking into account their specific geographic characteristics and the fact that no public order disturbances have taken place or are expected to take place.

9. The declaration of martial law in the districts of Aileu, Ermera, Bobonaro, Covalima, Ainaro, Liquiçá and Manufahi and the declaration of the state of emergency for the others, for a period of 30 days, starting at 10:00 PM of 23 March and ending at 10:00 PM of 22 April, should suspend the following fundamental rights, liberties and guarantees of citizens:

   a) Restriction of the right of free circulation, with curfew from 10:00 PM to 6:00 AM in the districts where martial law is declared; and restriction of the right of free circulation, with curfew from 11:00 PM to 5:00 AM in the districts where a state of emergency is declared;
   
   b) The rights of demonstration and of assembly;

c) The right to inviolability of residence, allowing house searches during the night, subject to the relevant warrant.
10. During exceptional states, security operations shall comply with the provisions of Decree-Law no. 4/2006 of 1 March — *Special Arrangements within the Criminal Procedure Framework for Cases of Terrorism, Violent or Organised Crime*, as well as of Decree-Law no. 2/2007 of 8 March — *Special Crime Prevention Operations*.
11. The Government is pleased with the model adopted by F-FDTL / PNTL for this mission, as it proves once again that defence and security forces can be effective when they work together.
12. The Government is pleased with the collaboration of the people and the manner in which they have respected the declaration of exceptional states. There is no data of populations contesting the decision of the sovereignty bodies. On the contrary, populations have requested the continuation of an exceptional state, as the latter has enabled public tranquillity and confidence in the democratic institution, while enabling people to perform their normal daily activities.
13. It is in the national interest to adopt at this time exceptional measures and forms of organisation that can solve the problem permanently, in order to prevent new cases of disturbance of the democratic institutions, public life and society life in the future. Additionally, it is necessary to ensure the restoration of public order and to return the right of every citizen to security, since these are vital prerequisites for individuals and institutions to safely re-enter the path to economic and social development, without any type of threat.
14. Lastly, I urge all citizens to respect the legal normative included in the Constitution and in the legal diplomas of Timor-Leste. The State is working hard to bring stability back to the Country, and the moral and political support by citizens to the defence and security forces is very important for them to be able to perform their tasks efficiently.
15. In view of this, I ask that any weaknesses detected in the actions of the 'Forces' be reported so that they can be corrected. This should be done without destructive criticisms or attempts to increase instability. The errors/abuses by security and/or defence forces detected during martial law are being investigated and disciplinary sanctions will be applied.

16. I ask everyone not to judge the whole by the parts. Sporadic situations of breach of rights, freedoms and guarantees are being suppressed. They have not taken place in a significant number, but that does not mean that a single case is to be tolerated. The Government is confident that the awareness-raising and clarification campaign conducted within the armed forces and the security forces, making them more knowledgeable of laws and regulations, as well as of their rights, responsibilities, obligations, and power limitations, will ensure compliance with the laws and with the Constitution (namely, in what concerns the provisions of sections 25.5 and 30).

# Reception for the Indonesian Minister of Defence, Mr Purnomo Yusgiantoro

Hotel Timor, Díli
19 August 2011

> Your Excellency the Minister of Defence of the Republic of Indonesia,
>   Mr Purnomo Yusgiantoro
> Distinguished Guests
> Ladies and Gentlemen

Your visit, distinguished Minister, particularly on a date so full of symbolism in affirming Timor-Leste as a sovereign and independent State, fills us with gratitude, and represents another important step in the strengthening bonds of friendship between our two peoples.

Wounds that in the past may have pulled Timorese and Indonesians apart have long been healed. Now, Timor-Leste and Indonesia are, without question, friends with great respect for each other and that cooperate closely across a broad range of areas that are critical for our economic and social development. With our strong relationship as friendly neighbours, we have a shared commitment to resolving, as soon as possible, and to everyone's satisfaction, the small technical issues that remain in regard to our common land border.

Indonesia has been our main and most active supporter in our bid to join ASEAN. We profoundly appreciate the remarkable effort and determination by Indonesian leaders, particularly President Susilo Bambang Yudhoyono, in pushing our cause with ASEAN members so that Timor-Leste may move towards membership of this important regional body.

> Dear Minister Purnomo Yuisgiantoro,

It is with great satisfaction that we all witness increasingly close bilateral cooperation in the area of Defence between Timor-Leste and Indonesia. Our Armed Forces, the successors of FALINTIL, the 36th anniversary of which we are celebrating, have merited special attention by their Indonesian counterpart, particularly in the important aspect of training. F-FDTL officers have taken part in courses provided in prestigious military education institutions in Indonesia, including the National Defence Institute of Jakarta. Joint exercises have also taken place involving naval forces from both our countries. In September 2009, we had the great pleasure of receiving the visit of the TNI Commander, General Djoko Susanto, and, in May 2010, the Chief of the Defence Force of Timor-Leste, Major-General Taur Matan Ruak, visited Jakarta in a reciprocal sign of goodwill.

We are firmly committed to strengthening the ties of cooperation between the F-FDTL and the TNI. As such, this very afternoon we signed a Memorandum of Understanding between our two governments regarding further Defence cooperation activities. We want to institutionalise regular consultation and dialogue meetings concerning common interest strategic and security issues. We also want to exchange relevant Defence information, promote cooperation between the Armed Forces of both our countries and establish logistical support cooperation arrangements. We would also like to look at expanding this cooperation to other priority areas for National Security. I am sure, Minister, that we can rely on your goodwill and determination to support projects that are vital for the valorisation and modernisation of the Armed Forces of Timor-Leste.

Indonesia is a vital strategic partner for the political and economic interests of Timor-Leste. In addition to sharing a large sea border, we also share this island. In recognition of this we are enabling the populations on both sides of the border to live in peace and harmony, strengthened by significant family ties that have been established throughout the centuries. For us Timorese, the Indonesians are not rivals or competitors in our legitimate claims to be acknowledged by the international community as a modern and fair State. On the contrary, we see the Indonesians as brothers and sisters and we seek to maintain and to build on the bonds of friendship that bring our two peoples increasingly together.

Dear Minister, I wish you, your wife and the delegation that accompanies you a very pleasant stay in Timor-Leste. I also hope that you may return soon so that you are able to enjoy all that this Country has to offer.

# Ceremony Dedicated to the Promotion of Senior Officers of F-FDTL

Nicolau Lobato Training Centre, Metinaro
14 January 2010

> Your Excellency the Secretary of State for Defence, Dr Júlio Tomás Pinto,
> Your Excellency the Chief of the Defence Force, Major-General Taur Matan Ruak,
> Distinguished Guests,
> Officers, NCOs and Privates of F-FDTL,

This military ceremony to witness the promotion of four senior officers of our Armed Forces should be a time of joy, however, we are all still grieving because of the premature disappearance of our dear comrade, Major Ular.

Major Ular is one of the heroes of our Motherland. He fought throughout the entire Resistance period as few did, displaying exceptional skills as a fighter and as a leader of men. More recently, already under F-FDTL, he shone in the command of the operations that led to the capture of the armed rebels that sought to overthrow the democratic Rule of Law. All through his life he was an exemplary officer and he contributed very significantly to make the Military Institution so prestigious in the eyes of the Timorese society. He is a role model for all those who choose to enter the Armed Forces. May he rest in peace.

> Colonels Filomeno Paixão de Jesus, Falur Rate Laek and Mau-Nana and Naval Captain Pedro Klamar Fuik,

Your thoroughly deserved promotion represents the recognition by the State of the valorous services you have been performing in favour of the public cause, as well as a reward for your dedication to the Armed Forces. The Military Institution owes you a great deal. As such, this promotion is entirely merited and rewards a whole life in the service of the Motherland, first fighting the occupier and subsequently building Armed Forces dedicated to ensuring peace. It should be said that this is the first promotion in eight years to the highest positions in the category of senior officer. This indicates the will to start preparing F-FDTL for the future. The top of the Armed Forces hierarchy now has very prestigious officers, acknowledged by their peers as the most able to hold the highest positions of command and leadership. Upon their shoulders rests the hope that, in a not too distant future, they will lead the Institution they serve.

Soldiers are by nature disciplined and dedicated. They do not get themselves involved in any activities that do not befit the mission they are given. However, they are also demanding, indicating to the political leaders that they must provide the defence forces with the necessary conditions for them to be able to play smoothly the role they have within a modern and sovereign State. Career progression is a legitimate aspiration for any officer, NCO or private, and it is an incentive for the persons who dedicate themselves fully to the profession they have chosen, being certain that they will be progressively rewarded for that dedication. On the contrary, undeserved stagnation in a certain rank results in loss of motivation and consequent neglect of military duties, causing serious breaches in terms of internal discipline and of the esprit de corps that characterises military life.

Therefore the State has the obligation to ensure all those who serve in the Armed Forces normal access to the position immediately above, regardless of any financial difficulties. As such, this Government is firmly committed to the regular and normal processing of the F-FDTL promotion regime, rewarding those who merit such distinction. The promotion of these four senior officers opens vacancies in the positions they had been holding, thereby unblocking progression to the positions immediately below. I hope that this act is an incentive to all the other soldiers, showing that it takes hard work to rise one day to the highest positions in the categories where they are inserted.

I salute the officers now promoted and wish them the best in their new positions.

# Tenth Meeting of the CPLP Ministers of Defence: Review of International Issues and Political and Military Implications within the Regional Context for CPLP Member Countries

Hotel Timor, Díli
17 May 2008

> Your Excellencies the Ministers of Defence of CPLP
> Your Excellency the Executive Secretary of CPLP
> Your Excellencies the Members of the Delegations
> Ladies and Gentlemen,

The issue of defence has specific individual and regional features depending of the continent and regional wherein each CPLP member country is inserted. However, defence today also has a more globalised and strategically more complex dimension. What can a Community consisting of countries that are physically distant from each other and geographically scattered contribute to world peace?

The last decades of recent history have signalled an ongoing and growing involvement of peace interventions beyond borders, in order to restore normality. Timor-Leste has benefitted from these interventions and, unfortunately, continues to be viewed under this light until it can prove that the values we all share are respected by leaders, rulers and the population. Interventions, whether bilateral or multilateral, mostly show the need to suffocate the instability points of a certain region, since no country wishes to have as a neighbour a country that is unstable and undergoing conflicts.

The events that radically transformed the world at the end of the twentieth century and that led to the end of the Cold War also changed the challenges that modern society has to deal with. The classic divide between West and East, based essentially on the adoption of different political and economic models, has disappeared. In its place came a vast array of latent conflicts, the consequences of which have in a certain way tied us all, from Europe to Africa, from the Americas to Asia, and may end up being far more serious to world peace and stability. Overall, terrorism has become a plight that started off by targeting western powers and has since become a means to rekindle internal disputes resulting from ethnical or religious differences, as well as political, social, cultural and other issues.

Its geographic location makes Timor-Leste potentially vulnerable to this new threat. Being located between two regional powers, Indonesia and Australia, which are potential targets of this unpredictable foe that is terrorism, Timor-Leste is not totally immune to possible damage resulting from terrorism. Indonesia has been the victim of these cowardly attacks by radical Muslim movements, some of which are considered to be close to Al Qaeda. These groups have carried out terrorist attacks with dire consequences, as the ones that took place close to Timor-Leste, in Bali.

Consequently, and in what regards defence perception or design, Timor-Leste urgently needs to look inside itself and to reformulate our internal capacity for ensuring peace and stability within our territory. The required capacity building must be developed in such a way as to respond to the new demands of globalisation and to transnational threats. Other factors that can threaten the stability of the country are drug trafficking, human trafficking and, in particular circumstances of the country's development, money laundering.

Your Excellencies
Ladies and Gentlemen,

Although Timor-Leste does not face any short-term threats of aggression to its territory, we cannot overrule the existence of non-military threats that can jeopardise national security. We remain a vulnerable country due to our small size, our low economic development and the inexperience of our political, administrative, legal, security and defence institutions. The country has large wealth, particularly in terms of oil and gas. These are essential commodities for economic and social development in today's world, and vital for ensuring the pressing needs of the populations. As such, we may be the target of foreign greed, which can hinder the cohesion and solidity of our institutions.

Our maritime fauna is also incredibly vast and valuable, with Timorese waters being easy prey for illegal exploration. It is necessary to promote the efficient protection of our maritime space through proper patrolling and surveillance, so that we do not lose important sources of food and revenues. As I said before, we need to give a new boost to the prevention of eventual illicit activities, such as piracy, smuggling, people trafficking and drug trafficking.

We also face new threats and risks in addition to the ones I mentioned, namely, criminal organisations, capital laundering, weapon trafficking, illegal immigration, ethnic conflicts, environmental problems and possible shortness of some resources that are abundant today, like water and rice, which is the cornerstone of our people's nourishment. These threats and risks have become globalised and weaken today's societies. The volatility of the country's security conditions, as is normal for a State that is still very young, may allow terrorist groups to enter the national territory and to carry out attacks against the security of the State, as well as to go after foreign citizens and interests.

Presently, defending the borders and the maritime space of a country against any external threat is not limited exclusively to that country's defence and security forces. It entails a broader field of play, which we call regional defence. Timor-Leste, being located both in Southeast Asia and in the Pacific, cannot be isolated from its regional partners. This is one of the reasons why we have been seeking to join ASEAN as a full member for some years now. At the same time, we also want to maintain a healthy cooperation in terms of national security with Australia, which is a dominating power in the region and indispensible for ensuring stability in the Pacific.

Indeed, this is a true challenge for Timor-Leste. We need to be well inserted in the region, without Timor-Leste being a factor of disturbance between Asian and Pacific States (or even between Indonesia and Australia), and we need to remain free from interferences by any party. This means that the Timorese policy must be able to promote good relations with our neighbours, based on values of mutual respect and peaceful relations, so that neither of the two feels that Timor-Leste is growing apart from them.

Our privileged relations with Portugal, based on a common past of nearly five centuries, as well as Timor-Leste's adhesion to CPLP, have opened the doors of Europe to us and have enabled us to channel indispensible support to sustain our State and our national sovereignty. Similarly, the privileged relations Timor-Leste has with its two powerful neighbours, Indonesia and Australia, may serve to bring the CPLP countries closer to the Asian market and to strengthen friendship ties with Asian and Pacific nations. For instance, free from the constraints of the past, Timor-Leste, which was once a factor of separation and conflict between Portugal and Indonesia, now brings these two countries together and is an asset for the relationships between Indonesia and the European Union.

Because of its external vulnerability, Timor-Leste needs a strong State, with democratic and stable political institutions, so that it may be better protected against external forces and that it can unite the Timorese and meet their varied interests. My Government is aware of this, and therefore seeks to promote balance between the State, Defence Forces and Civil Society (particularly the Church), to strengthen internal cohesion and to develop the spirit of Timorese national identity. Choosing Portuguese contributes to this, as it differentiates us from our neighbouring States. CPLP, to which we are proud to belong, will certainly continue to play a leading role in terms of cooperation in the areas of defence and security. As such, we rely on its prestigious assistance to strengthen and build the capacity of our Armed Forces and our Police.

Recently, the authority of the Timorese State has been seriously shaken and jeopardised, as a consequence of the attacks against the President of the Republic and the Prime Minister. This act was possible due to the conjugation of several factors, with the guilt being shared by all entities with authority in terms of ensuring internal order. This led the Timorese State to substantially change its policy concerning the capture and dismantling of armed groups, which at first were not considered a serious threat to the stability of the Country, allowing them to create a strong support network. This recent incident, which cannot be separated from the sequels left by the 2006 crisis, caused constraints in two fundamental democratic institutions: F-FDTL, which endured serious problems leading to the departure of almost a third of its members, and the near collapse of PNTL. This showed how frail the foundations of these institutions were.

As such, the Government has taken stronger measures, proposing the declaration of martial law and applying restrictive measures so as to carry out special measures for preventing episodes of violence by support groups and to conduct the necessary investigations to capture those responsible for the attacks. We have also strengthened confidence in the national military and law enforcement institutions. For this purpose we created a Joint Command consisting of the Defence Force of Timor-Leste (F-FDTL) and a considerable part of the National Police of Timor-Leste (PNTL). These two institutions, which are tasked with ensuring national defence and internal security, had been at cross purposes almost all the time. There had been several records of conflict between soldiers and police officers, which did nothing to benefit national stability. However, it was the creation of this Joint Command that enabled the success of the operations seeking to capture and seize the weapons of those who threatened national cohesion and sovereignty. Consequently, the authority of the State was restored throughout the entire national territory.

If, during the most controversial periods, one can draw positive aspects, then here I must highlight the reconciliation between these two institutions, proving that, when confronted with common goals, they can work well and in a coordinated manner for the good of the Nation. This served to clear the doubts of those who said that these two agencies would never get along in the pursuit of the goals of consolidating a Democratic State under the Rule of Law. It was mostly with this purpose, as well as to enable both Institutions to carry out their activities in close cooperation towards a common goal, that the Fourth Constitutional Government I have the honour of leading decided to concentrate the areas of defence and internal security into a single Ministry, the Ministry of Defence and Security, with myself as Minister.

Unfortunately we still have some security problems to solve, starting with the issue of the so-called petitioners who departed from the F-FDTL ranks. However, the recent adoption of actual measures tending to respond to those problems efficiently, without reducing State authority, will enable the prompt resolution of this case that has been afflicting us for the past two years. All petitioners are already concentrated in a camp created for this purpose. Soon, there will be financial compensations for those who chose to return to civilian life and abandon for good the desire to being reintegrated in the Armed Forces. Those who still aspire to wear the military uniform will be given conditions to apply for the selection procedure in the next recruit, being aware that the criteria now applied will be very strict and that the Government does not ensure their immediate acceptance.

Another adversity inherited by this Government and caused by the conflicts that hatched in 2006 relates to the IDP camps. Thousands of people who saw their houses burned down or who feared for their lives concentrated in makeshift camps have since become a permanent source of difficulties, such as resistance to the public order, physical confrontations between diverging groups and proliferation of epidemics. The ongoing providences have mitigated the nefarious effects of this potential public calamity, and so far a significant percentage of IDPs has already returned to its places of origin. I was pleased with the recent dismantling of the camp near National Hospital Guido Valadares, as a solution was found for resettling the people who were there, thus putting an end to a situation of latent danger to public health.

We are aware that the complete normalisation of the Timorese society through the efficient development of the policies needed for ensuring security conditions to the people, as is indispensable for the economic growth of the country, will still require some time. As such, we are firmly committed to having F-FDTL and PNTL continue working together to build on the success of the operations already carried out and to consolidate the democratic order of the Rule of Law.

It is also with this purpose that the reform of the Sector of Defence and Security and the capacity building and professionalization of F-FDTL and PNTL are not being developed as autonomous and watertight processes, subject to their specific competences and to their competences given by the Constitution. This is a purpose that goes beyond the Government and covers the remaining sovereignty bodies. In terms of national security policies, all relevant decisions must be assumed together by the President of the Republic, the National Parliament and the Government.

Under the power given o him by the legislative electoral process, the President of the Republic has concentrated under his direct dependency a Group for the Reform and Development of the Security Sector. In partnership with the other two main security bodies, and particularly in close cooperation with the Government, this group will have as key mission to enable the review of all legislation in the areas of defence and security considered to be pressing, as well as to reform and develop defence and security forces and services.

Before I conclude, I would like to state my heartfelt desire to see the Defence cooperation strengthened between our countries. I am absolutely convinced that the exchange of experiences and the harmonisation of concepts and practises may contribute to improving individual security in each of the CPLP member countries. Even more so, I believe that as CPLP we can aspire to the noblest sentiments of Peace, Harmony and Solidarity, contributing to the defence of our countries and perhaps humanity itself.

# Strategic Framework Module for Timor-Leste within the Pilot Course on Defence and Security — Reviewing Resistance and Understanding the Present

9 November 2010

A — Lessons from the Resistance

1. The Indonesian intelligence services started to operate in our territory after the Portuguese revolution on 25 April 1974. Military intelligence offices, disguised as traders, were infiltrating in order to collect a wide range of information on our political, organisational and military capabilities. They also observed and understood our weaknesses, which were apparent and included:

- our political immaturity
- our inconsistencies
- our continuous misunderstandings
- our lack of consensus on matters of strategic interest
- our internal divisions

All of these factors were carefully watched and analysed. Indonesia then began to undertake small test raids, in order to prepare for larger scale action.

2. Although we were aware of these preparations, we were too busy with the quarrels among ourselves to give necessary attention to them.

After three weeks of fratricide war, the Indonesian incursions at the border in September to November, 1975, increased in firepower and strength, with the use of artillery and cavalry, and were pushing our forces back.

On the afternoon of 28 November, during the ceremony of unilateral proclamation of the RDTL, we could see the smoke from the Indonesian frigates near Ataúro, as if to show how unprotected our sea was.

On 7 December, in Díli, and subsequently in Baucau and Lospalos, the dropping of paratroopers also showed that we had no air security.

During the first few weeks, the warships in the bay of Díli and the cannons in the mouth of Comoro vomited fire on the entire slope of the capital.

3. In the first two years, and although outnumbered in terms of soldiers and materiel, we managed to hold the enemy advances, by carrying out a war of defending positions, so as to safeguard large areas, which we called liberated areas and which were the support bases where all the population moved and worked.

During that time, we had to endure raids that caused material and logistic damage, as well as human losses and the impact on morale. The defence of these large areas that housed the population required all our Forces and prevented us from carrying out significant offensive initiatives that might turn the tide of the struggle, and worked against a fundamental military principle that attack is the best defence. This was a struggle that we were fated to lose, since we could not resupply and renew our military materiel and had to deal with communication and coordination problems due to the lack of an integrated command.

Soon the successive annihilation of our military regions forced us to resort to guerrilla warfare. By learning to fight like this, we managed to overcome our main weakness: [lack of] self-sufficiency in terms of materiel, namely weapons and ammunition. This was essential for us to be able to continue fighting at all.

B — Country's Defence and Security — present time

In order to understand the country's defence and security, we must look at the legal and political framework that ensures the legitimacy of the actions of the State in that sector.

This takes us to Part V of the Constitution of the Republic, on national Defence and Security.

Section 146, on Armed Forces, reads as follows:

'FALINTIL-FDTL shall guarantee national independence, territorial integrity and the freedom and security of the populations against any aggression or external threat, in respect for the constitutional order.'

On the other hand, section 147, on Police and Security Forces, says that: 'The police shall defend the democratic legality and guarantee the internal security of the citizens...'

We understand that the 'democratic legality' expressed in section 147 has the same connotation as section 146 when it talks about 'respect for the constitutional order'. Its legal sense can be seen in section 85 (g) and (h) on the 'exclusive competencies' of the President of the Republic.

Sub-paragraph (h) says that it is exclusively incumbent upon the President of the Republic: 'To declare war and make peace following a Government proposal, after consultation with the Council of State and the Supreme Council of Defence and Security, under authorisation of the National Parliament', while the previous sub-paragraph states that these same conditions are required to 'declare the state of siege or the state of emergency'.

This is reinforced in section 87, on 'Competencies (of the President of the Republic) with regard to international relations', with sub-paragraph (a) reading the following: 'To declare war in case of effective or imminent aggression and make peace, following proposal by the Government, after consultation with the Supreme Council for Defence and Security and following authorisation of the National Parliament or of its Standing Committee', with only the lapse that the State Council does not have to be heard.

However it must be said that this entire process of proposals and consultations will not work in practise in situations of 'imminent aggression' and even less in situations of 'effective aggression'. As such, we believe that these restrictions of competencies are meant to safeguard the democratic rule of law by preventing unconstitutional propensities.

Thus we could ask: What is defence? What is security?

Is talking about 'defence' the same as talking about 'preparation for war'? Let us recall section 146, which reads the following:

'FALINTIL-FDTL shall guarantee national independence, territorial integrity and the freedom and security of the populations against any aggression or external threat...' and this only means that the Armed Forces should be prepared for the eventuality of any war.

Will there be war in the future? Why should we think about that, when section 8.2 of the Constitution of the Republic, on 'International Relations', says that: 'The RDTL with all other peoples, aiming at the peaceful settlement of conflicts, the general, simultaneous and controlled disarmament (and) the establishment of a system of collective security...' which can be assumed to mean the entire world.

Section 8.4 also states that: 'The RDTL shall maintain special ties of friendship and co-operation with its neighbouring countries and the countries of the region'.

Will there or will there not be another war in the future? From a very personal standpoint, I would say that one should never cast aside the possibility of armed conflicts, whatever their nature may be. Our own history has shown us, as well as all the other wars that have been fought and that are still being fought, that wars can be caused for a great many reasons, including to take control over the natural resources of other countries.

What would then be the mission of the F-FDTL? Already in section 146 of the Constitution, the legislative stated that in the event of 'aggression or external threat' our Forces should dig trenches along the border to 'guarantee territorial integrity' and thus guarantee 'the freedom and security of the populations'. In the first few years of the resistance, the defence of the territorial integrity was based on the effort to ensure 'freedom' of movements and 'the security' of the populations in the controlled areas.

Still, upon reading the Constitution, we see that section 6 (a) identifies as one of the main goals of the State: 'To defend and guarantee the sovereignty of the country'.

And the State, in order to defend and ensure the sovereignty of the country, will need an agent, which would obviously be the F-FDTL. As such, should 'sovereignty of the country' be seen only as 'national independence (and) territorial integrity', as stated in section 146 on the mission of the Forces?

No, because when one speaks about territorial integrity one is speaking about territory and this is covered in section 4.3, which says that: 'The State shall not alienate any part of the East Timorese territory or the rights of sovereignty over the land, without prejudice to rectification of borders'.

Here we need to understand what sovereignty is, since section 49 reads the following: 'Every citizen has the right and the duty to contribute towards the defence of independence, sovereignty and territorial integrity of the country'.

The three concepts are presented separately here, which helps us to understand section 8.1, which says that: 'The Democratic Republic of East Timor shall govern itself by the principles of ... permanent sovereignty of the peoples over their wealth and natural resources ...'

Their wealth and natural resources! Sovereignty is, after all, the right of possession and enjoyment. Very recently, when the Naval Component of the F-FDTL arrested an illegal fishing boat, there were voices reminding us that this should have been a task for the Police and not the Armed Forces. I believe these to be thoughtless opinions that seek only to shake the dust off from the mantle that covers the cynicism of good intentions, as is already the standard in the modern world, in which the largest threat to populations is the policy of two weights and two measures that is still going strong today.

### C — Threats in the age of globalisation

1. Lately, I am horrified whenever I watch the news. There is an open war against the drug cartel in Mexico and there are pirates seizing oil tankers off the shores of Somalia. In Africa, there continue to be internal problems that seem impossible to solve, while in some regions there are problems caused by ethnic tensions, political ambitions or the economic motivations of large multinationals which all convey images of insecurity and fragility across the entire continent. However, the wars in Iraq and Afghanistan give us food for thought as to the reasons for this all.

I am also very frightened by the terrorist attacks by suicide bombers and very recently by the explosive packages sent by mail to European heads of governments, not to mention the cancelling of flights, which is becoming routine in airports. There is much talk about the meeting of civilisations and about the global village, but the truth is that human civilisation is reaching the peak of insanity in terms of political, religious and sectarian intolerance.

The strong continue to want to rule the world, imposing their own standards and imposing duties on others. The wealthy do not cease to try to maintain their economic supremacy by any means, and reject any models that may come along to level the playing field.

In this imbalance of options, humanity is vulnerable to the threats that arise, either as spontaneous reactions or as planned responses and backstage moves, to give reasons to justify actions over others.

In the troubled setting of today's world, we can see that people are becoming increasingly aware that the real cause of problems is not religion in itself, or an ethnicity or sect in themselves, or human rights in themselves, or democracy in itself, or underdevelopment in itself, or poverty in itself. The real cause of all existing problems is the cold war mentality that still subsists, namely that:

- you can only survive by imposing yourself,
- you can only impose yourself if you threaten someone,
- you are only safe if you attack and destroy, and
- in order for one to be strong, there must be those who are weak.

And all of this finds its reason for being in the need to maintain economical and financial hegemony as the basis for political hegemony, which after all is the greatest battle by the so-called civilisations, which have much more room for quarrels today than they did before.

The billions of dollars spent on wars in the name of democracy would have been better used to reduce world poverty, within a spirit of solidarity and equality among peoples. I believe that someday an atmosphere of global security may become a joyous reality.

### 2. And how is Timor-Leste inserted in terms of defence and security?

Being a territory inserted in the crossroads of Asia and Pacific, between Australia and Indonesia, giant neighbours with different backgrounds that adopted a common policy regarding our destiny in the past, Timor-Leste must strive to steer away from political ingenuities, thinking that its Constitution alone may ensure national independence, territorial integrity and sovereignty over its resources. Even worse would be to assume that others will respect our Constitution.

The future adherence to ASEAN, which should not be rushed, must be viewed more in economical terms than in what regards policies and security.

Also, we are not yet ready to meet the great expenses that will result from it, without immediate or medium-term benefits.

3. **On Destabilisation Threats**
    a) *Internally,*
    - we must be prepared against surprises that could be avoided if we all could have a common perception of how fragile we seem in the eyes of others, thereby reducing acting discrepancies, normally under the banner of democratic differences, which only serve to divide.
    - we must strengthen our capability to understand emotional agitation and its connections by agents operating in our country, who make use of the full freedom of movements that we ourselves grant to them.
    - we must put an end to our present complete ineffectiveness of not knowing who may be controlling our communications and how. Nowadays, technological sophistication puts us at the mercy of the large economic interests that always guide political interests.

In order to solve all of this, we must invest heavily in internal security. In democratic countries established hundreds of years ago, national intelligence services are areas that are not debated. In our Democratic Republic, there is not yet this awareness and this sense of State security, which means that the biggest constraint is always the possibility of public debate by Parliament on the amounts to be allocated. It is necessary to change this attitude because, truth be told, other people know what we say, whom we say it to, what we want and what we do not want. On the contrary, it is we who do not know if the person talking to us, whether they are a Timorese citizen serving the interests of our country or trading their allegiances for a hefty salary.

b) *Also internally,*
- we must maintain a fast pace in the recruitment of police officers, so that our community police has enough personnel to carry out the task that the Constitution has already given to the PNTL to 'guarantee the internal security of the citizens'.

For this, we need to use technical assistance to teach our police officers to work in the communities or to be coast guards, while the State must be ready to invest much more on facilities and working conditions, so that our men and women may carry out their duties with efficiency.

In the last ten years, much of the generous technical assistance provided by our development partners has not achieved the desired effect, since our agencies still lack the proper operational conditions. It is time to change this policy, and change must involve investment by the Timorese State. In this matter, all Timorese must have the same approach.

For all of the above, the State must invest:
- in increasing the personnel and in improving conditions and facilities for the border patrol Police;
- in training more soldiers and in establishing more posts throughout the border, so that they can act better, in coordination with the patrolling police unit;
- in increasing the personnel and in improving the action of our maritime police, so as to enable better control over the movements of people and commodities;
- in a better intelligence service, so as to enable previous detection of attempts to infiltrate drugs, weapons and illegal persons.

4. **How can we protect the country?**

The principles listed in section 8 of the Constitution seek, in an ideal and idealistic manner, to ensure security for the State, by saying that it 'is ruled by relations of friendship and cooperation with all other peoples', 'by the mutual respect for sovereignty, territorial integrity and equality among States' and 'by the establishment of a new international economic order capable of ensuring peace and justice in the relations among peoples'.

In terms of international relations, Timor-Leste must:

- Understand the scope of the regional and / or sub-regional forces in order to be able to identify its contextual objectives and our role within that framework;

- Understand the impacts in decision-making processes that do not obstruct the security of the country itself, taking into consideration the weaknesses that are inherent to the State building process;
- Continue to monitor processes throughout the world in terms of military actions, political reforms and adjustments, and inequality of economic opportunities; and
- Avoid running to the arms of cooperation that would hinder our movements and prevent us from issuing legitimate opinions.

However, we all know that Timor-Leste signed in 2005 the Treaty on Friendship and Cooperation, under the ARF (Asian Regional Forum), where it participates and discusses issues of Defence and Security every year.

Independence is a relative political process when viewed under the sphere of the interdependency of States, but sovereignty is an absolute concept.

The same way that democratic and developed countries have been worrying about their defence and security for hundreds of years, investing in those vital areas, Timor-Leste cannot hesitate to invest in its Defence and Security, so that it may protect the sovereignty of the country!

# Visit to the National Defence Academy of Japan

Tokyo
10 March 2009

> Your Excellency the President of the National Defence Academy
> Distinguished Officers of the Armed Forces
> Distinguished Teachers
> Dear Cadets,

It is a great pleasure for me to be at this National Defence Academy, and I appreciate the invitation to address you young cadets who seek through advanced education to join scientific knowledge with military training, so as to best prepare to meet your responsibilities and mission as future officers of the Japanese Armed Forces.

As you are aware, I was a soldier myself, although not exactly by choice or as a result of natural ability. As a matter of fact, at the time, both my colleagues and I did not care for the army, and tried for as long as we could to avoid serving in the military. Timor was then a Portuguese colony and Portugal was at war with three African provinces — none of us wanted to be deployed somewhere in Africa, most of all to take part in a war! However, military service was compulsory, and therefore an order was made providing that those who did not report for military service would be sought out and conscripted for war.

This way, I and many others ended up at the Training Centre to be prepared to integrate into the Army, which, oddly, was the best way to avoid being conscripted to go to war. I found many of my high school colleagues there who, despite not having finished their education, were nevertheless sergeants. Because I was only a first corporal, I had to salute them. From the memories I have of the time, of those three years of mandatory military service, I remember that we learned the meaning of organisation and obedience. It was without doubt a School on Discipline!

When we completed our duty to the Portuguese Motherland, we returned to our civilian lives and, after a while, we were allowed to dream of our true Motherland, Timor-Leste. However, in December 1975, Timor-Leste was invaded by Indonesia. This meant a war we could not escape and a war in which I ended up being an active participant. I started out as Platoon Commander and, afterwards, because it was necessary to provide political assistance to our people, I left the military field and joined the political cadres for three years.

In 1977, Indonesia carried out large operations and began to destroy the resistance sectors one by one, from the west to the east. Because I was located in the eastern-most part of the country, the furthest sector from Indonesia, we were the last to dismantle, and consequently I lived through many wartime experiences.

Dear Cadets,

During the guerrilla activities, we had to make many tough decisions. We had to provide for the safety of our people, and at the same we had to fight the enemy. We were completely cut off from the world and without military support. In situations like this, decisions must be obeyed, not discussed, since they are matters of life and death. Discipline is therefore essential.

The military superiority of Indonesia reduced our human and material resources dramatically, weakening our ability to resist. From around 30,000 armed members, we were reduced to just over 1000 guerrilla fighters with only 700 weapons. Most Timorese leaders were killed during the first three to five years of the occupation. In view of this situation, and with my superior officers having already fallen, I ended up being appointed as leader of the guerrillas in 1978 and given the difficult task of reorganising the struggle. Going from the political cadres to the leadership of the Resistance, I had the opportunity to reflect on the changes needed to lead our People to victory.

For one year, we analysed the defeats we had suffered, we studied the errors we had made and we learned from these lessons — and then we changed our guerrilla strategy to make our Resistance stronger. During that period, we studied guerrilla tactics used all over the world and realised that none suited the situation we were in. We therefore worked to understand our own war and to learn to survive as guerrilla fighters. This was the turning point for our Resistance! We reorganised the few guerrilla fighters we had left, we restructured the struggle into small mobile forces that, little by little, covered the entire territory, and we relied on the selfless participation of the People. This was the birth of the 'Clandestine Front'.

By this time, our motto was no longer 'Destroy the Enemy' but, rather, for the Clandestine Front, it was 'The Art of Living with the Enemy'. On the other hand, our Armed Resistance took inspiration from the motto, 'Conserving Our Strength, Destroying the Enemy — To resist is to win', through adopting new tactics and actions to recover weapons and reduce human losses. This was especially critical given our weapons came from the opposing army.

However, the difference in military power between us and the Indonesian army was still enormous. As we lacked the capacity to drive the enemy from our country, we started trying to destroy it psychologically, morally and militarily, through small but incisive actions. The success of these actions depended a great deal on our collective efforts with greater participation by the people, especially in terms of donations: money, food, clothing, intelligence and even war material.

Finally, we joined our strategy with a greater coordination with the Diplomatic Front, which maintained the case of Timor-Leste in the International Community as a cause that was not a lost one. With my arrest in 1992 by the Indonesians, a new leader of the Resistance was chosen, Commander Taur Matan Ruak, who is here today and who is now the Chief of the Defence Forces of Timor-Leste. Commander Ruak continued the effort to give our actions greater operational capacity and efficiency, keeping the flame lit, so that we would not despair or give up as a result of the losses we suffered at the hands of the opposing army until we gained our freedom.

Today we are an Independent Nation! Our Armed Forces come mostly from the guerrilla forces, but also include the younger generation. Nevertheless, we are still some way from having a fully professional and disciplined Force.

In 2004–2005, the new generation of soldiers were shown to lack military discipline, and in the following year they started a rebellion within the Institution, which resulted in about 600 soldiers abandoning their barracks. This situation caused an environment of insecurity in the country and a series of difficult problems, which ended up leading to confrontation between police forces and military forces. The lack of resolution of the crisis culminated in 2008, when an armed rebel group, led by a former officer who could never understand the concepts of discipline and military responsibility, conducted attacks against the lives of the Head of State and myself as Head of Government.

If, on the one hand, this act was unacceptable, on the other hand it turned out to be a necessary evil, as it contributed to the restoration of normality to the Military Institution, as well as to the Police, which also suffered with the events that led to the crisis, and to society in general. The attacks of last year were ultimately a final warning on the need to correct and reform our national policies.

In this sense we reorganised and, in a more coordinated manner, looked for the right model for Timor-Leste, gaining the consensus of the Timorese and respecting the steps and time needed given our reality. As a result, we have managed to solve the problems that resulted from the 2006 crisis, namely, that of the so-called petitioners who left their barracks, the internally displaced persons and the armed rebel groups.

Today we are strongly committed to reforming the security sector, which includes internal security, national defence, intelligence and civil protection. We have a project called Force 2020 that sets the guidelines for our national defence strategy, which includes the construction of a naval component. This force shall be created not so much for protection against a foreign military threat, but rather to defend our national resources, such as our maritime fauna and fisheries. We will also be setting up a Maritime Authority, through which the coordination of work by the people, the Police and the Armed Forces will enhance our country's security, as well as combat the transnational threats of today's globalised world.

In order for these goals to be realised, it is essential that our Armed Forces have access to more and improved education and training — vital components for our reform. The challenges of our Military Institution require the presence of professionals with not only scientific, technical and military skills, but also with capacity for critical thought, leadership ability, tolerance and respect for human rights. The dreams of better opportunities through education, which were denied to my generation due to our historical circumstances, now belong to our new and future generations.

Dear Cadets,

Addressing this National Defence Academy of Japan, I am pleased to see students of several nationalities. The opening of this Academy to foreign students gives me great pleasure. I hope that, with the scholarship support to young Timorese already agreed upon between our two countries, it will be possible to improve our Armed Forces.

If we learned something from those 24 years of fighting for our freedom, it was that, with cooperation, with cohesion and with a collective vision, we can look forward to a better future for our Nation. The current struggle that Timor-Leste faces is different from that of the past, but it is not necessarily easier, and once more requires the engagement of all Timorese. The barriers to sustainable development and national stability are not enemies that can be overcome without the creation of strong and organised Institutions, including the Defence Force of Timor-Leste.

Finally, I would like to conclude by sharing with you one of the noblest lessons that we learnt from our war experience — the value of gratitude and friendship. Japan has been providing invaluable support to Timor-Leste, and for this I would like to say, 'arigato' to our Japanese friends, from the bottom of my heart.

# Homage and Recognition by the State of Timor-Leste to the Veterans of the Armed Front

A state tribute to 205 former Guerrilla fighters who fought for national independence for over 15 Years.

UNTL Gymnasium
Díli, 2 December 2007

We are here today so that the Nation can publicly recognise our heroic Armed Front Resistance. The former Guerrilla Fighters, both men and women, to whom we have the honour to pay homage and to present this award, have fought in the woods for over fifteen years, defending our independence.

To be able to institute the 'Fundamental Constitutional Principle' of 'Valorising Resistance', we began five years ago to register former fighters and veterans of FALINTIL. This enabled Parliament to draft a law on the Status of National Liberation Combatants. This law, dated April 2006, created the legal regime for recognising and valorising the National Liberation Combatants, presenting the legal definition 'Veteran Combatant' and determining that the 'recognition of the quality as National Liberation Combatant' is dependent of registration. It was at this time that Timor-Leste fell into a deep crisis that affected us all.

Despite the difficulties, the process for recognising Resistance was started on 28 November 2006 and the State of Timor-Leste succeeded, from the records featured in the Database and up to last 12 November, in paying homage to around 13,000 National Liberation Fighters. Out of this number, more than 90 per cent died as a result of having fought for national liberation. In line with the Programme of the Fourth Constitutional Government for the first four months,

Parliament approved in October 2006 a proposal for 'payment of allowance to veterans' up to the end of the present fiscal year.

The two government agencies responsible for the veterans, the Secretariat of State and the Homage Commission, an ad hoc commission consisting of three members of Parliament, one representative from the Chief of the Defence Force and two former Commanders of the Struggle, selected, with the assistance of the database, the 205 beneficiaries of the tribute that we will be presenting today.

I am very proud and honoured to preside over this act as the Prime Minister of the IV Constitutional Government.

Eight years after the end of the war, most heroes and veterans of the Liberation are still living in poverty, without minimum conditions of dignity. If, today, we live in a free country and we can be the masters of our fate, we owe it to them. Without them, many of us would still be in the jails of Cipinang or in the Diaspora in Mozambique, Lisbon or New York.

Still, better late than never. And, today, 2 December 2007, we are awarding them this tribute, paying them our homage and conveying to them the gratitude of the State of Timor-Leste for their heroic efforts in the Fight for National Independence. For most of them, this is the first time in thirty-two years that they will receive financial assistance to help them meet serious needs and enable them to fulfil old desires. We will continue to acknowledge and to dignify the Resistance, respecting the constitution, the law and the history of the Liberation of the Fatherland. Ceremonies such as this one will be held when all the truth has been ascertained and the true Combatants have been separated from the false ones.

Ladies and Gentlemen

Dear Countrymen and Countrywomen

Youngsters of Timor-Leste,

The brothers and sisters to whom we are paying homage today had to endure many difficulties, watched thousands of their brothers and sisters die and did not know whether they would be alive in the next hour. Still, they knew that, dead or alive, the Day of Independence would come. Despite the lack of weapons, the patriotic spirit overcame all difficulties and we gained our independence. Independence was achieved as a result of determination, selflessness and sacrifice, but also persuasion, timing, discipline and courage. It was their persistence that led our cause to victory. Without the courage, selfless dedication and total commitment of the FALINTIL combatants to the liberation of our People, frequently giving up their lives in the process, Timor-Leste would never have seen the day of its self-determination and would never have had its Independence acknowledged by the international community.

The FALINTIL veterans and the Resistance veterans, both individually and as the representatives of all those who gave up their lives for the Fatherland, deserve the utmost recognition and respect of the Timorese Nation and even the international community for the values of liberty and dignity they fought to protect in conditions of extreme hardship and difficulty. May their example be a reference of courage to today's youngsters, as well as a factor of national unity.

Follow their example! Honour their difficult past and participate in the building of our Nation. After all, it was because of the people and so that our youngsters could live in a free country that they have fought for 15 to 24 years in the mountains of Timor.

# 66th Session of the United Nations General Assembly

New York
23 September 2011

> Your Excellency President of the General Assembly
> Your Excellency the Secretary-General
> Excellencies
> Ladies and Gentlemen,

It is a great pleasure for me to be back at the United Nations Headquarters. Last February, I had the honour of taking part in the Security Council meeting, where I took the opportunity to thank the permanent members and all other nations that have been part of the Council for the generosity and care that have always been present in the resolutions on Timor-Leste. Today, on behalf of the people of Timor-Leste, I want to take this opportunity to thank all members of this forum for the support they have given to Timor-Leste in the promotion of peace and security and in the building of our national institutions.

I am pleased to inform the General Assembly that we have come a long way as a people and as a state, replacing intolerance with constructive dialogue, and the right to protest with the duty to protest responsibly. We have taken firm steps away from the difficult circumstances of the past and we have renewed the confidence of the Timorese people in the institutions of the State. As such, we have already endorsed the Joint Transitional Plan for the withdrawal of the United Nations Integrated Mission in Timor-Leste by the end of 2012.

We are in the last year of the five-year mandate of the Coalition Government that I have the honour of leading — the Parliamentary Majority Alliance (AMP) Government that includes five different political parties. Under the Constitution of Timor-Leste, the Government is determined either by the party with the most elected representatives, or by an alliance of parties with a parliamentary majority, as it is the National Parliament that is elected directly by the people and not the government itself.

A government can only be constituted if it is supported by a parliamentary majority. Following the 2007 elections, the party with the most parliamentary representatives did not have a majority in its own right, so the President of the Republic, after formally meeting with all parties, endorsed a coalition government in order to provide the best opportunity for a stable government. This constitutional option served the best interests of the nation, as we were living in a period of great fragility at that time, as demonstrated by the instability and violence that were consequences of the 2006 crisis.

Having inherited an unstable domestic situation, the AMP Government focused on restoring peace and stability and resolving the many social and political problems that stemmed from the 2006 crisis and that continued into 2008. We were determined to put an end to the violent outbreaks that began in 2000 and that were repeated every two years, as though Timor-Leste was trapped in a vicious cycle of violence. The key to breaking the cycle was to acknowledge and to admit that we had failed. We had to address the root causes of our problems and learn to deal with the frailty of our State institutions. Fortunately, we were successful in conveying a strong political message about the need for stability.

The AMP Government committed itself to a reform agenda and, by governing through dialogue, was able to:

1. Initiate vital reforms in the defence and security sectors, including capacity-building and professionalising the police and the defence forces;
2. Implement structural reforms in the state administration's management;
3. Create systems and structures to ensure good governance, while continuing to support the capacity building in the justice sector;
4. Introduce fairer social policies to reduce the imbalance that existed in society, taking into account the physical, moral and psychological damage of a twenty-four-year long war. I am speaking about veterans and the elderly, who sacrificed themselves for our independence and who, directly or indirectly, have suffered the consequences of a devastating war;
5. Encourage structured policies on education, health and agriculture;

6. Promote a coherent economic policy throughout Timor-Leste to encourage the fledgling private sector.

In 2009, on the Tenth Anniversary of the Referendum, the Government launched a new motto, 'Goodbye Conflict, Welcome Development'. The people of Timor-Leste embraced this motto wholeheartedly. Looking forward to the period 2011 to 2020, we are confident that we are now truly becoming a more stable and tolerant society that is peaceful by nature. We also have the necessary optimism to initiate a bolder period of development.

Excellencies
Ladies and Gentlemen,

Over the last four years, we have been strengthening the institutional capacity of our public administration to defend the best interests of the state, to improve public service delivery and to promote good governance. We have introduced reforms in the area of public finance management and we have created a Civil Service Commission. We have also created an Anti-Corruption Commission and begun to establish a Chamber of Accounts to promote transparency and accountability in our public accounts.

Earlier this year, we launched both an on-line Transparency Portal and a Procurement Portal, providing access to data that is updated daily on the process of the Timor-Leste State General Budget and its execution. These portals also allow public consultation on advertised public projects. We have begun to develop the capacity of our private sector by promoting competence, professional honesty and technical skills. Our aim is to transform the private sector into a strong Government partner at this crucial period when we are building our country. Across the country we have invested in agriculture to increase the productivity of the sector, as well as Local and Decentralised Development Programmes, focused on minor infrastructure projects to promote employment for young people in rural areas.

These measures have contributed to our economic growth and helped create jobs in the capital, Díli, and in rural areas, and they have encouraged confidence in our state institutions and led to a spirit of optimism that has contributed to a change in mindset.

Ladies and Gentlemen,

Timor-Leste is a country blessed with great natural wealth, which means that we have the financial capacity to improve the living conditions of our people. However, we know that countries rich in natural resources often perform below their economic potential and that they are more vulnerable to conflict and more susceptible to bad governance. As such, transparency and good governance, which are essential in any country, become even more imperative for countries that are rich in natural resources. Currently, the Timor-Leste Petroleum Fund of Timor-Leste has a balance of $8.9 billion. We are the first country in Asia, and the third in the world, to be compliant with the Extractive Industries Transparency Initiative.

As a result of our good governance and prudent use of revenue, Timor-Leste has had double-digit growth in the last few of years. We believe that we are on the path to maintain this growth and we are confident that the institutions we have established to support the Fund will become stronger, ensuring responsiveness and greater quality of work and execution. We will diversify the investment of our petroleum fund equally in bonds and equities to guarantee long-term sustainability, so that future generations will benefit in the same way as the current post-war generation.

Having achieved our goal of stability, we were in a position to prepare a 20-year Strategic Development Plan that would substitute the annual plan for each fiscal year. The Strategic Development Plan covers three vital areas: social capital, infrastructure and economic development. In terms of economic development, we are focused on three strategic industry sectors — the hydrocarbon industry, the agriculture sector and tourism. We want to shift from an oil dependent economy to a non-oil dependent economy.

The strategies and actions set out in the Plan aim to transform Timor-Leste from a low-income country to an upper-middle-income country, with a healthy, well educated and safe population that is prosperous and self-sufficient in terms of food by 2030. This new paradigm requires public investment in infrastructure and services and a dynamic private sector. Many emerging economies, particularly in the Asian region have been growing, despite the serious international financial crisis.

Mr President

Excellencies

Ladies and Gentlemen,

Next year will be very important for us to consolidate our State building process and to affirm ourselves as a sovereign, tolerant and democratic Nation. In 2012, we will hold presidential and legislative elections — the third democratic elections in Timor-Leste — which I am confident will be conducted peacefully.

Next year we will also celebrate vital historic dates that connect us to the more recent past of the struggle for independence and to the older roots that make us unique within the region and the world. In addition to celebrating the Tenth Anniversary of the Restoration of the Independence, in 2012, we will celebrate the centenary of the Manufahi Revolt and the 500-year anniversary of the arrival of the first Portuguese navigators in Timor-Leste. I would like to take this opportunity to invite you all to take part in these celebrations, in the same spirit of thanks and solidarity that we extended the invitation to our independence celebrations on 20 May 2002. After all, we were not alone on that important date and we continue to benefit from the generosity and support of nations throughout the world, as we pursue the challenge of nation building. We are pleased to continue to strengthen and expand our ties of solidarity with friendly countries from various continents with different stories, different beliefs and different ethnicities.

We are trying to be more active in our region and in the world, showing that it is possible to leave behind, or to close a period of conflict, even when it was long, and to focus our energy on humanist ideals of political and social tolerance for the dignity and development of all. This is why we are intent on joining the Association of Southeast Asian Nations, ASEAN. Timor-Leste desires peace and shares the spirit of co-operation that led to the creation of this regional organisation.

We are also continuing to build upon our relationships with other friends in Asia and the Pacific, including China, Japan, South Korea, Australia and New Zealand. Timor-Leste is strongly committed as well to our membership of the Community of Portuguese-Speaking Countries, which is formed by nations and peoples from the four corners of the world. We are observers in the Pacific Islands Forum and we have a good relationship with the European Union, which provides us significant support and assistance.

Next week, I will be conducting an official visit to Portugal. Portugal shares ties with Timor-Leste that go back hundreds of years. Despite being in one of the worst economic and financial crises in its history, exacerbated by the global and European financial crises, Portugal remains a steadfast partner to Timor-Leste, strengthening its bilateral cooperation in several areas. The first Timorese military personnel are being trained in Portugal to integrate into the Portuguese contingent that will participate in the peacekeeping mission in Lebanon under UNIFIL.

Ladies and Gentlemen,

Timor-Leste is part of fifty States classified as 'Least Developed Countries', or 'LDCs' for short. We are also called 'fragile States'. This classification as fragile States results from institutional, political, economic, social and other factors.

In April last year, we had the honour of hosting an International Dialogue in Díli on the subject of 'Peacebuilding and Statebuilding', with the participation of LDCs from the g7+, which is presently chaired by Timor-Leste. It is a forum that allows fragile and post-conflict countries to come together and to talk about themselves, to learn from each other's experiences and to create new possibilities for facing the future with determination and optimism. The g7+ consists of 17 member countries, covering around 350 million people from Africa, Asia, the Caribbean and the Pacific. The g7+ also aims to improve the transparency and efficiency of international aid. It provides member nations with an opportunity for dialogue with each other and the international community about aid programs and aid effectiveness.

It should also be noted that fragile States require a period of transition with greater flexibility in donor funding; a 'one size fits all' policy approach can interfere with the individual processes of each country.

Mr. President

Excellencies

Ladies and Gentlemen,

A High Level Forum on Development Assistance is scheduled to take place next November, in Busan, South Korea. In this forum we will evaluate progress made in achieving the Millennium Development Goals (MDGs) and we will set new action frameworks. Developing countries focus on meeting MDGs every day; however it will be very difficult to meet them by 2015. These countries face daily challenges and difficulties in pursuing objectives to combat mal-administration and reduce poverty.

Democracy is a process and not an end in itself. Most of these countries are young democracies and have the arduous task of changing the mindset of their people who have been scarred by conflict. They must also deal with internal and external pressures that prevent them from paying too much attention to a series of "universal" criteria that are too idealised or standardised and not adjusted to the actual situation of those countries. Understanding the specific circumstances of each developing country and motivating the people to cultivate a spirit of hope and belonging will surely yield more results than forcing situations where receiving countries cannot meet the conditions imposed on them immediately, thereby being put in a situation of moral, psychological, political and financial dependency that does little to help them move towards development.

It is in this context of balanced and sustained development that I raise the issue of aid effectiveness. Poor countries also need a message of confidence, since all they hear about is transparency and accountability. Still, the international economic recession proves that the lessons taught by those that have all the power, the knowledge and the money may not always be the best. Therefore, I believe that we must all change our attitudes — poor countries and donor countries. And, ladies and gentlemen, the UN has a vital role to play here in terms of correcting and adjusting aid to actual and local realities.

We remain divided into North and South, into rich and poor, into westerners and Arabs, into Asian and African, into Muslims and non-Muslims, into Christian and non-Christian. Even today, many of the people who hold or influence power still have a cold war mentality. We need a new world order that is also political and economic, where conflicts and discord are replaced by dialogue, where democracy is used to give voice to the weak and vulnerable, where aid and solidarity are used appropriately to mitigate the suffering of the people. We have to give voice to the peoples of the world and listen to their aspirations. Only through dialogue can we fight violence, which causes all kinds of misery. Only through peaceful solutions can we prevent the massive destruction caused by war. The people of Timor-Leste, who have experienced the pain caused by destruction and violence, hope that their brothers and sisters throughout the world who are suffering today because of conflicts, may find peace.

Peace is not merely the absence of war. Peace, real peace, comes from within — the spirit of peace. Thus, I appeal to the United States of America to show great spirit and humanity and lift the embargo on Cuba, which has lasted for more than 25 years.

In 1991, I was still in the mountains leading the resistance when the Referendum for the Western Sahara was first proposed. I was in prison in 1995 when Yasser Arafat, Shimon Perez and Yitzak Rabin received the Nobel Peace Prize. Two prominent Timorese citizens also received the Nobel Peace Prize, and Indonesia accepted the Referendum result, just as North Sudan did. We hope that the people of Western Sahara and Palestine can find more viable, just and realistic ways to resolve their conflicts, which are sadly becoming the oldest conflicts in the world.

We all need to reform our mindsets, attitudes and institutions. We all must start these reforms within our own nations, but I would like to suggest a common challenge: that these reforms begin right here in this building in the headquarters of the United Nations!

# Reception by the Council of Ministers to the Special Representative of the UN Secretary General

Government Palace, Díli
13 January 2010

> Members of Government
> Your Excellency the Special Representative of the UN Secretary General, Ms Ameerah Haq

It is a great honour to receive you today in this meeting of the Council of Ministers, and it symbolises the respect and appreciation that we have for the United Nations Mission, which, since last week, has been headed by Your Excellency. From our part, you can rely on our full collaboration and assistance, so that together we can work towards solutions to ensure that Timor-Leste achieves peace, stability and improved living conditions for our People.

Your task presents an exciting challenge, however, I caution that you are sure to face various difficulties, none the less so because you are replacing someone who was respected and will be missed by all those who worked alongside him. Mr Atul Khare always listened to the Timorese, to understand our longings and to respect our wishes. He learned our weaknesses as well as our strengths, and in this way his decisions were based on the deep understanding he had of our Country and of our People.

We are confident that you will show the same enthusiasm for dialogue and for finding solutions as your predecessor, so that together we can overcome difficulties that lie ahead of us.

The State of Timor-Leste is absolutely dedicated to providing its armed forces and its police with the essential human and logistical support so that they may carry out efficiently and effectively the mandate given to them by our Constitution. The importance we give to Defence and Security is reflected in the decision by this Government, made immediately on coming to office, to place these two areas under a single Ministry, to enable soldiers and police officers to undertake their roles with close coordination and cooperation.

The State of Timor-Leste also embarked upon a reorganisation and restructuring of the Defence and Security Forces, with the establishment of the Group for the Reform and Development of the Security Sector, under the oversight of His Excellency the President of the Republic, and with the participation of the National Parliament and the Government. As such, in all matters concerning national defence and internal security, it is not the will of the Government that is imposed, but rather decisions resulting from a broad consensus involving the above three organs of sovereignty.

We would be most appreciative if Your Excellency would always take into consideration the will of the State of Timor-Leste in the performance of your duties. This should, however, of course in no way be seen as an attempt to constrain or interfere in the tasks that are your exclusive responsibility.

We may have limited experience as an independent and sovereign Nation, but we have culture, customs, history and tradition that go a long way back in time. And we know well what is the best way forward for us; we just lack sufficient human resources to be able to implement the policies that we set. This is exactly the role that we hope the United Nations will play, particularly the mission now under your charge: providing us with the necessary tools so that we may carry out the reform of our security sector.

We are fully aware that the PNTL still has a long, and sometimes challenging, way to go before it is able to operate without the external assistance that has been provided to it by the various missions, and which have been vital to ensuring the safety of our People and the protection of their assets. But we are also aware that we can only learn by doing. Ms Ameerah Haq, I call upon your understanding and good sense, so that we may achieve the goal agreed between the State of Timor-Leste and your predecessor: that is, transferring all executive responsibilities for the Country's internal security to the PNTL by the end of this year. We know that there are still various constraints that need to be overcome so that we can reach this goal, but we are determined to work hard in order to fully resolve these issues.

In my view, it is the common and consensus opinion that the UNPOL mission should be extended up to 2012. And we all hope that this year the PNTL will have reached a level that enables it to operate and undertake its responsibilities without multilateral cooperation. A number of mistakes have been made in the past. This has included the selection of a policing model that proved to be inconsistent with Timorese society. We sought to correct these errors, and that is why we prepared a new Organic Law setting out a police model we consider appropriate for our Country. This was of course our prerogative, based on the legitimate right we have to be masters of our own fate. We hope that this decision, therefore, will be understood and respected, rather than challenged, by those from abroad whose assistance we have requested and that we greatly value. The basic training to be provided to the PNTL must be undertaken in accordance with these considerations and by the police force of only one country, which has a similar policing model to that of the PNTL.

We believe that this training can be perfectly accommodated within the framework of multilateral cooperation, thereby also involving UNMIT. The FPU/GNR may make available part of their personnel for this mission, subject to the full execution of the mandate that led to their establishment. Of course we leave this preference of ours to your consideration, trusting that you will take it into account.

In addition, I would like to inform you that the Council of Ministers has decided to create a Commission representing the Office of His Excellency the President of the Republic, my Office (the Secretary of State for Security) and the PNTL, which will seek to negotiate with UNMIT the revision of the Supplementary Agreement. This is an important measure to safeguard our legitimate aspirations and to enable the State of Timor-Leste and UNMIT, in full cooperation and working side by side, to successfully execute the reform of the Country's security sector. I would be pleased if you could give this Commission the proper attention in addition to you establishing direct contact with the sovereign bodies and State agencies with responsibilities in the security sector.

Ms Ameerah Haq, welcome to Timor-Leste. I wish you the best both personally and professionally in this new stage of your life.

# Meeting of the UN Security Council

New York
22 February 2011

> Your Excellency the President of the Security Council
> Distinguished Members of the Security Council
> Ladies and Gentlemen,

First and foremost, and on behalf of the people I represent, please allow me to thank this great Council, its permanent members and all others who have walked through these halls for the generosity and concern that you have shown in your resolutions on Timor-Leste.

After more than five years, I must say it is a great pleasure to be back here at the United Nations Headquarters. I must also recall that, in May 2006, the then Minister of Foreign Affairs of Timor-Leste, Dr Ramos-Horta, came before this Council to plead for the support that our people needed at a time where intolerance trumped constructive dialogue, so that we might find proper solutions. My presence here today follows that SOS we sent five years ago.

I am also pleased to be accompanied by the Special Representative of the Secretary-General, Her Excellency Ms Ameerah Haq, since, thanks to her commitment and dedicated leadership at UNMIT, the relationship between Timor-Leste and the United Nations remains strong as ever.

I am also honour bound to thank my good friend, Mr Atul Khare, for everything he did, in very trying circumstances, both for the Timorese and for the Mission he led. My friend, Atul Khare, always showed great responsibility and care in his work, as well as great understanding and cooperation, so that together we could achieve our duty: to restore confidence in the Timorese society.

Since UNMIT's establishment in 2006, both our President of the Republic, Mr Ramos-Horta, and the Vice Prime Minister, José Luís Guterres, as well as Mr Atul Khare and Ms Ameerah Haq, in their due time, have been reporting to this Security Council on the progress achieved in Timor-Leste.

Ladies and Gentlemen,

I would like to underline a few of the steps we have made since the five-party Coalition Government I lead entered into office on 8 August 2007:
- for the first two years, we focused our efforts on restoring peace and stability and solving most of the social and political problems created by the 2006 crisis, which continued up to 2008;
- we implemented and continue to implement structural reforms in regard to management of the administration of the State;
- we have been creating systems and structures in order to ensure good governance, continuing to provide support in building institutional capacity and that of the agents of the Justice sector;
- we have been implementing social policies in order to reduce the imbalances in our society, taking into account the physical, moral and psychological damage caused by a war that lasted 24 years;
- we have been nurturing structured policies on education, health and agriculture;
- we have been promoting a coherent economic policy throughout the country in regard to our nascent national private sector.

The restoring of peace and stability in the Country was primarily a result of the reforms started in the PNTL and F-FDTL, which, by 2008, finally ended the cycle of friction, overcoming the petty differences that divided both institutions. Since the Joint Operation in 2008, the PNTL and F-FDTL have been activated here and there to continue the exercise to restore normality in the Country, in full compliance with the values of a Democratic State under the Rule of Law.

While one of the main factors in the 2006 crisis was the inability of State Bodies to manage problems collectively, in February 2008, at a time of extreme gravity and threat against the constitutional order, we saw all State institutions working in a coordinated manner and in close collaboration, thereby meeting all legal and constitutional requirements for overcoming that prolonged crisis. The result was the creation of a political precedence of enormous significance and scope, which shows to the Timorese that there are proper instruments they can use to save the country from anarchy and disorder.

Nevertheless, I must acknowledge the extremely important role played by civil society, including the Church and NGOs, as well as the political parties, the youth and, most of all, our people, in this process for consolidating National

Unity and Stability. In 2009, the year marking the Tenth Anniversary of the Referendum, this enabled the Government to issue a new motto: 'Goodbye Conflict, Welcome Development', which the people embraced with all their hearts.

Thus, on 31 December 2010, after the first decade in which the Timorese People were truly free, we saw off the year in a festive atmosphere, knowing that we are on our way to becoming a friendly and, most of all, tolerant and peaceful society. It was in this mood that the fireworks in Díli greeted the 2011– 2020 decade, during which we will be strengthening these values and starting a bolder development period.

I did not come here to praise the progress made by my Government, so as to correct some reports on Timor-Leste that tend to sound more like verdicts. We regret those reports, but we try to understand their reasons. I also did not come here to underestimate the difficulties and the challenges that still lie ahead of us.

We are aware that we still have many needs as a nation. We are fully aware of the efforts we will have to take in order to build State and country. Still, we have not been alone in meeting these challenges, for we have benefited from the generosity and support of Nations from all over the world. And you, the distinguished members of the Council, you represent that generosity and support, because you represent those Nations from all over the world. Hence, we continue to strengthen and, little by little, to expand our ties of solidarity with friendly countries from various continents and with different histories, different beliefs and different ethnicities.

Most of all, we are taking our due place in our region. We are currently formalising our application for membership of ASEAN, during the Indonesian presidency of this regional forum. We believe that having Timor-Leste join ASEAN during the Indonesian presidency will have great symbolism not only for Timor-Leste and Indonesia, but also for all the members of this Association.

We are also continuing to strengthen our relationship with other friends in the Asia Pacific region, including China, Japan, South Korea, Australia, New Zealand, among others. Timor-Leste is also strongly committed to the Community of Portuguese-Speaking Countries, which includes countries from the four corners of the world.

We also have ties of cooperation with India, where dozens of Timorese are studying in the areas of IT and Oil.

We are also fortunate to have strong support and assistance from the European Union and its member States. After this important visit to the United States, I will also be travelling to Cuba, where over 700 Timorese are studying medicine, as well as to Brazil, a country with which we are also cooperating in several areas.

Ladies and Gentlemen,

Timor-Leste is truly committed to having dialogue with several countries so as to enable a critical review of processes. As a Nation, we have received much from the international Community; currently we hope to be able to reciprocate, in a genuine manner and within the same spirit of solidarity, by sharing experiences, both sweet and sour, with other fragile countries throughout the world.

As such, in April 2010, we had the honour of hosting the International Dialogue under the motto 'Peacebuilding and Statebuilding', with the participation of LDCs from the g7+, which is currently chaired by Timor-Leste. The general goal of the g7+ is to awaken leaders and peoples so that they may reacquire ownership of their processes, viewed within a long-term perspective without losing sight of the characteristics of each country and their priorities, and without forgetting to focus also on the need for a better control and adjustment over outside help, requiring greater transparency by donors and beneficiaries, so that the real impact of that support can be seen in the development of the countries. The g7+ is enabling countries that are fragile and affected by conflicts to gather and to speak about themselves, to learn from their mutual experiences and to create new opportunities to face the future with determination and optimism. The g7+ currently includes 17 member countries representing 350 million people, from Africa, Asia, the Caribbean and the Pacific.

Timor-Leste has also been involved for the third consecutive year in the Bali Democracy Forum, which has been gaining participants every year. Countries like India, Iran, Bangladesh and others have also chosen to give their important contributions to this Forum, showing that the world wants to discuss the subject of democracy.

I would like to convey my respect and admiration for my friend, Mr Susilo Bambang Yudhoyono, the President of the Republic of Indonesia. Under his leadership, the largest Muslim country in the world is taking steady steps towards consolidating democracy and has managed to gather representatives from various governments in Bali to discuss the values of peace, non-violence and tolerance, and particularly the connection between democracy and development.

Today we are witnessing an inevitable movement by societies and peoples who demand freedom of expression and fundamental rights. In all that is taking place, as well as in the g7+ and at the Bali Democracy Forum, people are becoming aware that they must be sovereign in terms of the decisions that concern them, rather than remaining subject to the imposition of programs of others and, worse still, subject to the interests that are not their own.

While we Timorese fought alone for 24 years, we never lost sight of what was going on in the world. The objective awareness that the world was changing, both in our region of the world as well as others, was something that nurtured our aspirations to be free, even in extreme situations. And the world continues to change, fortunately! In all of this, the most important thing is that people are the masters of their own fate.

Ladies and Gentlemen,

Changing topics, but remaining in this world we live in, the LDCs, of which Timor-Leste is one, are concerned with the continuous indecision by the large economies in drafting a new economic order. Time goes by and at best it generates anxiety, if not despair. And this is the truth: time goes by, as it has done ever since the first alarms on climate changes, decades ago. Today, all over the world, it is meaningless to talk about preventive measures, since all that can be done is invariably to bury the dead and to calculate the amount of damage in order to create funds to mitigate the suffering of people. Therefore, countries like Timor-Leste, which yearn for development so as to improve the living situation of their peoples, face one of the worst challenges, uncertainty, in view of the adverse effects of the world economic recession and the lack of coherence in terms of measures to save humankind from hunger, disease, misery and all things that derive from that.

Accustomed to enormous challenges during their lengthy Struggle for Liberation, the people of Timor-Leste are determined to focus on their development. After a thorough review of the needs and challenges, we are currently drafting the Strategic Development Plan, which will be submitted to Parliament for approval. We are hoping to launch it at the next meeting with our Development Partners, scheduled to take place in July in Díli. In macroeconomic terms, the Strategic Development Plan is based on the following paradigm:

- production
- production capabilities
- productive employment opportunities

Only by creating employment can we improve the social and economic situation of our people, since only employment can generate income, and income results in the eradication of poverty. For that, the Timorese State will have to invest boldly on core infrastructure and on human capital development.

With your permission, I will go once more to the reasons that brought me here to New York.

On 25 August 2006, in response to a request by the then Prime Minister of Timor-Leste, the establishment of UNMIT was approved for an initial period of six months, with the possibility of renewal. December 2006 saw the signing of the Supplementary Agreement on the restoring and maintenance of public order, which regulated the relationships between UNMIT and the State of Timor-Leste, transferring leadership over the national and international police to UNPOL. Support to the reform, restructuring and rebuilding of the National Police of Timor-Leste was also defined. This enabled the start of the registration and certification programme for all PNTL elements, resulting in the final certification of all Police officers who did not have pending processes regarding crimes and human rights violations.

Meanwhile the PNTL Promotion Regime was also approved, which set a Promotions Committee with the goal of selecting PNTL officers and recommending them for promotion. The Committee was supported by senior police officers from friendly countries, enabling the creation of an international Jury to make the process more credible.

The transfer of executive responsibility from UNPOL to PNTL in the various districts began on 14 May 2009. This process should be completed by 27 March, the date of the eleventh anniversary of the PNTL, with the handing over of the Díli District Command and the PNTL General Command. From that point on, PNTL will be responsible for conducting, leading and controlling all police operations in Timor-Leste.

I acknowledge the concerns stated in the report by the Secretary-General of the United Nations regarding the final certification of the remaining PNTL elements. I only want to underline the Government's commitment to strengthening the leadership and control and to applying disciplinary procedures in a serious manner, so as to ensure the integrity of our Police.

Ladies and Gentlemen,

Next year will be a very important year in the consolidation of the building of our young State. Two thousand and twelve will be the year when we will hold presidential and parliamentary elections, the third democratic elections in our country. I am confident that they will take place in an atmosphere of tranquillity, as indeed they did back in 2007, when, despite the recent crisis and a few isolated events, the elections took place with greater normality throughout the national territory. And, for this to be possible, we are prepared to continue ensuring stability in the country. Here, the PNTL will continue to require assistance by their colleagues at UNPOL, who will perform only advisory and capacity-building tasks in various areas, according to the needs of the Timorese police and following the plan already drafted by its General Command. This matter should continue to be subject to consultation and coordination with the relevant Timorese authorities.

Allow me to remind that, in regard to legislation, training, administration, discipline and operations, it would naturally be ideal that the advisors to the PNTL have technical and professional skills in these fields. Also, if possible, we would like to see the advisors already cooperating in those areas to remain there until the end of their mandates.

Under the leadership of our President of the Republic, at high level meetings involving UNMIT and the Government, we will continue to study the post-UNMIT period, that is, the period after the 2012 elections when UNPOL may start to withdraw.

In the election period, namely March and April for the presidential elections and in June for the parliamentary elections, we seek to draft a special agreement with UNMIT so as to enable UNPOL to participate alongside with PNTL in the maintenance of public order in the country. In addition to this, and with an advance of one year, I would like to remind that UNMIT will also be requested to provide logistical support to the elections, as it has always done, more recently in the 2009 elections for local leaders. We are counting on the presence of the International Community through international observers, which we hope will come in sufficient numbers to cover the 700 polling booths, in order to anticipate any irregularities that may emerge and which we want to avoid.

The UN has been present from the moment our Nation started to be built, and as such I urge you to remain with us in solidarity, so that we may fulfil the dreams of our people. Today, those dreams are about peace and development. I thank the UN, the Security Council and the entire Community of Nations for their efforts and support for State building in Timor-Leste. The Timorese People vow to continue working hard towards peace and stability in our Country. Only by doing so can we help the United Nations to provide due assistance to other countries in crisis that have a greater need for aid than Timor-Leste.

On behalf of all Timorese, I thank all those men and women who have left their families and their countries to be part of the noble mission to assist the building of Timor-Leste throughout these five long years. I thank all governments that, during these years, were part of this Council and deliberated on the support to Timor-Leste, in the spirit of true friendship and solidarity among peoples and nations.

Speaking of friendship and solidarity, I could not end without congratulating the Governments and peoples of Sudan for their intelligent adoption of non-violence during the recent referendum process. The people of Timor-Leste, who have experienced the devastation of destruction and violence, hope that their Sudanese brothers and sisters, from both North and South, continue to engage in dialogue and in a pacific solution, which is the only way for the integrity and survival of both peoples.

2012 will also mark the tenth anniversary of the Restoration of our Independence and the realisation of our sovereignty. I would like to seize this opportunity to invite you all to take part in the celebrations, as we all did back on 20 May 2002.

In conclusion, I wish to thank His Excellency, the Secretary-General for his report and for the recommendation to extend UNMIT's mandate for one more year. In the consolidation phase of PNTL, the reconfiguration of UNPOL is important and I have every confidence that the PNTL will be well assisted in the process of building institutional and human capacity.

However, during this time of anguish, it would be remiss of me not to express my sincere and deepest sympathy and solidarity with the people and Government of New Zealand for the earthquake that hit Christchurch for the second time.

# Commemoration of the 9th Anniversary of Timor-Leste's Restoration of Independence

Díli
17 May 2011

>Excellency President of the Republic
>Excellencies
>Honorable Dean
>Lecturers
>Ladies and Gentlemen
>Dear Students,

First of all, I would like to thank you for this opportunity to speak a little about the theme that was given to me: Nation Building and State Building.

In three days time, we will celebrate the ninth year anniversary of the restoration of independence, which we declared on 28 November 1975. This unilateral declaration was our own self-declaration, however, the international community had yet to accept or recognise it. It was only on 20 May 2002 that the international community gave us the recognition that we needed, so that we could become a member of the community of nations in the world and, therefore, on September 2002, we became a member of the United Nations.

In the coming month of July, Southern Sudan will also go through the same process and the international community will be with them on this great day in which they will stand as an independent country and people. And also, in the coming month of September, their nation will have a place in the General Assembly as a member of the UN.

It has been nine years that we have governed our beloved country. Many countries in Africa and Asia gained independence after World War II, meaning 66 years have passed. Countries from the CPLP, in Africa, such as Angola, Mozambique, Guinea Bissau, Cape Verde and São Tomé and Principe, have had 37 years.

That is why it is very important for us to hold on to our thoughts as we have only recently established our nation and our State. When we do not measure correctly the time that each country has been independent, we make the mistake of comparing one country to another; we fail to see the challenges and difficulties that all countries faced in their first ten to twenty years of independence.

When we fail to understand a process, we have the tendency to expect more than what we are able to achieve under this process. In order to undertake an action with firmness (such that when we start something we have to finish it), to proceed with conviction (that is, if we do something, we believe that it is good), it is important that we do not lose sight of the process or its development.

And this process has to be our own — this is very important!

At the 3rd Bali Democracy Forum, where every year more and more countries are participating, and at Conferences, and also at Universities including some that are overseas, I always say that:

- democracy is a long process and it can only consolidate when everyone clearly understands the process;
- democracy is a process that each country practices, according to its own conditions and characteristics.

We can travel the world and see that, in many countries, they focus on elections, that is, they believe that if elections are good, everything else will change. In Africa and in Asia, many countries, more than 40 or so, still face problems which are the same or greater or more difficult than Timor-Leste. If we do not open our eyes, to do an extensive study of other countries' processes, we will not be able to see what we ourselves can do, what we ourselves must do, and what we ourselves know that is good for us.

The principle theory that I have mentioned above is the one we held by ourselves as we took action in the 24 years of struggle until we won. If we did not have this way of thinking to guide our thoughts, we would have lost the struggle, long after 1979. That is why we did not make a war in the dark, and we did not make a war without a theoretical base in which to place the process of war. All processes are the same, and have their own course. Social processes can find their own difficulties and find their own results. Economic processes will always find their own difficulties and come to their own results separately.

Political processes also have one way: they have their own challenges and when answering these challenges, the results will respond to its own process.

We are currently following the 'popular revolution' in North Africa as well as the Middle East. Egypt's physical development provides cities that are great and beautiful, however, the political process provided an autocratic regime. This is the same for Libya, Syria, Yemen and Saudi Arabia. In Asia, we see Laos, Myanmar, Bangladesh, as well as Papua New Guinea, which Australia granted independence in 1975, and it is not surprising that they have moved forward. If we do not know how to study these processes with their own difficulties, we will not find a way to strive forward. In doing so, we can identify a good process, where we can see how it functions and measure the steps that are being taken to achieve good results.

Processes of Nation Building are extremely complex, where all issues are together, yet at the same time separate, however interlinked or interdependent. Interdependent means that one area that functions well can influence the other. However, if an important area falls behind or is damaged, it can affect other areas, as well as have the ability to stop the entire process.

The process of State Building is a process with its own difficulties and with various challenges. And, more importantly, for our own understanding, it is a very long process. It is not a process that can be undertaken quickly.

That is why we can ask: What is a State? States have sovereign institutions, which are pillars of our independent Timor-Leste. Everyone knows the State Institutions: President of the Republic, National Parliament, Government and Judiciary.

We have recently achieved nine years in the process of self-government! That is why we have to agree that we are still in the construction phase. This means that these institutions already exist, however, we need to make a continued and greater effort to strengthen each year, until each one has its own capacity to deliver good service.

The President of the Republic is the highest institution in our State and is an institution that oversees national unity and democracy, as well as other functions, and oversees the actors of that State that need to obey the Constitution and the Laws.

The National Parliament is a sovereign institution, which is also critical. In the Parliament, where the representatives of the people present and defend the people's aspirations, the parliamentarians then debate and approve the turning of these aspirations into laws. This institution also has a duty to audit the government's policy, that is, the plans and measures of the government and review if all the government programs and plans have been implemented.

We also need to recognise that the Parliament, in its two mandates (2002–2007 and 2007–2012) has already achieved many things, however, there is still room for improvement, in order to truly represent the people's wishes. This process needs to be given time, to reinforce the institution's own capacity and institutional memory.

Government is an institution that has the responsibility to administer programs for five years according to its mandate, and, in each year, follows its mandate. The government also needs to oversee and improve the public administration capacity, and believe that, only through a public service that is capable and professional and full of spirit to serve, can our State function effectively.

For this, the State Inspector General has responsibility to identify any irregularities in the administration. The government also must give attention to the training of the inspectors and auditors in the institutions of government, so that they can better do their work.

We now have a Civil Service Commission, which oversees the recruitment process which must be transparent, the promotion process which must be based on merit and not on friends or family, or political affiliation or bribes, and instead be a process which is based on honesty and fairness in the evaluation for all public servants, and also to impose disciplinary measures when they are deserved. It has been not much over a year since we have started and we still need a place or facilities, as well as people with capacity and aptitude for this job.

In the self-government process, we also have a process to build and strengthen all the institutions. That is why the State needs to help find solutions that are good for various problems that arise, with an obligation to see all the mechanisms within our society. That is why we have the Provedor (Ombudsman) for Human Rights and Justice, which is currently performing its functions. We all need to accept that, if they are to work according to our wishes, it will take time, as the Government needs to improve their conditions and increase the number of people with skills and capabilities.

Another important institution is the Anti-Corruption Commission. Sometimes I hear that, one year on, there has still been no arrest. To speak like this is poor, because we cannot forget that, for an institution to function properly, human resources is a fundamental requirement. Investigation of corruption crimes is not the same as investigation of homicide. We first have to prepare our people.

Finally, the Courts are also one of our State pillars that uphold justice in our country. The Courts' responsibility is to make sure that everyone is under the law. According to our Constitution, this is our greatest value: everyone has access to justice and everyone is subject to the law. However, we move forward. Courts, which are institutions that are independent from the three above-mentioned institutions, must assure that there is no interference in their decisions. Recently we witnessed the Vice Prime-Minister going to Court as a defendant. José Luís Guterres, as a human being, suffered emotionally, morally and politically. However, our State won! However, our State was strengthened! This is what is important!

According to our constitution, we need to establish Courts as follows: a Supreme Court of Justice and other Judicial Courts, Administrative Courts of Fiscal Accounts and Administrative Courts and Military Courts. Today, we only have the Court of Appeals, which has the highest responsibilities and competencies. This only says that we still have processes to establish in our State. This process needs to develop slowly because, to establish it correctly, we need to consider our human resources. This is the factor that is still lacking in our country, which is like a measure of our capabilities in the process to establish a State. The Government has also approved and sent to the Parliament proposed legislation to create the Chamber of Accounts as a first preparatory step for our administrative and fiscal system in our State.

For all the citizens to have access to justice we have to establish a court within our country. However, this is not enough. We also need Prosecutors and Public Defenders; we also have to properly prepare the civil servants in the justice sector; we also have to better prepare police investigators and we also need more lawyers.

Even though it is small, let us begin to celebrate. Yesterday I participated in a ceremony for new judges, prosecutors and public defenders who took office. A recruitment process is also now in place. In this year alone, 45 more will receive training. Sixty investigators will also receive training. To understand all this we must not lose the sense that we are still in the process of establishing and strengthening the State's institutions.

Now we move to the other question: What is a Nation?

The nation is the country Timor-Leste and all its people, the State and the whole society. According to the 2010 Census Statistics, which we did ourselves, Timor-Leste has 1.064 million inhabitants.

Looking at these age group figures we can see that the situation is very complex. Timor-Leste's population is a very young population.
- There are more than 400,000 people up to the age of 15
- Up to the age of 25, there are more than 500,000

This data can be seen from two perspectives: one, that RDTL has great hope for its future because our population is still young. The other is a big challenge for the education and for their training and their capacity. This shows to all of us that the Education sector is the biggest and greatest priority for the future of this nation — education for all children and a quality education. Education that needs to be orientated to all the children to acquire skills so, in the end, they can find jobs. Because our greatest challenge for our nation in this time is work and jobs for all the Timorese.

According to our Constitution, the State exists to look over the livelihood of the people. When we mention livelihood we cannot move away from the health sector, which oversees the people's wellbeing. When sickness arises, it affects a lot of people, and there is also sickness that affects small groups, which they still look after. In order to look at all this sickness, the State needs to find ways to continue to attend and better plan so it can reduce or, in the end, eliminate some of the diseases from our country.

Many illnesses affect the population because of malnutrition and we can also mention food because there is still a lack of food. Therefore, the agriculture sector has the responsibility to improve, and slowly it will eradicate hunger in our country. It is not just our people that are suffering hunger. Many countries, millions of people in the whole world, have a shortage of food or are hungry.

I only mention the areas that are important and very basic for the people's wellbeing, for today and the future.

In the process of establishing our nation, what are the mechanisms that the State needs to oversee?

When we mention mechanisms, we are raising a big issue. Therefore, I will focus on two mechanisms that we need to really improve for the nation to move forward in a better way.

    a)    Political mechanism, an area which, whether you like it or not, is a part of our lives according to our Constitution.

A democratic system that provides freedom of expression, in which every person is entitled to their own opinion, and there is no one who will prevent you from expressing your opinion. However, when we begin to establish a democratic process, we think that democracy is used to shout at one another and put each other down, and think that freedom gives us a licence to do whatever we like.

Democracy is about the rights of every individual, however, it also about the rights of everyone. There is a very beautiful expression to help us understand: my rights are only until the boundary where another person's rights begin. In reality, we can say, my vegetable patch or my backyard is only until my neighbour's fence. When we have this understanding, we can begin to adopt the correct concept within a democracy. Because of this concept, we can be assured of our own understanding regarding obligations. I have the obligation to respect other people's rights, just as other people have the obligation to respect my rights.

Democracy does not only grant rights; democracy also gives obligations to each individual and everyone. When we are within a democracy we better understand obligations. Always within a society, the spirit of solidarity should be strong. Solidarity arises when we respect one another but it takes the whole society to love one another and to help each other.

    b)    Social mechanism

In this mechanism, we will look at the various organisations that bring together a lot of people who think and want the same things. We can mention religion in this context. Timor-Leste, while majority Catholic, respects other religions. In this area, we all should be proud because there is true tolerance within our society. However, because of this tolerance, in one or two years, some groups have taken actions, and later stolen other people's property and have became a problem. All this can happen because we are the ones who received them in our house and we extended our hands to receive some food or money.

Lastly, external groups brought their religion and books, which they distributed and which were radical. This can ruin us as a small nation, a nation that is still poor, and we ask for all the religious orders to keep an eye on this. Radicalism has entered our country so, if we are not vigilant, it will ruin us like it has done other countries in the world.

In the social mechanism, we also mention other organisations for the youth, for the women, for the professionals, for the vulnerable and for many others. Our State does not yet have the capacity to oversee all these mechanisms. After we see the general situation in the nation, the State has the duty to prioritise. However, we cannot also think that everything is a priority. If we think like that, we are not thinking correctly. In weighing up all the necessities, some became priorities to attend to in order to reduce these necessities.

Last Saturday, we met groups and organisations which are called martial arts or 'ritual arts', so that they can talk to each other and ask each other what each group can contribute to this beloved nation. They all made a promise that, as a group or organisation, they no longer want to be involved in violence in this country. The State's obligation is to oversee this, to assist and to improve a spirit of citizenship in each Timorese's thinking and action.

The State recognised that it has yet to give its maximum attention to the arts, to the culture, to the paintings, to the theatre, to the music and to the sports. However, we have to move slowly. We are in the process of strengthening our Nation and our State.

Last week also, the government met with the village chiefs to discuss their duties within their communities, to attend to the various problems that might arise and which will need to be resolved. The Government is also working with the Civil Service Commission to bring together all public servants to discuss with them their rights as well as to reinforce their conscience regarding their obligations.

In the past few years, the Government sought to meet with the private sector, because we need to oversee our private sector, so they can improve in order to be better partners in the development of this country.

The biggest foundation for this process is security, stability, peace and love within the whole of our society. We have already started and we still need to continue.

To conclude, I will talk a little about the construction of a citizenry. Our Constitution says all citizens are obligated to defend Timor-Leste's sovereignty.

University, as an institution of higher learning, has a big responsibility in the process to establish our nation, that is: to educate citizens that are good and knowledgeable for the future.

Citizens who are good are those people who look to hold firm the principles that are good.

Citizens who are good are those people who look to hold firm good values.

Citizens who are good are Timorese, which put the interest of people and nation above interest of individuals or other groups.

A citizen can be smart, however, and still become a citizen that is not good.

Last week, I received the Dean and the Directorate of University of PGRI from Kupang. They informed me about the plans for co-operation with UNTL, and they also wanted to implement a Portuguese language course as well as activities in the area of sports in their university. Our meeting was very positive. We discussed the responsibilities of the institutions of higher learning and we discussed the meaning of education. We came to the conclusion that education is to train people, to broaden their minds to be able to understand and respond to the real world which they will confront. However, we also reminded each other that, in Indonesia, rivalry between schools has created violence, created intolerance (which, in Indonesia, is known as braul antara sekolah-sekolah) and a phenomenon which is a bad thing, because it is contagious to a society which has found a place to breed intolerance and violence in the future.

Because of this, institutions of higher learning have obligations to teach and reinforce moral values and ethics, so that they can produce good citizens for a Nation. I proposed to them that, because this is a very important topic, the government is ready to lend support to the yearly seminars between university lecturers which are near us. To define what they all can see and need, so that universities can have the ability to better prepare the citizens for each other's country and for the world.

Citizenship does not mean to just obtain an ID card, to vote for a political party or vote on Election Day. Citizenship means an obligation to positively contribute to the Nation.

Sometimes, the Timorese can sidestep their obligations, can lose their concept of sovereignty. This person, this Timorese, considers himself or herself as an independent person and, therefore, the interests of the Nation have no value to them.

They consider themselves to be independent, because it is not the State that pays their way; rather, it is large organisations, such as perhaps UN agencies, where there are also questions of transparency and the effectiveness and results of the big budgets that they have spent. The BBC has reported that a UN agency has taken billions of dollars to Afghanistan to fix the living standards of the children, however, when the money was spent and the agency left the country, the children were worse off than before.

I will make a small intervention and I ask your permission to speak a little longer, because yesterday I also read a beautiful document from UNMIT. I am happy to read Timor Wikileaks, or UNleaks, which was released yesterday by Tempo Semanal. On 24 January this year, UNMIT made a presentation to their staff about 'Democratic governance in Timor-Leste'. In it, it said that Xanana Gusmão is a big obstacle to the development of democracy in Timor-Leste.

I was very happy because they showed that they do not know Xanana Gusmão. And now, I say to all of you, and also take this opportunity to inform them, just as in 2009 I informed Australian Intelligence when they asked me why I purchased the patrol boats from China: Xanana Gusmão was, before a Marxism-Leninist, a member of the Fretilin Central Committee, which claimed Marxism-Leninism as Fretilin ideology on 20 May 1977, in Laline. Those who participated in this decision who are still living are Abel Larisima, Ma Huno and Filomeno Paixão.

Xanana Gusmão, who could have become President of Fretilin and President of RDTL, on 3 March 1981, at the Conference of the Re-organisation of the Struggle, when the path was wide open for him. But he did not want to, because his preoccupation was to learn to direct the struggle to win independence. And, with his influence, Mr Abílio de Araújo, who at the moment is in Lisbon, was chosen.

In March 1985, Xanana Gusmão presented a plan for a solution to the struggle, a plan that only in 1999 was the UN able to apply.

In 1986, Xanana Gusmão took one year to study a better strategy for the struggle, withdrew from Fretilin so as to embrace other parties as well as to open the way for more parties. Friends of the Fretilin delegation outside the country wrote a letter to him, in the mountains, to say that they did not agree with this strategy; some even called him a traitor to the revolution, until even today.

UNMIT and UN Agencies have forgotten that, in 2001, after already approving the transition Plan for the Restoration, on the 20th of May, Xanana Gusmão no longer involved himself in the UNTAET process, nor did he involve himself in the political process for the Constituent Assembly Elections; he was sitting quietly, overseeing the veterans and receiving US$500 from the World Bank for the demobilisation of FALANTIL.

UNMIT and the experts, both Timorese and international, who work in UNMIT, consider Xanana Gusmão the biggest obstacle to Constitutionalism.

In February 2008, Xanana Gusmão did not read correctly the Constitution of RDTL to stop the non-activities of UNMIT and the non-operations of the ISF, when he decided to create a joint operation so that our sovereignty would not be alienated — a decision I can guarantee that, had it not been made, we would still be in a crisis.

But for UNMIT, this would have been good, because they could get to stay here longer! And I must say, that some Timorese defend UNMIT and do not want it to leave, because it greatly assists the economy of our people, and argue that, if UNMIT leaves, our people will be very poor. But this has already happened when, from 2000 to 2008, the international community spent almost US$8 billion in Timor-Leste and yet we do not see any physical development and even more poverty was created in our country. And because they are leaving, poverty increases, and this is our fault!

UNMIT also stated that my response to the 2009 State General Budget case was very hostile, meaning that I showed a lack of respect to the Courts. I agreed that UNMIT had a lot of knowledge, with its nationals and internationals, which is why they did not correctly study my response to the National Parliament.

UNMIT's knowledge cannot understand that I, as the Prime Minister of Timor-Leste, do not accept theories from politicians or academics in Portugal, that the Courts referred to and relied upon in their judgment, because I have followed the financial and economic situation in Portugal. (As before, I do not fight in the dark). In my response, I mentioned that if the theories which the

Court referred to in their judgment were correct, Portugal would not be falling down. Today, Portugal, with US$120 billion of debt, is looking for assistance from the European Banks and the IMF. If this is a response that UNMIT classifies as hostile, this means that the 'experts' in UNMIT are very clever indeed.

And UNMIT also mentioned the Maternus Bere case. Some Timorese also shouted, because people from other countries told them to shout. Saddam Hussein has been killed! Everyone was happy because justice has prevailed! In ten years, Iraq has had numerous elections according to international standards. In Iraq, the war still continues, and President Obama himself promised in his campaign to end the war. Today, I say there is no capacity to make a decision regarding this issue. In January 2006, I went to Washington, I spoke at the Center of Strategic Studies and I said: 'President Bush, until the end of his mandate, did not manage to establish a date to reduce or withdraw the American troops from Iraq'. And I said to the Americans, 'Do not kill Saddam Hussein. Use Saddam Hussein to make reconciliation in Iraq, or else the Iraqis will continue to kill one another.' And, today, May 2011, they continue to kill each other and this war will not end quickly, even though Osama bin Laden has now also died.

These experts have not followed the events in Libya where people are also looking for a compromise solution to Muammar Gaddafi, to convince him to go to another Middle Eastern country, some with promises that he will not have to answer to anything. This is not possible; however, when we reflect on this, the big problem that will arise is that any of the Middle Eastern nations which may receive all have problems of their own. Attempts such as this, have also arisen in relation to Hosni Mubarak, from Egypt.

That is why everything is relative. One thing is activism! Another thing is politics, where one has to defend the interest of the nation. And the interest of the nation is something that is very broad, from diplomacy to the aspects of practical relations, from economy to commerce, from security to sovereignty.

I also have my appreciation of UN agencies. My proposal is this: UNMIT and Timorese experts: offer your services to improve Iraq, Afghanistan, Pakistan, and give support to democracy in Yemen, Syria and Libya. However, in the UNMIT presentation, in January 2011, they said that only if the UN continues to be in Timor-Leste can this country improve.

I want to say to these Timorese, which have become experts for UNMIT, you do not need to show-off; you do not need to grovel for other people's money;

because this is a sickness, which we call mental colonialism or intellectual colonialism. In the Portuguese language it is alienation. In our Constitution it says: do not alienate our sovereignty; do not sell our sovereignty to other people.

I am happy that UNMIT has this view of me. Perhaps they are the ones who elected me as a good person. To UNMIT: the people have a right to suspect that I have already alienated the interests of the people, I have already alienated our nation's sovereignty. Therefore, I am happy because the nationals and internationals in UNMIT are not happy with me.

We know some people have become big 'experts' in our country; however, maybe they should now work together with President Obama to look to resolve the 14.5 trillion-dollar American debt, and the big fraud which the financial institutions and banks displayed in 2009 that damaged the whole world.

Some have become 'expert' in macroeconomics and finance in our country. They have yet to learn that they are well groomed to serve Europe to get it out of its big problems, such as €788 billion in debts from Ireland, Greece, and Portugal and a bailout in which the European Bank and IMF can only offer €322 billion.

These experts today hold RDTL ID cards, but they do not yet know that greater countries in the world need them. America and Europe need these Timorese experts and internationals, to correct the standards which they so dearly defend.

And the world needs reform that is indeed big. Big organisations in the world need reforms which are bold and clear, in order to clean the dirt from within, so that they can gain experience to clean other people's backyards. The UN itself needs this big reform.

In 2004, I and the current President Dr Ramos-Horta, at the time Minister of Foreign Affairs, went to visit Germany. German's President asked for Timor-Leste to support reforms in the UN and their candidacy to the Security Council. I said to the German President: 'Reforms in the UN cannot just be by providing new members to the Security Council. There needs to be a true reform because the UN is a big organisation and very bureaucratic, which spends a lot of money, and we all see that poverty continues to increase throughout the world.'

There needs to be a reform throughout these agencies, where they only communicate with each other, where they defend the standards that they profess but seldom practice. Big and rich countries cannot continue to impose their rules on the world. Small and poor countries cannot also remain silent when receiving these empty words in their ears.

In February, I participated in the Jakarta International Dialogue on Defence. In my intervention, I challenged the participants, civilians, politicians and military staff from Europe to Asia, from UN representatives to those from Africa and the Middle East, and said: 'Why do we not look for a way to end the many wars which cost billions of dollars each year, so that the international community can make a good plan to provide water to the places which are in drought, mostly in Africa, and therefore, money used for war can save thousands and millions of people and this provides real sustainability?'

The topic of transparency regarding assistance from overseas was also raised. I also raised this challenge there, because, why not? International agencies spend a lot of money and, in some places, take rice to distribute and write their own big reports that they have saved people from hunger in order to ask for more money to continue to distribute the rice.

Couple this with "sustainability", which today comes across as a new word to some of the experts in our beloved country. Some Agencies or NGOs have found money, have come to do something, and when there is no more money, they come running to the government asking for assistance or else they will close. However, every day they preach to us regarding sustainability. And the Timorese, which have already become experts, also mention every day to us "sustainability". Why is that? If they do not shout, people no longer give them money, and they also do not find sustainability.

My Dear Friends,

Because of this, Timor-Leste today leads the g7+ where 17 countries come together, representing a total population of more than 350 million people to talk or to say the right word to correct the systems that are currently used throughout the world.

All these things that we the Timorese need to look to understand, look to accompany, look to listen; or else every day we think that Timor-Leste is the worst in the world. If we did not know, we would think that the Timorese and international experts are right. To make us think that, in the world everyone has a job, everyone has liberty, everyone lives in peace, everyone has a full belly, their police do not hit their people, they do not have crime, there are no prisons, or that the hospitals are closed because there is no sickness, the rich people feed the poor three times a day — that governments do not have problems like in Timor-Leste.

We understand that we still have a lot of problems. We will improve. We all look to continue to make an effort. At an Indonesian University, I also delivered a speech last March and I said, 'In developed countries, there is a bad culture; the society does not value the efforts that their government is making to respond to the various necessities. People like to minimise these efforts which only strengthens other countries wellbeing.'

However, it is not only because of this that the State is surprised. The State cannot give value to the undeserved opinions of one or two individuals. The State needs to remain firm, to follow the road that it knows to be correct and good for the people. The correct way is this: during the war, we had one principle: 'Rely on your own strength', meaning 'Rely on your own capacity'. We kept in our mind, another principle: 'national unity through reconciliation', meaning, we only build unity when we make peace and live in peace.

We know what we want and the State of Timor-Leste knows what its people want.

# Presentation of the Legislative Proposal Concerning the 2012 State Budget

National Parliament
9 November 2011

> Your Excellency the Speaker of Parliament
> Distinguished Members of Parliament
> Distinguished Government Members
> Representatives from Civil Society
> Ladies and Gentlemen,

Today, we are here to present the State General Budget for 2012, the last budget of the legislature of the Fourth Constitutional Government, and as such one that fulfils the commitments made by this Government.

When this Government entered into office it adopted an ambitious agenda based on the Program approved by this Parliament. Acknowledging the many priorities, the Government set out a clear program for each year in order to achieve the necessary and desired outcomes. Importantly, we had the political will to improve the state of the Nation and viewed our economic, social and security difficulties as challenges we had to stand ready to overcome. The government team that has been with me for four years has responded with hard work and responsibility to the call for reform that was made by our people and succeeded in bringing about change. As such, reform is the legacy this Government leaves for the future! With bold reforms we succeeded in consolidating stability and security and beginning an effective process towards sustainable development, which in turn will provide Timorese with more jobs and more opportunities.

> Your Excellencies
> Ladies and Gentlemen,

Because we are in the last year of the mandate of the AMP Government, a pioneering five-party coalition, it is apt to recall that it is the Constitution of

Timor-Leste that dictates that the government is to consist of the party, or the alliance of parties, that holds a parliamentary majority.

In August 2007, when we came to government, our Nation was experiencing a delicate situation of fragility, with frequent episodes of instability and violence. It appeared as if we were on our way to becoming a failed State. At this time, the AMP provided the necessary governing stability, which was a necessary prerequisite for serving the best interests of the People and of the Country.

We are aware that we did not do everything. Furthermore, we know that we were not alone in doing the things we did. The Government has also relied on the active participation of His Excellency the President of the Republic and the dynamic and vital collaboration of Parliament, both from the AMP and the opposition, which has been a strong and informed opposition, to find solutions for critical problems faced by the State in its process of consolidation.

We have sought to govern in dialogue with all State Agencies. We have sought to listen to Civil Society and to engage all Timorese citizens. Therefore, it must be said that, if today we are living in a more stable situation and in a climate of greater confidence in the future, it is primarily due to our People. If we succeeded in conveying a constructive policy message to the Country, then our People succeeded in interpreting this message and embracing it to change the image of Timor-Leste.

In very brief summary, the change we have made in the Country is a result of the following measures that were implemented:

1. Thorough reforms to State administration and public sector management;
2. Vital reforms in the defence and security sector, including capacity building and the professionalising of the Defence and Police Forces;
3. Establishment of systems and structures to ensure good governance and transparency, including the capacity building of Justice agencies and their officers;
4. Development of key policies in the areas of education, health and agriculture;
5. Recognition of the veterans and the elderly, as well as other victims who directly or indirectly suffered physical, moral or psychological damage from our struggle for Independence, by way of more just welfare policies and the provision of financial support to address hardship;

6. Beginning implementing a plan of integrated basic infrastructure to enable the development of the Country's productive sectors;
7. Promotion of a coherent policy in regard to the development of the fledgling national private sector.

It was in this atmosphere of change that we concluded the year of 2009 with the motto, 'Goodbye Conflict, Welcome Development'. We then concluded 2010 with growing confidence and optimism as a result of our unprecedented economic growth. Now, as we approach the end of 2011, I can say that we have a clear vision of what we can be in 20 years: a strong and prosperous Nation, as set out in the Strategic Development Plan that belongs to and was welcomed by our People, since it reflects their aspirations.

Your Excellency The Speaker of Parliament
Distinguished Members of Parliament
Ladies and Gentlemen,

The year of 2012 will be very important for our young democracy and for our consolidation as a sovereign, tolerant and developing Nation. Next year we will be celebrating important dates that connect us with the more recent past of the struggle for independence as well as with our older roots that make us unique within both the region and the world. In addition to celebrating the 10th anniversary of the Restoration of Independence in 2012, we will also be celebrating the 100$^{th}$ anniversary of the Manufahi Revolt and the 500$^{th}$ anniversary of the arrival of the first Portuguese in Timor-Leste. Further, in 2012, we will hold presidential and parliamentary elections. These will be the third democratic elections in our Country.

In January 2011, when presenting the 2011 State General Budget, I urged everyone to 'socialise the values of moral policy and to build on the confidence of the People in the future, to consolidate social harmony and democratic tolerance'. Today, in this National Parliament, I urge all the people, and the youth in particular, as well as those who are responsible for the future of this Country, to show the world that we can exert our rights with responsibility, and that together, we will ensure that the electoral processes take place in an atmosphere of peace and social and political harmony.

Also in 2012, after the elections, and with our heartfelt thanks for their invaluable assistance, we will witness the departure of the International

Stabilisation Forces (ISF) and of the United Nations Integrated Mission in Timor-Leste (UNMIT). Regarding the latter, we have already endorsed the Joint Transition Plan, which means that at last we will regain full responsibility for our future.

We have many reasons to be proud of our Nation and to be Timorese. Now that we are living in an atmosphere of peace and tranquillity, it is heartening to see how tolerant and peaceful our people are by nature. We are living in harmony with our cultural and social diversity. Every day, in our institutions, streets and our homes, we live alongside people with different languages, cultures and social habits, coming from all corners of the world, who add to our diversity. We accept, welcome and have learned to live with this diversity, although unfortunately some countries still issue travel warnings that discourage their citizens from visiting Timor-Leste, as if we were Pakistan, Iraq or Afghanistan.

Speaking of foreign countries, allow me to say a few words on our international policy. During these past few years we have consolidated our privileged relations with the CPLP Countries. In 2011, we have also been busy with the process to formally join ASEAN, and we hope that soon we can access this important Regional Forum. We have been an active Observer in the Pacific Islands Forum, having already explored opportunities to cooperate. We believe that in the future there will be more areas of shared interests. We are also a founding member of the South-West Pacific Dialogue and enjoy positive relations African, Caribbean and Pacific States and the European Union.

As you all know, I have recently been to Juba, the capital of South Sudan. On the day we arrived, the South Sudanese were celebrating 100 days as an independent State, pleased with the fact that they were so soon able to host an international event, the g7+ Ministerial Retreat.

At the g7+ meeting, we were pleased to approve the entry of two more countries, Equatorial Guinea and Togo, bringing to 19 the countries represented in this group. Guinea-Bissau requested to host one of the next meetings of this group, so that the g7+ can assist them in better addressing their challenges.

The Retreat also discussed the proposal for a New Aid Deal, which seeks to improve the effectiveness of international aid. In July 2010, Díli held an International Dialogue on Peacebuilding and Statebuilding and a preliminary g7+ meeting. At the end of this month, Busan, in South Korea, will host the

Fourth International Forum on Aid Effectiveness, and the g7+, chaired by Timor-Leste, will also be present.

Ladies and Gentlemen,

From 2007 to 2011, Timor-Leste made significant advances towards good governance and transparency in the public sector, which included:

- Establishing the Civil Service Commission.
- Establishing the Anti-Corruption Commission.
- Strengthening the powers of the Office of the Inspector-General and the capacity of the Office of the Prosecutor-General.
- Establishing the Chamber of Accounts as the precursor to the Higher Administrative, Tax and Audit Court.
- Establishing an integrated financial system so as to better monitor budget execution and procurement processes, and enabling public access through the Transparency Portal and the Procurement Portal.
- Moving up nineteen positions from 2009 and 2010 in Transparency International's world ranking, measured by the Corruption Perceptions Index.
- Receiving full compliance status with the Extractive Industries Transparency Initiative, becoming only the third country in the world to achieve this status. This international recognition enabled us to be elected for a second term as Members of the EITI International Board.
- Being acknowledged in the first ever Revenue Watch index as a Government with Comprehensive Revenue Transparency.
- Improving petroleum revenues by 38 per cent from 2009 to 2010.
- Achieving strong budget execution rates, which have been increasing considerably since 2007. Budget execution in the capital development category alone, from 2006–07 to 2011, increased by 3,413 per cent. The budget execution rate was 89 per cent in 2009 and 91 per cent in 2010. It is estimated that the budget execution rate in 2011 will be at least 95 per cent.

These reforms, together with the increase in public investment, enabled Timor-Leste to have the highest economic growth rates, not only in the region but also in the entire world, with 12.7 per cent in 2008 and 12.9 per cent in 2009, despite the world's serious financial crisis.

Economic growth is only a valid sign of progress if it results in real improvements in the living conditions of the people. There are indicators that measure these improvements, such as:

- The scope of the Millennium Development Goals regarding the mortality rates for infants and children under five. Health indicators are improving fast, with 78 per cent of children currently receiving treatment for basic illnesses and 86 per cent of mothers receiving pre-birth care, a 41 per cent increase.
- The United Nations 2010 Human Development Index shows that Timor-Leste moved up 11 positions since 2005, being currently situated in the category of medium human development.
- UNDP's 2011 Human Development Report shows that Timor-Leste increased once more its Human Development Index, with a 22 per cent improvement from 2001 to 2011. The report highlights the positive and sustainable growth and development of Timor-Leste, including key indicators such as the increase in the average life expectancy.
- The United Nations Report on Human Rights in Timor-Leste showed advances in the justice sector, with Timor-Leste having the potential to become a regional and global leader in terms of human rights.

I know there are some doubts about the implementation of the MDG-Sucos Programme, with an investment of $65 million in 2011. In May, we promoted a general assembly with the heads of Suco from the entire territory to explain precisely the rational of this program. I would also like to take this opportunity to explain to the general public that housing under the MDG-Sucos Program cannot be built like the social housing built for poor families. MDG-Sucos' housing meets the Millennium Goals, which involves decent homes with water, sanitation, electricity and access to health, education and markets. It is precisely because of this that during discussions with communities we set the following criteria: a permanent water source as the number one criterion; land that is sufficient and accepted by the entire community; and good road access.

Land has been ascertained to be the primary obstacle, and as a result we decided to begin pilot projects to motivate communities to find collective solutions to problems. We believe that, by the end of 2012, and after presenting the outcomes of pilot projects, we will be able to witness positive changes in communities throughout the Country.

- The Decentralised Development Program I and II, with an investment of $44.3 million in 2011, funded the development of small-scale infrastructure and nurtured the growth of construction companies in the districts, sub-districts, sucos and villages of the Country.

In relation to this program, we have also heard concerns regarding the quality of the works. The NDA is involved in a process with small business people to demand greater responsibility from them. It should be noted that these local business people have agreed to undertake corrections and in doing so demonstrating their seriousness and a good attitude. By the end of the year, the Government will have awarded certificates to the best companies, so as to create healthy competition in the fledgling private sector.

I would also like to mention that the program Sensus Fo Fila Fali is currently taking place, to socialise the results of the 2010 Census at local and community levels. This data will contribute to providing sucos with greater knowledge about their own future needs, and to enable them to measure their relative development every year. As well, communities will also be better equipped to make their own choices and to set their own collective priorities.

- In terms of access to education, we now have 90 per cent of school-aged children enrolled in basic education, fulfilling the goal set for 2015. Additionally, in 2011 alone, we have built and rehabilitated around 35 basic and secondary education schools and over 250 classrooms.
- In 2011, the national literacy campaign made considerable progress, with the eradication of illiteracy in the districts of Manatuto, Manufahi, Lautém, Aileu and Covalima by the end of the year.
- Agricultural production and productivity increased substantially in regard to rice and corn with a cultivation of around 28,000 hectares producing 64,000 tonnes of rice (productivity of 2.97/ha) and

cultivating around 27,000 hectares producing 30,600 tonnes of corn (productivity of 1.41/ha).
- To promote food security, we developed the integrated information system database and the regular collection of information on food security through the communities of the 13 districts.
- We trained over 1,200 groups of farmers on improved agricultural techniques and we distributed over 12,000 information manuals for agricultural extension workers.
- We continued to pay Bolsas de Mãe to over 15,000 beneficiaries and strengthened the attendance and assistance to women who are the victims of abuse and to children at risk. In addition, we have been paying pensions to National Liberation Combatants and we have awarded around 98 scholarships to the children of martyrs.
- We have started to build the 20 Monuments to the National Heroes and the 12 mausoleums, and on 20 August we conducted the Demobilisation Ceremony for 236 National Liberation Combatants.
- We have integrated the 668 medicine students who returned from Cuba into the National Health System and we held the ceremony declaring Timor-Leste Free from Leprosy.
- The Vice Minister for Health currently holds and will hold for the next two years, the position of Vice President of the Executive Board of the World Health Organization.
- The transformation of the Banking and Payments Authority into a Central Bank, with specific responsibilities in the development of the financial sector, constitutes another important stride towards the consolidation of State Agencies.
- This Government has also invested in the largest infrastructure project ever in the Country, the creation of an electric energy production, transmission and distribution system, which is currently in an advanced stage of construction.

This project includes the Hera Generation Plant, with 119.5MW capacity, and the Betano Generation Plant, with a capacity of around 137MW. These projects also include transmission lines to establish a ring around Timor-Leste to enable all Timorese, even those residing in the more remote areas, to have access to electricity.

The entire National Power Grid will be completed by the end of next year. Already this month, Hera can supply Díli, Aileu, Manatuto, Liquiçá and Gleno. It is hoped that before Christmas, and upon completion of the Baucau sub-station, Baucau, Lospalos and Viqueque will also be supplied by Hera. The Generation Plant, which is starting its operations, as well as the Bobonaro, Suai and Cassa sub-stations, may be operational before late 2012.

The importance of this project is unquestionable. In addition to generating direct and indirect employment, it will create numerous business opportunities and attract foreign investment. The regular supply of electricity through the National Power Grid is one of the key achievements of this Government, and its impact will start to be realised between late 2011 and mid-2012.

Your Excellencies
Ladies and Gentlemen,

In January 2011, I came here to defend the 2011 State General Budget. Today I want to repeat what I said in January 2011 word for word.

'It is important to highlight the following:

1. This budget execution rate will be higher still, because, according to the applicable international standards, the closing of accounts is only fully recorded two months after the end of the financial year in question;
2. The Government no longer includes commitments in the financial execution reports. I should clarify that there are differences between obligations and commitments;
3. All funds not used revert to the State at the end of the year, in a transparent manner;
4. Expenditure is monitored through the FreeBalance system, in view of the expenditure approved by Parliament, thus ensuring greater transparency and real time adjustment to the contingencies of the Country, making public spending more efficient.'

There is a methodology, which may be archaic but is still very useful, to monitor any development process. The current development stage of the Country requires all actors, inside and outside the State, to understand the parts in order to be able to have a realistic perspective of the whole. Those development stages can be international, regional and national.

Your Excellency the Speaker of Parliament
Distinguished Members of Parliament
Ladies and Gentlemen,

The 2012 State General Budget was programmed in order to establish a launching pad to transform Timor-Leste into a medium-high income country within the next 20 years.

Once again, following the legal framework to the letter and using proper planning instruments, we have a budget program that is sound, transparent and displays vision.

As the Distinguished Members of Parliament will recall, on Friday, 4 November, the Government referred to the meetings that took place on 1-2 August at the Díli Convention Centre to demonstrate that it is committed to improving management practises and correcting mentalities in Public Administration, as well as implementing a better budget methodology. I stated here last January that the Government wants to reformulate the Budget into two major divisions: recurring expenses and development expenses. We are on the right path when we view the recurring expenses we want to stabilise, thus focusing more on capital development. In a stage when we are building and consolidating the institutions of our State, having a numerical methodology with set figures would only serve to show our inability to adjust, both mentally and critically, to the realities of the Country.

The international budgeting standards are probably not the best. When every day I see TV coverage showing the German Chancellor, Angela Merkel, French President, Nicolas Sarkozy, and British Prime Minister, David Cameron, trying to give advice, the Italian Prime Minister, Silvio Berlusconi, looking scared and waving the white flag to the IMF a few days ago, and the Greek nation in an unprecedented political crisis, I find myself thinking that the Member States of the European Community have not been paying too much attention to the international standards. Perhaps that was the reason why President Obama accused the European countries of not having been able to solve their own problems since 2008. Similarly, the G20 held last week in Cannes failed to deliver the sign of hope that so many were longing for. Today, many commentators say that Italy may become the next Greece.

Within this global context of economic and financial crisis, forgetting that we are part of the great region that is Asia, with strong and emerging economies, is failing to place ourselves in space and time.

Your Excellencies,

The 2012 State General Budget will be the first to reflect the development goals set out in the Strategic Development Plan launched in July. The Strategic Development Plan covers three vital areas for the development of the Nation: social capital, infrastructure and economic development. It has been informed by the valuable data from the 2010 Census, which captured the actual and objective situation of the population, and now uses this data to create sustainable development policies.

Investing in development in 2012 means investing $1,763.4 billion in sustainable policies for the Country, which will build on the achievements so far, and place Timor-Leste on the right path. This investment is designated particularly for the construction and maintenance of essential and productive infrastructure, to the building of the petroleum sector on the South Coast, to decentralised development at district and local level and, also to the development of our human capital. Knowing that three-quarters of our population reside in rural areas, we will continue to invest in agriculture projects so as to increase the productivity of the sector. Together with DDPs I and II and with the LDP, these projects will promote employment creation for young people and adults living in rural areas.

Ladies and gentlemen, I will now describe the key budget guidelines for 2012:

1. We intend to invest $1,054.4 million in Capital Development, increasing investment in this category by 209 per cent against the year 2011. This amount includes:
   - $746.2 million for the Infrastructure Fund;
   - $52 million for Decentralised Development Programmes I and II; and
   - $200 million for the Capitalisation of the Timor-Leste Investment Company.

The Infrastructure Development Fund, created in 2011 with an initial allocation of $599 million, and dedicated to multiyear projects to support a modern and productive country that is able to generate employment opportunities, will continue in 2012. If the Infrastructure Fund and the DDPs are not new (as they continue this Government's focus on infrastructure and rehabilitating more and better roads, bridges and ports, irrigation systems, schools, clinics and hospitals, power grids, monuments, houses and police and military facilities, as well as the important development of Tasi Mane and other basic infrastructure at national and district level), the capitalisation of the Timor-Leste Investment Company (CITL) is an innovative measure for the new fiscal year.

This company will promote investment and economic growth opportunities, by focusing on commercial strategic projects. This will be the privileged instrument by the Government to transform our petroleum wealth into a non-petroleum economy. In other words, we will be diversifying our economy and promoting the creation of industries and services, instead of relying on petroleum and natural gas. With an initial capitalization of $200 million, this company will start its activity with an autonomous management, similar to Singapore's Temasek. The creation of this company is a strategic decision by the Government, with a political and economic nature, that is foreseen in the Constitution. The State, as the sole stockholder, acts as an economic agent, supporting the market and enabling investment in certain economic areas.

Potentially, CITL will be dedicated to the following projects:
- An underwater cable providing internet connection to the rest of the world, using the best available technology and substantially improving internet access in Timor-Leste.
- Reference projects in the areas of tourism, particularly concerning hotel building and manufacturing parks producing quality products at competitive prices, through the exploration of partnerships with advantages for the development of the tourism sector;
- Building commercial offices to allow the provision of high quality services;
- Other strategic investments, such as supporting access by passengers and freight at fair prices.

2. We intend to invest $344.7 million in Goods and Services, including:
    - $30 million for the Human Capital Development Fund;
    - $87 million for the fuel required to supply electricity to the entire Country;

- $2.4 million for the professional training of teachers, to improve the skills and professionalism of teachers, which in turn will result in better education for the students;
- $6.5 million for the operational services of the Ministry of Education, to support primarily the school meals programme;
- $14.5 million for the operational costs of the presidential and parliamentary elections;
- $9 million for the Food Security Fund, so as to ensure national reserves of corn and rice;
- $1.6 million for the National Development Agency;
- $2.1 million for the National Procurement Commission.

The National Development Agency and the National Procurement Commission, also created in 2011 by Decree-Law, along with the Timor-Leste Investment Company, will contribute to a better implementation of the major strategic projects, ensuring proper management, monitoring and cost-efficiency of infrastructure works and assuring that the implementation of the Strategic Plan, in regard to capital works, is a success.

On the other hand, I would like to highlight in this expense category the considerable investment made in education and technical and professional training, including the Human Capital Development Fund, which foresees around $11.8 million in scholarships alone for key development areas such as the petroleum sector, public finance and management, and education. The Human Capital Development Fund, created in 2011 with a total of $25 million, to be increased up to $175 million during the first 5 years, is developing the necessary competences in the fields of education, professional training and technical capacity for Timor-Leste to have the labour required for the social and economic progress of the nation, particularly in strategic areas, such as natural resources, agriculture, tourism, infrastructure, education and health.

Lastly, in this expense category we would like to note the expenses required to ensure that the 2012 elections take place in a fair, democratic, participative and safe atmosphere. For this purpose we have allocated $8 million to STAE, $1.5 million to CNE, $4 million to PNTL, $0.5 million to F-FDTL and $0.5 million to RTTL.

3. We will invest $194.2 million in the category of Transfers, including:
   - $69.9 million for payments to National Liberation Combatants;
   - $32 million for payments to elderly citizens over 60 years old, covering around 89,000 beneficiaries;
   - $6.3 million to continue to implement the Local Development Program, supporting rural communities; and
   - $20 million for rural-based community projects, seeking to improve rural roads and to create employment in rural areas.

To invest in people is to invest in the future of the Country. This has been one of the mottos of our government. For this reason, we will continue with our public transfers program, including the payment of benefits to National Liberation Combatants, the elderly and other vulnerable groups.

Our governing experience has shown that this type of justice and these types of social stability programs provide an invaluable return for the country. Additionally, removing our people from poverty, either directly or indirectly, is a moral obligation for any Timorese leader, since it is to our People that we owe the Independence of Timor-Leste. This is a debt that can never be paid in full.

4. The 2012 Budget also includes $30 million for Minor Capital, particularly for purchasing multipurpose vehicles for health centres and for purchasing medical and hospital equipment.

5. Finally, we have allocated $140.1 million for Salaries and Wages. In addition to the recurring expenses in this category, we decided to:
   - Increase salaries in the area of education, in order to implement the teacher career regime, with an investment of $2.6 million;
   - Strengthen higher education through UNTL with an investment of $3.5 million;
   - Implement special careers for health professionals with an investment of $3.4 million; and
   - Convert temporary public servants to permanent staff with an investment of $23.2 million in 2012.

Your Excellency the Speaker of Parliament
Distinguished Members of Parliament
Ladies and Gentlemen,

The impact of the investment we have been making during these past few years on the living situation of the Timorese and on the operation of the State institutions is the best indicator of budget execution and encourages us to be even bolder when developing the country. For the first time, Timor-Leste will incur public debt, based on the Public Debt Regime approved by Parliament. Consequently this Budget presents the maximum borrowing threshold of $33.1 million for building strategic infrastructure for the Country. Nevertheless, the Government vows to manage public debt in a sound and sustainable manner, identifying from the start the projects to be funded in this manner and listed in the SDP:

- Construction and supervision of the roads linking Díli-Manatuto-Baucau; Manatuto-Natarbora; Díli-Liquiça-Tibar-Ermera; and Maubisse-Ainaro/Same.
- Construction and supervision of the motorway in the South Coast, so as to support the development of this region.
- Construction and supervision of the development of the Díli drainage system, resulting in a cleaner city that is less subject to floods.

We have started to fulfil the goal set in the Strategic Plan of developing an extensive road network linking communities, promoting rural development, industry and tourism and providing access to markets, as well as improving basic sanitation and drainage systems, by 2015.

In 2012 the Government may use Public-Private Partnerships (PPPs) to support projects included in the SDP, namely the construction of large projects such as Ports and Airports. The legal and political framework for this is being developed. However we know that these processes are very complex and consequently should only be used in cases where it is necessary to share risks and to have access to international expertise.

Ladies and Gentlemen,

These large infrastructure projects should be associated with the development of our banking and financial services, so as to maintain an environment that is attractive to national and foreign investment. For this reason, in 2012 we will continue to invest in long-term credit and funding systems, with accessible rates, in order to encourage the development of our private sector.

We will also continue to invest in the Commercial Bank of Timor-Leste, formerly the Microfinance Institute of Timor-Leste, focusing on providing micro and small loans. It is estimated that the number of clients in the portfolio will increase in 2012, as well as the number of deposits and loans, particularly at district level.

Your Excellency the Speaker of Parliament
Distinguished Members of Parliament

Domestic revenues have been increasing gradually and should increase even more as the economy grows and public administration improves. For 2012, we are estimating an amount of $136.1 million in domestic revenues. This represents a 23.6 per cent increase against 2011. As such, we continue to rely on petroleum revenues to fund our budget, but it is precisely to curb this trend that we programmed the 2012 budget with the priorities we have set out.

Up to 1 January 2012, we estimate that the total petroleum wealth that encompasses the actual net total from the future petroleum revenue is $22.2 billion. According to the latest Bank Payments Authority report, the balance as of 30 September 2011 is $8.9 billion, and it is estimated that by the end of 2011 we will have $9.4 billion and, by the end of 2012, $11 billion.

The revenue deficit is $1,627.3 billion. It is financed through the Petroleum Fund ($1,594.2 billion) and through public debt ($33.1 million). The withdrawal exceeding the three per cent of the Estimated Sustainable Income Budget is justified because the policies integrated in 2012 concern the long-term sustainable development of the Nation.

One of the conditions required for the ESI to be truly sustainable is that the real return rate of the Fund is three per cent. Because of this, and in order to protect future generations, the legislation proposal approved by Parliament changes the Fund's investment policy, so as to diversify its portfolio. This reform proposed by the Government will enable increasing the medium and long-term investment returns from our Petroleum Fund, in order to achieve three per cent or more, against our present return of two per cent. Consequently, the changes made to the Petroleum Fund Law state that the purpose of the investment policy is to maximize the return adjusted to risk, using the principle of diversifying the

Fund's investment portfolio. Changing the law also enables investing at least 50 per cent of the Fund's assets in Treasury Bonds and no more than 50 per cent in equities. The economic models estimate that this will give a reasonable probability of achieving a real return of three per cent over time, with a level of risk that is acceptable to the Government. This will align the Petroleum Fund's investment policy with the budget expenditure guidelines on the ESI.

Lastly, we will be able to present 10 per cent of the value of the Fund as collateral for borrowing money that can only be used to build strategic infrastructure for developing the Country. This enables us to negotiate borrowings under more favourable conditions and with greater security.

The Government continues to argue that the only way for us not to be eternally dependent from the Fund is by diversifying the economy. This is fundamental for us to achieve sustainable economic growth. The Government also considers that the responsibility to create jobs is part of the prudent and sound management of the Fund. Consequently, we cannot let our human capital go to waste. Human capital is the key factor for growing our economy. As such, we have been creating the conditions to generate employment. Still, the driving force for this employment creation should be the Private Sector, rather than the State alone. This is precisely the change we want to make in the Country. It is here that the Government assumes its responsibility to create the necessary conditions for facilitating private initiative and of making our economy stronger and more competitive.

The Government must take on an increasingly regulatory and oversight role, creating an environment that is conducive to investment and inducing our Country's business people to be more participative in the development process. As such, the first obstacle to the development of the business and industrial sector has already been removed. By ensuring security and stability in the Country, the Government has given the private sector more confidence to invest. Now, through the Strategic Development Plan, the Human Capital and Infrastructure Development Funds, the Decentralised Development Plans, the development of banks that provide credit to the Private Sector, and many other initiatives, we are creating the necessary conditions for multiplying economic development opportunities in the Country.

Your Excellency the Speaker of Parliament
Distinguished Members of Parliament

Ladies and Gentlemen,

The year that lies ahead will be important for Timor-Leste. It will be a year for reaffirming the democracy we have earned, a year for consolidating the development we have achieved, and a year for celebrating historical dates that make the Timorese identity unique in the entire world.

For next year we have big dreams and large challenges, as well as the start of a stage of major national investments. The implementation of the Strategic Development Plan entails the need for considerable investment, at least during the first five years of execution. Still, we know that making the dreams and aspirations of our people come true is an investment with a return that cannot be expressed in words.

I would like to conclude by reminding everyone that in 2012 we will receive guests from all over the world to take part in our celebrations. I know that these senior representatives have great expectations in relation to Timor-Leste, although it has only been 10 years since we have emerged from the debris of destruction and started to build our Nation. Many other young democracies that were created in post-conflict situations such as Timor-Leste cannot yet claim the same successes that we have achieved. Presently we are a success case at a global level! As such, let us welcome 2012 with hope, optimism and the will to build a better Timor-Leste for our children. It is in this spirit that I ask your collaboration and commitment, Distinguished Members of Parliament, so that we can make this State Budget a Budget for the future, a Budget for every Timorese citizen.

# Notes

1. *Report of the Committee of Rapporteurs* (Buyens, Calonder, Elkens) L.N. Council Doc B 7/21/68/106 [VII] 27-28 (1919). See discussion, P. Ditton, "Self-Determination' or 'Self Management" [1990] *Aust Int L News* 3, 4. Much of this analysis is derived from Ditton.
2. BCIJ, SER A/B No.64 (1935). Cited in AORC 31, 110. *Ibid*, 17.
3. A. Cassese, 'The Self-Determination of Peoples' in L. Henkin (ed) *The International Bill of Rights: The Covenant on Civil and Political Rights*, New York, Columbia, 1981, 92, 93.
4. United Nations *Charter*, Article 1 in I. Brownlie, *Basic Documents in International Law* (3$^{rd}$ ed), Clarendon, Oxford, 1983. 1, 3 (emphasis ended).
5. See also *ibid*, 18 (Art 55). Note also chapters XI, XII, XIII and cf. Arts. 73, 76.
6. M.I. el-Kayal, *The Role of the United Nations in the Protection of Human Rights*, 1975, 310. See also International Committee of Lawyers for Tibet, *The Right of the Tibetan People to Self-Determination*, Preliminary Report, July 1990 (hereafter Tibet Report).
7. Cassese, above n3.
8. L.B. Sohn, 'The Rights of Minorities', in L. Henkin (above) 276.
9. United Nations, General Assembly Resolution 1514 (XV), 14 December 1960.
10. H. Gros Espiell, 'Right to Self-Determination: Implementation of United Nations Resolutions', UN Doc E/CN.4/sub.2/405/rev/1 (1980.
11. J. Crawford (ed), *The Rights of Peoples*, Clarendon, Oxford, 1988. See esp. I. Brownlie, 'The Rights of Peoples in Modern International Law', *ibid* at pp.1ff.
12. K. M'Baye, 'Human Rights in Africa' in K. Vasak and P. Alston (eds), *The International Dimension of Human Rights*, 283; Ditton (above) 8f.
13. UNESCO, 'International Meeting of Experts on Further Study of the Concept of the Rights of Peoples', November 1989, *Final Report and Recommendations*, SHS/89/CONF.602/7 p7.
14. I.A. Shearer, 'The decision in the East Timor Case' (1995) 69 *Australian Law Journal* 949.
15. Portugal, Assembleia da Republica, *Lisbon Declaration*, 2 June 1995 with annexed Action Plan. See also Parliament of Portugal, *Obligations of Portugal as the Administering Power of the Non-Self-Governing Territory of East Timor*, Lisbon, 1992.
16. Catholic Institute for International Relations and International Platform of Jurists for East Timor, *International Law and the Question of East Timor*, 1995, CHR/IPJET, London.
17. Amnesty International, *Indonesia and East Timor – Power and Impunity – Human Rights under the New Order*, Amnesty, London, 1994. See also Amnesty International, *Indonesia – 'Shock Therapy' – Restoring Order in Aceh*, 1989–1993, 1993, London.

www.ingramcontent.com/pod-product-compliance
Lightning Source LLC
Chambersburg PA
CBHW052132070526
44585CB00017B/1794